D1201135

THE SOVIET ECONOMY

STRUCTURE
PRINCIPLES
PROBLEMS

THE SOVIET

NEW YORK

ECONOMY
STRUCTURE
PRINCIPLES
PROBLEMS

Revised Edition

Nicolas Spulber
Indiana University

W · W · NORTON & COMPANY · INC ·

Library of Congress Catalog Card No. 68-8296

Published simultaneously in Canada by
George J. McLeod Limited, Toronto

PRINTED IN THE UNITED STATES OF AMERICA

1 2 3 4 5 6 7 8 9 0

For PAULINE
and DANNY

Contents

Part II: Sectoral Management and Planning

Part III: Social Accounting and Finance

Preface

Close to seven years have passed since the first edition of this book was written. In the meantime significant changes have taken place in socialist management and planning and in socialist systemic organization in general. The socialist camp resembles not a monolith, but a disorderly mosaic. From a period of faithful emulation of the Soviet model as it emerged under Stalin, we have come to a period in which experimentation becomes the hallmark of "socialist guidance" of the economy. The revised edition of this book pays close attention, first of all, to the changes which have taken place in the Soviet Union itself, and, secondly, to the possible direction of these changes in the socialist world at large.

One cannot understand the rationale and direction of change without a good grasp of the underlying assumptions, the fundamental structures, and the working principles of Russia's Soviet economy. It was the first, and in numerous respects, still is the pacesetter and the key economy of the socialist camp. The Soviet system remains characterized by interlocking political and economic leadership, nationalization of non-labor factors of production, and a combination of centralized decisions on main investment and key outputs with market mechanisms for carrying out its goals. This system is the outcome of a complex process of shifts and adjustments made over a number of decades. Like any living organism, it undergoes, and will continue to undergo, organizational changes. Although its institutional arrangements have been reshuffled in various ways, one should note that vast reorganizations are not an everyday occurrence; they take place only at historical junctures that end one phase and begin another. The vast organizational, political, and economic rearrangements of the 1930's carried out under Stalin remained basically unchanged until the mid-1960's. The much more cautious, but no less methodical, reorganizations carried out by his successors, will likely also provide, relatively lasting frameworks in a number of respects. I do not seek to foresee each specific change, but to examine the rationale and the working principles of the system as a whole. So long as the Soviet leadership's specific goals, priorities, and main steering methods do not change, such an analysis should, by and large, remain valid.

What is the most appropriate way to approach the study of the Soviet economy? Should one set it against the geographical, historical, and ideological backdrop of Russia? Should one organize it in the perspective of the Soviet Union's own economic evolution since 1917? Are our economic tools applicable to an economy that combines centralized commands and the play of market forces? What is the relevance of Marxian economic theories for probing the underlying assumptions of the Soviet economy?

I certainly think that geographical, historical, ideological, and economic factors all are important and interrelated. This interrelatedness is just as significant for the Soviet economy as for any other. The province of economics is well defined, however; one need not include in it what clearly belongs to other disciplines. Furthermore, much can certainly be said in favor of examining *seriatim* each of the phases of the USSR's economic development (notably, *War Communism*, 1918–1920; the *New Economic Policy*, or *NEP.*, 1921–1928; the *Comprehensive Administrative Planning* era, 1929–1965; and the *New System of Planning and Economic Incentives* or *New Economic Management*, *NEM*, 1965–   ) in their specific historical-institutional setting. I have, however, chosen a different approach. The present edition of this study is primarily focused on structural and operational aspects of the Soviet economy in the *NEM* period and on its prospects for future developments. While this approach may convey the impression that the USSR is treated, as it were, *sub specie aeternitatis*, the deemphasis of historical-institutional material has, however, a subsantial advantage. It allows the key structural elements of this type of system to be isolated better and facilitates the application of the ensuing analysis to the study of the various permutations of all socialist economies. As for our usual tools, some are fully operative in the case of the Soviet economy, whereas others are not. Interactions between saving and investment, for instance, differ in certain respects when the decisions concerning them are taken jointly, as in the Soviet economy, and when these decisions are taken separately, by heterogeneous elements, as in the free-market economies. On the other hand, it seems to me that some of the underlying Soviet assumptions and conceptual and statistical definitions cannot be understood without direct reference to certain Marxian economic concepts. Only in relation to the labor theory of value can one understand Soviet pricing; only in relation to the Marxian two-sector model can the Soviet strategy of economic development be clearly delineated. All these choices are the author's, of course; the reader must decide how useful and relevant they are.

For a long time, in economics, as in other fields, there was no real "dialogue between East and West." The political climate under Stalin and the divorce between Marxian and non-Marxian methods and concepts in economics (notably, concerning value and price, and hence the key question of allocation of resources) have prompted Soviet economists to show an ostentatious indifference toward what Western economists said about efficient allocation of resources in either a planned or a free-market economy. Since the death of Stalin, however, Soviet economists have turned their attention to econometrics and to the Western "techniques" of input-output and linear programming, even though the latter rest on some specific non-Marxian assumptions concerning relations of value to price, economic equilibrium, etc. Soviet economists believe that they can use the techniques and reformulate the assumptions. Thus, some Western economic tools have now been granted official Soviet citizenship.

On their part, Western economists have for many years shown a lofty indifference to the work of Soviet economists. One should note, however, that the Soviet economic literature is cast in a normative framework, is either historical and descriptive or narrowly pragmatic, and always uses a peculiar jargon with which one becomes familiar only after a long and tedious apprenticeship. Before the Soviet Union came into being, some Western economists had studied the problem of efficient allocation of resources under socialism, i.e., in an economy whose land and capital are nationalized. A classic example of such work is the famous study by Enrico Barone, *The Ministry of Production in the Collectivist State* (1908). The development of Soviet planning gave a new impetus to studies centered on the problems of rational allocation of resources, and price and income distribution in a planned economy. A whole set of theoretical studies of this nature appeared in the 1930's, but only a few writers paid close attention to the ways in which the Russians themselves were pragmatically manipulating the economic variables. After World War II, the interest of a newly emerging group of Western "Sovietologists" focused on the measurement of the Soviet Union's economic performance. This required a close look at the Soviet economic and statistical literature since it was the only material available. This interest produced a host of studies on the quality and nature of information under planning, on the plan itself, on the management of the Soviet economy, on its statistics of industrial output and of national income, on its underlying concepts, etc. To arrive at meaningful measurements, the Soviet data had to be fully explored, evaluated, and finally recast into more appropriate and more familiar frameworks. Thus a large body of economic literature was produced—most of it during the 1950's. Many of these materials shed a direct light not only on performance but also on the *modus operandi* of the Soviet system.

In this book, I try to integrate some of these materials, to weld some missing links, and at the same time, to examine the basic assumptions and the working principles of the Soviet economy as viewed by Soviet economists themselves. Although these economists have not formulated an integrated theory of their own planning, one should not overlook the fact that Soviet practice has provided them with a vast body of experience. The Soviet methods of physical allocation of resources along with deliberate distortions of cost-price structures have, by and large, achieved the aims of Soviet policy makers. Soviet solutions to problems of physical planning, the Soviet strategy of development and the Soviet concepts of social accounting need to be carefully explained and examined alongside the theoretical constructs formulated in the West. It is hoped that this book will fulfill this need.

This study comprises five parts: the first deals with the main steering and coordinating mechanism of Soviet economic activity, namely, the national economic plan; the second shows the relations of the main economic sectors and of their component units to this steering mechanism; the third examines the planning and accounting of income and money flows; the fourth discusses the problems of efficiency and of planning procedure from the standpoint of both Western and Soviet economic theory; and the fifth deals with the problems of Socialist cooperation and of competition with capitalism. Discussion of Russia's geographical setting and resources and examination of each specific phase of Soviet economic development are topics outside the scope of this book; in my opinion, these should be dealt with extensively in specialized works. Here, I attempt to place study of the Soviet economy within a simplified analytical framework—though certainly an imperfect one—rather than to detail its institutional changes in historical perspective. As much as is feasible, I use Western frames of reference in order to explain concrete connections in Soviet practice between, for instance, priority quantitative allocations and distorted price-wage structures.

By presenting a broadly based comparison of Soviet and Western concepts, from social accounting to efficiency theory, and by examining some of the main problems that arise when a comparative appraisal of Soviet and Western performance is attempted, this book will, I hope, provide the basis for a better understanding of the operation of the Soviet Union itself and of other economies structured on the Soviet pattern. In numerous respects the USSR still remains a model for socialist economies. It is with this "model" that I am primarily concerned. The study of the structure, principles, and problems of the chief socialist economy is, it seems to me, indispensable today, not only to economists, but also to social scientists, public officials, and the educated public.

A detailed bibliography of English materials keyed to each section and chapter will help the reader find material on each theoretical discussion alluded to in the text. Footnotes have been used only for factual data for Russian technical terms, or for specific references. For further research, additional materials, mostly in Russian, are listed in a bibliography of foreign sources.

In writing this book, I have benefited from the advice, criticism, and help of numerous persons. I am particularly indebted to Professors Franz Gehrels of Indiana University, Holland Hunter of Haverford College, Robert Lekachman of the State University of New York, and Charles L. Schultze of the University of Maryland, who read the original manuscript and made many valuable suggestions. I am very grateful to a number of colleagues from various institutions—too numerous to mention—who have kindly sent me valuable observations and comments on the first edition of this work. I am also indebted to Professors Robert W. Campbell, Louis Shere, and Roger Jeffrey Green—of Indiana University

—who have read parts of the revised edition and have helped with various criticisms and remarks. Mrs. Lorna Mory corrected the early drafts and significantly improved the general readability of the text. The editors of W. W. Norton & Company reviewed carefully and skillfully the final draft and helped in innumerable ways its preparation for publication.

I am grateful to the Ford Foundation for a Faculty Research Fellowship, which enabled me to give all my time to complete the earlier version of this study, and to the International Development Research Center of Indiana University for the help it extended to me in the preparation of the current edition.

The statements and conclusions presented in the book are mine alone. They do not necessarily reflect the opinions of either the persons who helped me nor the Ford Foundation, and I, of course, accept full responsibility for them.

Nicolas Spulber

Bloomington, Indiana

Part **I**

The Economic Steering System

INTRODUCTION TO PART I

Every economy faces and solves in its own way the problems of what to produce, what production processes to employ, how the goods produced should be distributed among its members, and how much should be currently consumed, used for increasing the production capacity, or stored. A capitalist free-enterprise economy solves these problems through a system of markets and prices; a collectivist economy of the Soviet type, through a combination of administrative commands and market mechanisms.

Institutionally, the Soviet-type economy may be likened to a single, giant, multibranch, multiplant corporation whose organizational component units are, however, autonomous within certain limits as far as their current operations are concerned. The theoretical "owners" — or nominal shareholders of this giant complex — are the Soviet workers. They sell their services to the state-owned enterprises through the market, and as consumers, are free to buy consumers' goods at the established prices. Management of this complex is deeply entwined with administration of the country. The corporation owns the land and capital but "leases" a large part of its cultivable land to agricultural collectives for an undetermined period. In the sphere of management of non-labor factors a dichotomy is thus created between state and collective farms. As in any corporation, programs of activity (plans) are drawn up at each level of the complex for implementing centralized decisions, i.e., the stated aims of the management, its priorities and methods of directing operations and of allocating resources. The programs are then adjusted and consolidated in a unitary (national) economic plan. Decision about the division of national income into saving, collective consumption, and individual consumption — which is analogous in our frame of reference to the decision about the ratio of profits (plowed back or distributed as dividends) to costs — is a top managerial decision. Hence, standard studies on the management of some corporations furnish useful clues to the operation of the present-day Soviet economy and to Soviet organization and activity in such areas as centralization and decentralization, departmentalization, devices of control, planning and coordination.

The opening chapter of this section identifies the principles underlying the structure of the economy and defines the basic ends of the top Soviet leadership and the relation between its over-all strategy of economic development, its programs of activity, and its instruments of execution. Soviet decisions concerning the courses of action for the economy as a whole, embodied in the national plan, are based on a strategy emphasizing industry and the priority development of certain branches of industry; Soviet techniques combine direct and indirect controls, administrative commands, and certain utilizations of the market mechanism. Chapters 2 and 3 focus on the nature, scope, and method of plan construction and implementation, i.e., on relations in respect to range, coverage, and execution among plans formulated at every level of the organizational setup and covering various time periods. Chapter 2 shows how these plans are interconnected, how consistency among goals set for each sector branch and enterprise is achieved, and how coordination between flows of goods and flows of money is programmed. Chapter 3 deals with the interplay between centralized allocation of non-labor resources and the price and wage system and examines the devices used for implementing the plan.

1.

Management of the Economy

PARTY-STATE ORGANIZATION

The characteristics of the Soviet economy are interlocking political and economic leadership; nationalization of non-labor factors of production; and the planning, coordination, and control of economic activities on the basis of a unitary plan for the economy as a whole.

Subordination of economic activity to the politically motivated decisions of the Communist party is a consequence of communist ideology, the Soviet political setup, and the locus of power within Soviet society. For the Soviet leadership, politics is "the most concentrated form of economics, its generalization and conclusion." The leadership does not regard the Soviet state as an instrument of arbitration among social groups — but as the class-warfare weapon of the factory workers "allied" with the peasants. According to the Soviet Constitution, in the Union of Soviet Socialist Republics (USSR) power belongs to the "working people," represented by soviets (councils) of workers' and peasants' deputies. Since the Communist party claims to be the organized avant-garde of the workers, it assumes, without putting its claims to the test of free elections, complete command over the Soviet state.

The proclaimed objectives of the Communist party have been the building of socialism and, eventually, of communism. In the Marxian frame of reference, communism represents the supreme stage of human economic development in which the level of production attained would be such that the society as a whole would pass from the realm of necessity (i.e., of scarcity) into the realm of plenty. By definition, socialism, the first phase of communism, implies a higher technological level than that attained by capitalism, which in turn outproduced feudalism. Since obviously, and paradoxically, the

Soviet system had been implanted in one of the most backward areas of Europe, from the early years of its seizure of power in Russia the Communist party set out to industrialize the country on a large scale, to raise its economy to the alleged advanced level of the Soviet political setup, and to catch up with and surpass the most advanced capitalist countries. A high rate of investment is systematically maintained, year in, year out, for the purpose of achieving this vast industrial expansion. From the beginning of its acquisition of power, the Soviet leadership has had both the will and the means to gather into its hands a vast share of the available resources of the country in order to carry out its chosen economic tasks. Soviet policy makers have unwaveringly had as their goals maximizing industrial growth, reconstructing the key branches of the economy on the highest possible technological plane, and hence organizing the most powerful industrial-military complex in the world, capable of both defense and expansion. The will to surpass the most advanced free-enterprise economy of the world, the United States, is the mainspring of Soviet economic policy.

Party and state hierarchies are distinct entities. The party is the engine driving the Soviet state. Its "cells" function within each plant, administration, and mass organization and are organized at successively rising levels; the committees or commissions at the top shadow all governmental departments.[1] In 1966, the party had some 12.5 million members and candidates, or roughly 5 per cent of the population. In principle, the party's highest authority is its congress. Actually, the latter does not always meet regularly as provided by party statutes. Between congresses, power is vested in the central committee. This committee, a body numbering between 200 and 300 members, elects a small policymaking political bureau, or *politburo*, of ten to fifteen full members and alternates and an administrative secretariat of some ten members, most of whom are also members of the *politburo*. Decision-making power is in the hands of the latter; administrative controls are in the hands of the secretariat. Within the party structure power lies in the hands of the first secretary. The *politburo* formulates the general political and economic tasks of the party and of the country as a whole. Its poli-

1. *As Carl Beck has noted in the case of Communist Czechoslovakia, this type of parallel organization lets the expert participate in state affairs "with a minimum increase in his power position;" on the other hand, it leaves the party free to intrude "at any level of decision-making without crossing well*

cies are periodically presented to the central committee plenums, and eventually to the party congress. The party adopts economic directives, which are implemented by the state under the form of laws. Since the party is the seat of power, all state questions are solved in complete conformity with party decisions. Any party-state conflict will be resolved in the favor of the party since the latter holds the crucial levers of control, because state officials of any significance are party members.

The state's highest organ is the Supreme Soviet, which consists of two elected chambers: the Soviet of the Union and the Soviet of Nationalities. The first is elected on a district basis; the second on the basis of administrative units (republics, autonomous regions, national areas), each with a given quota of seats. The Supreme Soviet exercises the legislative power, elects a presidium, which, among other functions, interprets the laws of the Union, and appoints the Council of Ministers of the USSR, which is the state's chief executive and administrative body. The Council consists of a chairman, deputy ministers, ministers, chairmen of certain state committees, and, ex officio, the chairman of the council of ministers of each union republic. Some Soviet ministries are similar to those functioning in any other country, for example, the ministries of finance, foreign affairs, defense, culture, health, and communications. Others are specifically Soviet, created by the all-pervasive economic role of the Soviet state, for example, the ministries of foreign trade, of electric power stations, engineering (general machine building), transport equipment. Also included in the Council of Ministers are the chairmen of various key state committees (e.g., for science and technology, for labor and wages, for economic and cultural relations with foreign countries), the chief of the State Planning Committee, the chief of the Central Statistical Administration, and the chairman of the board of the State Bank. The Soviet ministries are either All-Union or union-republic ministries: the first direct the branch of administration entrusted to them throughout the territory of the Union; the second direct their branches through corresponding ministries of union republics. The

established and codified lines of jurisdiction." The Journal of Politics, *Vol. 23 (1961).*

"One of the fundamental tasks of the party," states L. I. Brezhnev, "is the selection, placement, and rearing of cadres. Work with cadres is a key question in the work of the party, its chief task." Pravda *(Sept. 30, 1965).*

council of ministers of a union republic is appointed by the supreme soviet of the union republic and consists of the chairman of the council, deputy ministers, ministers, and the chairmen of certain state commissions (notably those for planning and building). Some ministers, called *union-republic* ministers, are subordinated both to their council of ministers and to the corresponding union-republic ministry of the USSR; other ministers, called *republic* ministers, are responsible only to the council of their republic. Finally, local administration is in the hands of local councils (Soviets). The activity of industrial and construction enterprises of national significance is supervised and regulated by all-union ministries; of all-union and republic significance, by republic ministries; of local interest and of the cooperatives, by republic ministries and by the local Soviets.

NATIONALIZATION OF NON-LABOR PRODUCTION FACTORS

State ownership is the only form of ownership in the USSR in the case of land.[2] However, the state assigns some of its land for use either by collectives — e.g., for farming — or by individuals — e.g., for personal-dwelling construction. In the case of productive capital, three forms of ownership are present: state, collective-cooperative, and private. State ownership encompasses (besides all the land and its mineral wealth, waters, forests, etc.) the mills, factories, mines, railroads, water and air transports, banks, communications, and state farms, as well as the municipal enterprises and the bulk of city dwellings. The collective-cooperative ownership exists in agriculture and in the sectors where small-scale ownership was widespread before the Soviet regime; it includes ownership of agricultural machinery, implements, livestock, farm buildings, and equipment of small-scale industry and handicrafts. The state and collective-cooperative ownership together form the so-called socialist sector. Private property [3] is limited to income and savings, some dwelling houses, household articles, and goods for personal use. In addition to its basic income every household in a collective farm is allotted a small plot of land and owns some live-

2. *In some socialist Eastern European countries, a significant part of the land is still privately owned. In Yugoslavia, the line between state and collective ownership is less clear-cut than in the* USSR.

3. *In Russian,* lichnaia sobstvennost' (*personal property*) *rather than* chiastnaia sobstvennost' (*private property*).

stock, poultry, and minor agricultural implements. The sphere of personal ownership includes the right to inherit personal property.

In the mid-1960's, the state sector accounted for almost all of the gross value of industrial output; only a small fraction of the output was produced by workshops and other industrial enterprises of consumers' cooperatives and of the collective farms. The state sector — the state farms and the state institutions — encompassed over 57 per cent of the agricultural land; the collective farms, 41 per cent; the subsidiary plots of the collective farms, less than 1 per cent; and the plots of workers and employees, roughly 0.5 per cent. The state farms sowed 46 per cent of the total crop land, and the collective farms sowed 54 per cent. The state retail trade shop networks accounted for over 68 per cent of the trade turnover; the cooperative trade, for 28 per cent; and the collective farm markets for less than 4 per cent. Thus, except in agriculture, the role of either private or collective ownership is sharply restricted.

The division of the national product between investment and consumption is determined by the government. The basic composition of each of these categories is likewise decided on by central fiat. Furthermore, the distribution of scarce raw materials, intermediate products, and capital goods is specified centrally in physical terms. Except for some agricultural machinery and handicraft equipment, no market exists for capital goods.[4] Most capital goods, along with minimum working capital means, are granted to state-owned enterprises. After provision is made for the level of investment decided upon, the remaining physical resources are made available for outputs of consumers' goods and for services. The government fixes prices for most inputs and outputs, but these prices do not directly affect the pattern of investment, the physical allocation of scarce supplies, or the key economic decisions of the party-state.

In order to ensure that the planned objectives of recruitment and deployment of labor will be met, the Soviet government relies essentially on wage differentials. A variety of administrative measures is also used when wide population shifts are envisaged, or when certain bottlenecks occur. Incomes received are spent freely through the markets for consumers' goods and services, at prices determined by demand and supply for certain agricultural produce and at ad-

4. This is one of the key differences between post-1951 Yugoslavia and the USSR; in Yugoslavia, all these goods are distributed through the market.

ministratively fixed prices for all other commodities, but production is influenced by consumer demand to only a limited degree.

ECONOMIC POLICY: OBJECTIVES AND INSTRUMENTS

The party-state guides the Soviet economy as a single, huge, multibranch, multiplant enterprise. The government's directives for action are called *economic plans*. These plans are, simultaneously programs of action and means of unified management. Although each enterprise operates on an autonomous accounting basis, to a great extent, its activities are charted by the plan and coordinated with those of all the other enterprises.

Any plan presupposes a number of *policy* decisions concerning the over-all pattern of development set by the policy makers. What should be emphasized — the growth of industry, agriculture, or both? Should productive activities take precedence over the expansion of strict economic overhead capital (e.g., transportation) or not? Which regions and areas should be developed? What policies should prevail concerning manpower, technology, housing, market expansion, or prices? The combination and attempted integration of these policies by rank of priority form what might be called the *strategy* of development adopted by the policy makers. On the basis of this strategy and the various hypotheses and forecasts, plan targets are established. The stressing of these targets implies that they will be "defended" against the impact of future aleatory conditions. The measures envisaged for coping with these uncertainties thus form a part of the strategy chosen. The carrying out of the targets requires the utilization of various *instruments* — of either a direct or indirect nature. The direct instruments are primarily commands addressed to the managers of branches or enterprises; the indirect ones are primarily fiscal, monetary, and credit instruments.

From the late 1920's, when the Soviet Union began to implement plans for the economy as a whole, and until the early 1960's, when, as we shall see, it ran into serious snags in its economic growth, the main emphasis of the Soviet strategy of economic development had been on industry as opposed to agriculture; on heavy industry as opposed to light industry; and finally, within heavy industry, on machine construction, which was regarded as the ultimate determinant of the place of development of all other branches toward sustained technical progress. Available investable resources were systematically allocated to secure a fast pace of development for industry, a faster pace for heavy industry, and the fastest pace for machine construction. Since the early 1960's, the original emphases have been temporarily blurred in favor of the simultaneous growth of both heavy and light industry. Further temporary shifts in favor of light industry and agriculture are possible because of possible sluggishness in economic growth, the expansion in policy makers' priorities as higher levels of development are reached, and the incapacity of the existing capital goods industry to cope with these new priorities. Originally designed primarily to reproduce itself on an increasing scale, the Soviet capital industry ultimately was too rigid when (particularly since the mid-1960's) the need arose for re-equipping and expanding the consumers' goods industries.

For plan implementation the Soviet policy makers and planners rely on positive central commands and a centralized system of allocation of supplies of capital goods and key raw materials; on the other hand, they depend on market mechanisms and various financial and monetary instruments to encourage or discourage the utilization of certain inputs, to orient labor resources according to planned objectives, and to distribute the goods produced. (See Figure 1.)

According to Soviet economic textbooks, the basic Soviet economic policy options and instruments are determined jointly by two objective "laws": (1) the law of "continuously raising the material and cultural requirements of the society"; and (2) the law of "planned proportional development." Actually these alleged laws are simply the obverse of the Marxian laws concerning capitalism. The first is the reverse of the so-called increasing "immiseration of the masses" under capitalism, and the second is the opposite of the "anarchy" allegedly characterizing the market. Neither the actual differences between a free-market and a centrally planned economy nor the mainsprings of the Soviet economy are much clarified by these "laws." The Soviet economy is guided by its policy makers and planners with the goal of maximizing over-all industrial growth rates while developing certain industrial branches as related to others. The manager of each Soviet enterprise aims to fulfill certain plan targets within the planned restraints, although, in order to meet his objective, he may have to diverge from various indices set by the planners. A free-market economy, however, has no such thing as an overriding objective. Each producer and consumer tries

FIGURE 1. *Diagrammatic Presentation of Soviet Objectives*

INSTRUMENTS			OBJECTIVES							
			Short-term			Long-term				
			Full Employment	Control of Pressures of Demand	Improvement in the Balance of Payments	Expansion of Production*	Improvement in the Structure of Production	Improvement in Working Conditions	Improvement in Income & Wealth Distribution	Other Objectives
Instruments of Direct Control	A. Enterprises	Control of type, size, location	+			+	+			
		Control of investment	+			+	+			
		Raw material allocation	+	+		+	+			
		Price fixing, cost & profitability controls	+	+		+	+		+	
		Wages and work conditions controls	+	+		+	+	+	+	
		Quality and standard controls			+		+			
	B. Branches and Sectors	Control of investment	+	+	+	+	+			
		Raw material allocation	+		+	+	+			
		Prices & wage controls	+	+		+	+	+	+	+
		Output & distribution controls								
	C. Foreign Trade	Imp. & exp. trading (prices and mixes)	+	+	+	+	+			+
		Exchange control	+	+	+					
		Immigration & foreign travel control	+							
Instruments of Public Finance	A. Related to Direct Controls	Direct and indirect taxes on, and subsidies of, enterprise	+	+	+	+	+			
		Public consumption	+	+		+	+			+
		Financing central investments	+			+	+			
		Payments to banks for loan financing	+	+		+	+			
		Budget surplus or deficit	+	+						

* *Within narrow limits, this could, of course, be relevant also in the short run*

and Instruments and of Their Main Connections

INSTRUMENTS			OBJECTIVES							
			Short-term			Long-term				
			Full Employment	*Control of Pressures of Demand*	*Improvement in the Balance of Payments*	*Expansion of Production**	*Improvement in the Structure of Production*	*Improvement in Working Conditions*	*Improvement in Income & Wealth Distribution*	*Other Objectives*
Instruments of Public Finance	B. Other	Taxes on households	+	+					+	
		Taxes on collective farms and cooperatives		+			+		+	
		Transfers to households							+	
		Foreign aid								+
		Custom duties		+	+					
Instruments of Money & Credit	A. Related to Direct Controls	Legal imposition of interest rates		+			+			
		Govt. guarantees of loans				+	+			
		Control of state enterprises borrowing				+	+			
		Control of collective farm and cooperative borrowing				+	+			
		Other directives				+	+			
	B. Other	Lending abroad				+				+
		Borrowing from abroad				+	+			
		Devaluation			+					
		Revaluation			+					
Changes in Institutional Framework	A. Affecting Other Instruments	Changes in the system of direct controls				+	+			
		Changes in the system of subsidies to enterprises				+	+			
		Changes in the tax system				+	+			
		Changes in the court system				+	+			
	B. Affecting the Production Framework	Changes in extent of public ownership				+	+			+
		Changes in labor's role in management				+	+			+
		Creation of new institutions				+	+			+

Based on: E. S. Kirschen *et al.*, *Economic Policy in Our Time*. Amsterdam: North Holland Publishing Co., 1964.

to maximize his own satisfaction, which, for the former, may mean maximizing profits. The contrast between the goals of over-all planning and the alleged goal of an atomistic economy is thus not very meaningful. Soviet practice, moreover, has been at sharp variance with the laws alleged to prevail under socialism. Significant increases in prevailing low consumption levels are postponed until after the key sectors of the economy have been fully "reconstructed" on the basis of up-to-date technology. Furthermore, Soviet planning has striven not toward a harmonious development among all the branches of the economy, but toward a deliberately skewed development which has often led to severe stresses and strains. According to official statements, this obvious discrepancy between the alleged operation of the second law and Soviet practice is to be accounted for by distinguishing between the plans and the law: as worked out by the authorities, the plans reflect the law more or less faithfully. If the plans violate the law too drastically, serious disturbances are bound to arise. This distinction between planning practice and the alleged law reduces the latter to a sort of generalized warning against inconsiderate policies and against the planners' assurance that everything is feasible because of their control over the state.

As such, these oft-repeated principles throw little light on the ways in which output targets are selected, the labor force is distributed, and price ratios are determined. The laws provide only a tenuous link between the prevailing official doctrines and day-to-day management of the economy as a whole.

EXECUTIVE AND OPERATIVE MANAGEMENT

The functions of executive leadership, involving planning, organizing, and controlling the basic directions of economic activity, are assumed by the top echelons of the party-state. The top management of the huge, multibranch, multiplant USSR consists of the Central Committee of the Communist party, the All-Union Council of Ministers, and the executives of the specialized economic committees for planning, labor and wages, and so on.

The table of organization of large corporations usually exhibits five managerial layers: 1) Board of Directors, i.e., *Trusteeship Management* safeguarding the stockholders' interests and determining basic policies; 2) Executive Council, i.e., *General Management* directing, coordinating, and controlling the operations of the business *as a whole;* 3) coordinating committees, or *Departmental Management* accountable to the Executive Council for various aspects of company's operation (wages and salaries, personnel, etc.); 4) branch leadership, i.e., *Sub-Departmental Management,* responsible to Departmental Executives; and 5) plant management or *Operational Management.* In the case of "USSR Inc.," the party's top organs discharge the first role; the Council of Ministers, the second; the ministerial committees the third; other committees and certain ministries the fourth; and the enterprise directors, the fifth. Alternatively, we may think of the first, second, and part of the third layer as forming the executive leadership or the "top management" of "USSR Inc."; part of the third and the fourth, as representing the actuators of the enterprises, i.e., their "supervisory agencies"; and finally the fifth, as representing operative management, i.e., the enterprises' directors.

Although the domains of executive, or so-called administrative, management and that of operative management overlap in many countries, their relationships may be neatly distinguished in the case of the Soviet Union. In principle, Soviet top management has no operative functions. On the other hand, executive and operative managerial functions are mixed in different proportions through the tiers of managing agencies down to the level of plant management. (See Figure 2.) Currently, the basic organs of supervisory

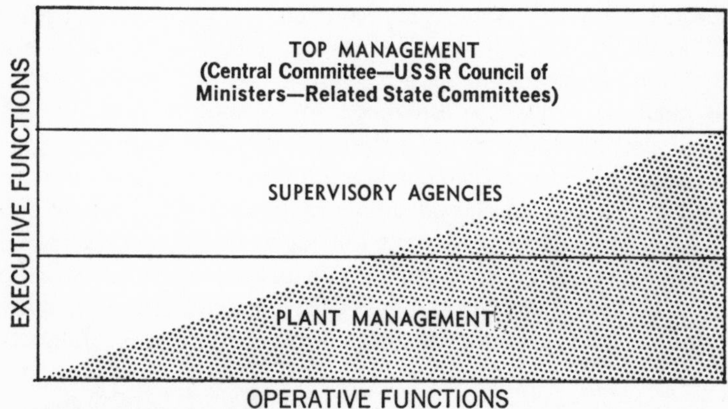

FIGURE 2. *Executive versus Operative Functions at Various Levels of Soviet Management*

agencies in industry are the economic ministries, to which the activities of plant managers are subordinated. In the case of agriculture, part of the executive managerial functions devolves upon the republic ministries of agriculture, while the operative managerial functions are discharged under their supervision and control by the directors and chairmen of state or collective farms. Thus, in industry, the scope of top management's economic authority is far larger in the USSR than that of any cabinet minister in a mixed economy or of the executive board of any corporation in a free-enterprise economy. Conversely, the plant manager's scope of authority is far narrower than in the private-enterprise framework.

Because top management reserves for itself such a wide field of decision making, a process of *functionalization* — i.e., of differentiating and relating functions at the top as is usual in any big corporation — has led to the establishment of a number of chains of command (or "lines") reaching down from the Soviet summit to operative management. At regular intervals, enterprises receive centralized directions concerning the volume and basic assortment of their current production. The central authorities also plan and sanction the output and allocation of capital goods. Special administrative bodies channel and control all key domestic or foreign supplies for industry. Others plan and control the size of the wage bill, forecast the distribution of the labor force, and prepare and introduce measures of technological change.

In order to construct such a vast program, to determine its practical aspects, and to control its implementation, the Soviet leadership must maintain not only detailed records of past performance but also a continuous flow of information on the work in progress in each and every part of the economy, on resources available, prevailing and possible shifts in production functions, impending bottlenecks, etc. Unified management requires the services of an army of statisticians, bookkeepers, and accountants and of a far-flung and complex machinery of both statistical reporting and programming. These functions are discharged by two central organizations: the Central Statistical Administration (CSA) and the State Planning Committee (SPC).[5] Both are rather similar in structure. Immedi-

5. *The former, called* Tsentralnoe statisticheskoe upravlenie — *or TsSU — has at various times been subordinated and then separated from the second, the* Gosudarstvennaia planovaia komissia — *or Gosplan. The title of the latter has at various times changed back and forth from a commission to a committee.*

ately below the CSA are the statistical administrations of the union republics, subordinated both to the CSA in Moscow and to the republic council of ministers. Still lower in rank are the statistical administrations of the autonomous republics, provinces, and principal cities, and finally, at the bottom of the pyramid, district and municipal statistical inspectorates. Immediately below the SPC are the planning committees of the union republics, which are also subordinated to the republic councils of ministers. The planning organs of the executive committees of the local soviets function directly under the republic planning committees. Through subordinated organs in each enterprise, agency, and institution, both the CSA and SPC pervade the whole economic administrative structure of the country.

Information is the lifeblood of planning. The CSA plays the cardinal role of centralizing a continuous flow of information concerning production, consumption, plan fulfillment, labor, population, etc., of processing the data and feeding it to the SPC, councils of ministers, and other executive organs. The CSA is supplied with this information by all enterprises, agencies, and institutions. On the basis of these data, its own information and estimates, and the government's directives, the SPC draws up the draft plans for the economy as a whole and for each of its branches. After discussion of the drafts throughout the operational levels of the economy, it consolidates and correlates the information returned by the production units and the instructions received from the executive party-state organs into a final economic plan. The SPC determines in detail the new investments and the interchanges between the republics; it controls the allocation of scarce supplies of both producers' and consumers' goods, moreover, it fixes most prices. The SPC thus establishes the schedules of activity of the economy as a whole and of each of its sectors and branches. Each enterprise must draft in the normal course of its activity programs of work for the immediate period ahead and submit the draft to its hierarchical links — the head office of a ministerial department or of a "trust" joining nationally or technologically related types of enterprises. For each operational plan period, i.e., for each specified segment of an unfolding program of action, production conferences of managers and technicians at the various hierarchic managerial levels contrast and correlate the production possibilities as evaluated from below and the direction and pace of activity as mapped out above. The actual plan is thus shaped to some extent through a process of give and take that operates within the vast reaches of the economic apparatus of the country as a whole. As projects and programs are passed upwards, they must be consolidated and systematized in various ways. As instructions and schedules of activities are handed down from the center, they must be interpreted, made specific, and finally adjusted to each plant. Centralized planning and unified management cannot and do not exclude the need for adjustment in the very process of formalizing the centrally determined tasks. Once a decision is reached, however, it becomes the fixed standard against which performance is checked and judged.

The CSA, the state committees, and the economic ministries consist of departments organized, as in any big administration or corporation, according to functions and according to branches or territorial subdivisions. Within the SPC, for instance, the first — or functional field — comprises the departments of planning, capital construction, labor and wages, the technical department, the financial department, and some others; the second — the operational or production-territorial field — involves the correlation of all information and instructions concerning investment, supplies, and prices by sectors, branches, and regions. In the economic ministries, the functional departments concern themselves mainly with planning, technology, capital construction, payroll, and finance; the operational departments, or chief administrations,[6] supervise the industrial or commercial branches. An obvious difference between the planning committees and the economic ministries is that committees put the main emphasis on the functional departments, with most of the operational departments reduced to the role of grouping, comparing, and collecting incoming data and channeling instructions, whereas the ministries place their main emphasis on the operational departments which transmit specific orders and exercise direct surveillance over the activities of enterprises.

As might be expected, both overlaps in lines of command and gaps in delegation of responsibility from one echelon to the next are inherent in the huge Soviet organizational setup. Certain lines, like those involving the direction of material supplies, play the leading role; others, like those concerning technological change, only sporadically occupy dominant positions. Interferences occur between crisscrossing lines and their expanded staffs at various levels. The

6. Glavnoe upravlenie, *or* Glavk.

lines descending from the top of the Soviet managerial pyramid, from the Council of Ministers of the USSR and from its committees down, through the supervisory agencies to the plants, link the executive management in a variety of ways to the activities of operative management in the enterprises.

2.

Plan Construction and Coordination

THE HIERARCHY OF PLANS

The plan is a program of action that coordinates information, forecasts, and directives concerning output and capital formation for a stated period. In Soviet planning, key outputs, employment targets, and main consumption objectives are expressed in physical terms on the basis of a system of input-output and consumption balances, which we shall examine below. In addition, producers' or consumers' goods are accounted for in monetary terms: production generates income, which in turn is either spent on goods and services or saved.

We may distinguish two basic types of plans: long-term expansion (capital formation) plans and yearly working plans, which deal with outputs, relation of production to consumption, etc. Both types of plans must be coordinated and subdivided for operational periods (quarterly or monthly) and for sectoral and geographical (regional, district, local) operational levels. Thus, plans are differentiated and then coordinated according to objective, time span, and the structural (i.e., organizational) setup of the Soviet economy as a whole — a process that, in many respects, resembles the planning procedure in any big business in the U.S. economy.

The expansion plans for ten, fifteen, or twenty years, called *general* plans, lay out a tentative sequence of main projects to be constructed in some leading industries considered significant for both defense and economic growth, for example, electricity, electronics, nucleonics, petrochemicals, and plastics. The Soviet method for preparing the specialized branch plans is in no way different from that customarily used anywhere for planning new factories. These branch and sector plans are then combined into a schematic structural model of the economy of the future. Until now, Soviet preference has been for "intermediate" plans, called *perspective* plans, of five to seven years' duration and representing a detailed scheme that provides concrete bases for scheduling yearly orders to the capital construction industries, i.e., to machine construction, building, and related activities. The five-to-seven-year period was selected as corresponding to the length of time needed for engineering, planning, constructing, and commissioning new industrial aggregates. Since capital construction may actually be begun in any given plan year, Soviet planners are now looking toward the implementation of a sensible suggestion, first made in the 1920's, concerning flexible, instead of rigidly established, perspective planning. According to this suggestion, a new five-to-seven-year perspective plan would be compiled each year. The initial and terminal points of the projection would be moved forward annually. The procedure would allow Soviet planners to modify the path leading to the completion of the general plan and would continuously illumine a moving period of five to seven years ahead.

The detailed yearly plans and their quarterly or monthly subdivisions are called *operational* plans. They aim to gear the economy to the targets ahead. The shorter the operational period, the stronger, of course, is the impact of existing capacity on the amount and nature of the product mix. The longer the perspective taken, the larger the possible changes in both quantity produced and output mix as new plants or even whole industrial branches come into being. Thus, the operational plans must be implemented under the restraints of the past and the spur of the tasks set for the future.

The starting point for all plans is the formulation of political directives by the party and government. These are based on the performance of the economy and each of its branches — the so-called achievement balance, which is prepared by the Central Statistical Administration. The directives express the prospective changes desired in the economy during a given period with respect to expansion and output. The choice between the various basic tasks (i.e., the scale of priority) expresses the preferences of the policy makers within the limits of the economy's estimated possibilities (i.e., resources present and prospective, exports, and imports). Once the directives are formulated, it is the task of the State Planning Committee to translate them into concrete and coordinated plans and projects. Like the final plans, these first drafts include data in both physical units and value terms and specify such magnitudes as output targets by sectors, branches, and key commodities, rates of development and sector proportions, volume of gross investments by sectors and regions, and volume of consumption.

The SPC submits the draft plans, called *control figures,*[1] to the economic ministries and administrations for detailed working out of the scheduled tasks and for modification and adjustment. These bodies, in turn, transmit detailed targets and indices to their enterprises. The enterprises work out their specific plans and determine their claims within the established framework for equipment, raw materials, fuels, and the like. In working out these projects, all sections, branches, combines, trusts, and enterprises are strongly urged to depend as much as possible on their own internal resources and possibilities so as to reduce their claims upon central resources. The projects worked out at the bottom of the pyramid are then submitted back through the hierarchy, corrected, and consolidated for all the supervisory agencies (ministries, etc.). On the basis of these projects, the Union SPC prepares the final program in which it aims at keeping in check regional tendencies toward autarky and at achieving, as much as is feasible, internal consistency between the various parts of the plan. The final document is not meant to be a technical summary of various projects, but a unified program for the whole economy. The consolidated blueprint is then presented to the party-state for approval. After its approval, the plan becomes the law of the land, compulsory for all economic organizations.

Quarterly layouts or shorter plans are not submitted to the government; the tasks scheduled by them are directly apportioned to each enterprise by its superior administrative link.

MATRIX PLANNING: CONSISTENCY AND RELATED GOALS

For consistency, the over-all expansion and output plans depend on the ways in which the various enterprise, branch, and sector plans are interrelated. For efficiency, the output plans depend upon the precision with which the production functions (i.e., the relation between outputs and inputs) are defined for the present and determined for the planned period. The problems involved can be

1. Kontrol'nye tsifry.

more easily grasped if we combine all interindustry relationships into an input-output matrix, i.e., a right-angled table with n rows and n columns. The familiar input-output analysis devised by Professor Wassily Leontief of Harvard reveals both the interdependence between production sectors and the relation between inputs and outputs. In the so-called open model, the national economy is divided into a production sector, encompassing all interindustry flows, and an autonomous sector, absorbing the net output or "final demand," i.e., consumption, investment, stocks, and exports. Assume that there are n productive branches with $X_1, X_2, \ldots, X_n$ as their producible (physical) outputs, and $x_1, x_2, \ldots, x_n$ as their net outputs flowing to the autonomous sector. Let a symbol, such as x_{ij}, represent the *input* of the *i*th good used in the production of *j*'s *output*. The total of any output, such as X_1, will hence be equal to $x_{11} + x_{12} + \cdots + x_{1n} + x_1$ (where the first subscript indentifies these elements as parts of the output of industry 1, whereas the second subscript indicates their destinations, that is, industries $1, 2, \cdots, n$). The production system as a whole can then be represented by Figure 3.

FIGURE 3. *Input-Output Structure of the Economy*

Sectors	Interindustry Demands						Autonomous Sector*	Total Gross Output
	1	2	.	j	.	n		
1	x_{11}	x_{12}	.	x_{1j}	.	x_{1n}	x_1	X_1
2	x_{21}	x_{22}	.	x_{2j}	.	x_{2n}	x_2	X_2
.	.	.	.	.	.	.	.	.
i	x_{i1}	x_{i2}	.	x_{ij}	.	x_{in}	x_i	X_i
.	.	.	.	.	.	.	.	.
n	x_{n1}	x_{n2}	.	x_{nj}	.	x_{nn}	x_n	X_n
Autonomous Inputs†	Y_1	Y_2	.	Y_j	.	Y_n		
Total Gross Outlay	X_1	X_2	.	X_j	.	X_n		

* *Final demands: consumption (private and public), investment, accretion to inventories, exports.*

† *Decreases in inventories, imports, depreciation, wages and salaries, and "surplus."*

The total output of a branch i and its distribution may be summarized in the generalized form:

$$X_i = \sum_{j=1}^{n} x_{ij} + x_i \quad (i = 1, \cdots, n)$$

Thus, the matrix allows us to visualize both the relations between each particular output (or supply) and its allocation, as well as the structural interrelations between all industries in the economy as a whole.

Leontief treats the flow of goods from an industry i to a sector j as being specific to the production process of sector j; this means that he assumes that each input χ_{ij} is required in *fixed proportions* for the output of X_j. The ratios x_{11}/X_1, x_{21}/X_1, and so on, can be written in the generalized form:

$$a_{ij} = x_{ij}/X_j \quad (i,j = 1, \cdots, n)$$

where a_{ij} represents *technical* (or input) *coefficients*.[2] Thus, the whole technological structure of the economy can now be presented under the form of a square matrix:

$$A = \begin{bmatrix} a_{11}X_1 + a_{12}X_2 + \cdots + a_{1n}X_n \\ a_{21}X_1 + a_{22}X_2 + \cdots + a_{2n}Xn \\ \cdots \\ a_{n1}X_1 + a_{n2}X_2 + \cdots + a_{nn}X_n \end{bmatrix}$$

These coefficients express the phenomenon of interdependence in the economy, and constitute its structural parameters. The core of the input-output system can now be represented by the following linear equations:

$$\begin{aligned} X_1 &= a_{11}X_1 + a_{12}X_2 + \cdots + a_{1n}X_n + x_1 \\ X_2 &= a_{21}X_1 + a_{22}X_2 + \cdots + a_{2n}X_n + x_2 \\ &\cdots \\ X_n &= a_{n1}X_1 + a_{n2}X_2 + \cdots + a_{nn}X_n + x_n \end{aligned}$$

Let us designate the column vector of production of individual branches, X_i, by X and the vector of final demands, x_i, by x. We can thus summarize the system of equations in the following form:

$$X = AX + x$$

Now we can define x by shifting AX to the left:

$$(I - A)X = x$$

By solving a system of equations related either to X or to x, it will be possible to plan either the level of production of individual branches so as to increase the output needed for the "autonomous sector" (consumption plus "accumulation") or plan the amount of the autonomous sector at various levels of output.

On the other hand, the structural interdependence in the economy can be expressed in terms of *costs* of *factor inputs* plus value added, i.e., purchases from other sectors or firms, and wages plus taxes plus profits. Sector *j*'s total *purchases* from other firms are given by the equation $x_{1j} + x_{2j} + \cdots x_{nj}$, while wages plus taxes plus profits are designated as Y_j. We can then define X_j, the value of output, with the formula:

$$X_j = \sum_{i=1}^{n} a_{ij}X_j + Y_j$$

This can also be used in multiple ways in planning: for example, we may establish a set of equations which can be solved either with unknown price indices or with unknown production indices.

Input-output techniques are extremely adaptable for planning in either physical or value terms; for scheduling given shifts in accumulation or consumption, or in the relationship between "productive" and "non-productive" spheres, between given branches ("A" versus "B" departments), or in zonal and interregional programming; or for determining given proportions at the level of a "combine," trust, or enterprise. Hence, definite avenues for applying these techniques are open in all the preparatory phases of any comprehensive plan.

In the input-output system, it is assumed that there are no joint products and that each product is obtained through a *unique* process with fixed proportions. These assumptions are discarded in the models devised by the allied but distinct method called *activity* (or *process*) *analysis* or *linear programming*. Although the concept of linearity (i.e., of constant returns to scale) is adhered to in linear programming, outputs are assumed to be obtainable by a variety of processes. A *process* is defined as a functional relationship in which inputs and outputs are dependent variables, and the "level" of the

2. *Hence,* $a_{11} = x_{11}/X_1$; $a_{12} = x_{12}/X_2$, *etc.; from which it follows that* $x_{11} = a_{11}X_1$, $x_{12} = a_{12}X_2$, *etc., that is, the input of* i *in sector* j *is equal to the corresponding coefficient* a_{ij} *multiplied by the gross output of sector* j, *namely:* $x_{ij} = a_{ij}X_j \quad (i,j = 1, \cdots, n)$.

process is the only independent variable. In the input-output model there is no scope for finding an optimal solution (or a set of optimum "levels"). In linear programming, the problem is precisely that of optimizing the results by choosing among processes and combinations of proportions to be used, given prevailing limitations on inputs. Thus, linear programming implies the study of the maximization (or minimization) of a function subject to linear inequalities. A linear programming model, then, will consist of a set of equations indicating quantities of inputs and outputs as a function of the levels of the various processes considered. The avowed object of the technique is close approximation of the practical problems of the entrepreneur and the policy maker by taking into account that, typically, different processes are simultaneously employed for using a set of inputs.

Linear programming also provides a fruitful approach to the study of alternatives for consumption and investment programs and for determining maximal steady growth. In the context of planning, given an initial capital structure, if growth is to be maximized, it is suggested that policy makers aim first at changing the initial conditions so that maximal steady-growth proportions (compatible with the given technological possibilities) will be achieved. After performing in this way during most of a given period, the system's capital structure could then be altered again in accordance with the planners' desired terminal proportions.

THE SOVIET APPROACH TO PHYSICAL PLANNING

Soviet plans are formulated in both physical and value terms, but the various balances involved are not fully interconnected. On the one hand, the material (physical) balances are not united into a single system which solves all the problems involved in intersector connections. On the other hand, the balances in value terms — i.e., the national accounts — establish broad relations between total product consumption and investment, but are not concretely coordinated with the intersector relationships of production and distribution. The gaps in the plan and the divorce between its two aspects have occurred, among other reasons, because planners have both needed and been able to concentrate only on certain key branches of material production, because enormous practical difficulties are involved in going beyond first-order inputs for the determination of technical coefficients (production functions) even for key products, and because the price system is distorted.

The core of a Soviet plan consists of selected *physical* targets for output, employment, and main consumption objectives by sectors, regions, etc.; the output and employment targets aim at using all available resources. The plan is built around output goals and the expansion in capacity needed for leading industries (the leading links of the plan), their supporting branches, and lastly, the other sectors of secondary priority including the consumers' goods industries. Annual Soviet plans utilize between 7 and 10 thousand physical balances; some 700 major product groups are used for supply planning. A balance in physical terms shows current, or intended, *supplies* of specific commodities or for a group of goods and their principal users. We can present an example of such a balance, using the notation of the preceding section:

If X_i is total (physical) supply of a given good, x_{ij}, the parts of this output used either in the same producing sector or in another sector (say j), and x_i, the surplus available for households, exports, and reserves, the planners must adjust the items of the two sides of the balance to produce equality between total supplied (X_i) and total allocated ($x_{ij} + x_i$) (see Table 1). The allocation of supplies depends on the input schedule of each industry according to its own

TABLE 1. *A Soviet Balance of Resources and Allocation*

Resources		Allocation	
Production	X_i	Used by the producing firm and by other firms	x_{ij}
Imports			
Reserve and Inventories			
		Marketed	x_i
		Exports	
		Reserve and Inventories	

$$X_i = \sum_{j=1}^{n} x_{ij} + x_i \quad (i = 1, \cdots, n)$$

output targets and the scheduled shifts in its production function, i.e., in its technical norms of utilization of machinery, materials, fuel and power, and labor per unit of production. In Soviet planning, the volume of inputs is worked out each year on the basis of a sort of crude aggregation of the input coefficients computed directly from the balances of the enterprises. In drawing up perspective plans, the planners adjust the coefficient in a variety of ways, assuming that the longer the planning period, the more significant the reduction in certain norms will be, on account of the planned shifts in capital-to-labor ratios and of projected increases in labor productivity. The breakdown by users is made by remembering the concrete requirements of a few key consuming ministries or administrations; the requirements of the other consumers appear only in aggregated form in the balances.

On the basis of the investment and output programs, the SPC elaborates the balance of capital construction — the so-called balance of "fixed funds" — and the procurement (supply) balances. The balance of capital construction details volume, structure, and location of capital installations and specifies in itemized lists the main projects and the timetable for their completion. Although this balance is an autonomous part of the yearly plan — since such installations are planned separately from the current production activities of the enterprises — it is the fulcrum of the plan because it determines the changes scheduled with respect to growth and sector proportions.

The balances of procurement of equipment, fuels, and raw materials cover two types of goods: those which are considered of paramount importance and are scarce and rationed; and those which have either a lesser priority or are more plentiful. The first category consists of the so-called funded commodities. The second category comprises two subgroups: "centralized planned" goods, whose allocation is under planned surveillance, and non-rationed goods, which are sold freely. Funded commodities include most equipment and basic industrial materials, namely, numerous kinds of machinery, all types of fuels, electricity, ferrous and non-ferrous metals, the most important construction materials, selected chemicals, and rubber products. Also included in the funded group are the principal agricultural raw materials. Funded commodities and part of the centralized planned commodities are not put on the market. They are distributed centrally, by branches and enterprises via the special channels of the so-called material-technical supply system. The rest of the centralized planned goods and all other non-rationed goods are sold through the regular distribution channels to collectives or to the public. Because of the enormous multiplicity of products in an industrialized economy, goods are grouped into certain conventional classifications by using technical conversion factors, such as steel content, horsepower, or some other physical common denominator. Fixing physical output targets for key commodities and for classified goods may be crude but it does have substantial validity since, in a complex industrial society, the most common combinations are reducible, as in chemistry, to a small group of basic elements, namely, iron, coal, coke, steel, rolled metals, cement, fuels, electricity, and the principal non-ferrous metals. For consumers' goods also, there is a relatively small list of significant items, namely, wine, meat, fats, fabrics, and shoes.

The manpower balance is a basic component of the Soviet plan. It is regarded as necessary for ascertaining the present employment pattern, the shifts required within it by scheduled planned development, and the volume of wages, a fundamental magnitude of the monetary balances, which we will discuss later. The manpower balance consists of an inventory of the labor force by age and sex (from sixteen to fifty-four or fifty-nine years for female or male labor respectively), actual employment by economic sectors (state and collective), forms of production (productive or "non-productive" sphere), territorial subdivisions (republics, regions, and districts), and types of skill. In establishing the sources of labor supply for any specific industrial branch, factors taken into account include recruitment by the enterprises themselves, organized recruitment of workers in villages, state "labor reserve" schools, intermediate and higher educational institutions, the possibility of redistributing manpower between branches, and the "planned" transfers of skilled personnel from one place to another. The necessary employment of factory workers is derived from the past and projected gross value of output, scheduled employment time, average levels of productivity, and defined amount of necessary equipment. Again, through grouping into a number of broad skill categories and through utilization of progressive output norms, the number of "norm" hours is calculated and the theoretical number of available jobs derived. The indices are refined by introducing correcting factors for absenteeism, seasonal fluctuations, etc. The number of white-collar workers and technical engineering personnel is ascertained on the basis of standard ratios of management to factory personnel. Clearly manpower planning is not in the Soviet context the same thing as forecasting manpower demand in market-directed economies. The latter requires knowledge (or estimates) about wage rates for various occupations, which in turn reflect the schedule of the marginal value productivity of each category of manpower, and the available supply. The Soviet system, however, considers the composition of employment necessary to carry out the goals set; its concept is technological rather than economic.

The key physical balances of capital installations, equipment, fuel and power, raw materials, and manpower are all based on planned outputs for some key industries — the so-called leading links of the plan. These outputs, in turn, have been established by taking into account the past and potential growth of the key industries and related branches under the assumption of full employment of all available resources.

THE SOVIET APPROACH TO FINANCIAL PLANNING

Centralized decisions concerning the size and nature of capital construction (i.e., the intensity of industrialization), choice of growth branches, determination of their outputs, preferences among a number of processes, gradation of plants' efficiency, and so on, may all be made solely on the basis of technological considerations, i.e., independently of prices. Direct allocation of scarce supplies may then guarantee fulfillment of the established capital and output programs. But more than technical manipulations are needed to broaden the range of choice among processes and alternative uses of inputs and to attempt to optimize returns in the use of factors. The essential requirement is knowing the scarcity coefficients of these factors, i.e., their relative prices. Plants could not be compared as to efficiency without reference to prices, except under severely limited assumptions about homogeneity of product and identity of productive circumstances.

In the absence of a market mechanism for non-labor factors, Soviet pricing — deliberately adapted to the regime of centralized physical controls and to various restrictions of choices imposed on both producers and consumers — is seriously impaired as an instrument for allocating resources. Later, we shall discuss in detail the numerous consequences of this fact. Let us note for the present that although decisions concerning output, employment, and consumption targets are set forth in physical terms, the capital goods used are accounted for in monetary terms, wages are paid out in money, and commodities are sold for money; in short, Soviet production within, as well as outside, the state sector generates income, which, in turn, is spent on goods and services or is saved; hence, the need for financial planning and accounting and for coordinating the latter with the physical planning.

In Soviet social accounting, total value of the material goods produced and of services not connected with material production are accounted for separately. The starting point in the construction of financial balances is the computation of the value of gross output for each enterprise (and then for each branch and sector), which is taken to be equal to the value of finished or semifinished goods produced for sale (commodity production), or for the firms' own requirements, plus the value of changes in stocks. As far as is feasible, gross output must be derived from the production plan expressed in physical terms.[3] Until 1949, gross output was computed in 1926–27 "constant" prices, i.e., sales prices of that base year, as well as in current prices. Since 1952, it has been computed in "comparable" prices (i.e., wholesale factory prices established centrally after comprehensive price revisions or reforms, viz. of 1955, 1963, and 1967), as well as in current prices.

The government sets prices by taking into account the planning of costs and of profits in each economic sector and branch, and the planning of taxes. The relationship between the value of commodity output (i.e., the value of goods for sale computed at realized wholesale prices, that is factory prices f.o.b. or c.i.f.) and, the gross value of output varies from branch to branch according to the specificity of the production cycle of each branch and of the volume of its unfinished production. The gross value of output contains numerous double countings under the form of intermediate products (see Table 2).

3. *Physical planning and the passage from physical to financial balances for each branch and for the economy as a whole are in numerous respects akin to the processes of planning, programming, and budgeting for defense occurring in any economy. As in Soviet economic planning, defense planning and programming precede budgeting (the programs for defense are established first on the basis of military concepts and are costed afterwards only). Furthermore, the whole process of budget formulation — with its incredible complexity and its relentless pressure for immediate and final decisions without close regard to optimizing results — raises a variety of problems similar to those with which Soviet economic planning has to cope. See Arthur Smithies,* The Budgetary Process in the United States *(New York: McGraw-Hill, 1955), pp. 108–114 and 240–252.*

TABLE 2. *A Product Account*

Stages of Production:	Outlays on Materials	Value Added	Gross Value of Output
1. Extraction of primary materials	A	B	$A+B$
2. Output of semi-manufactured goods	$A+B$	C	$A+B+C$
3. Manufactured goods	$A+B+C$	D	$A+B+C+D$
Totals	$3A+2B+C$	$B+C+D$	$3A+3B+2C+D$

By excluding the interindustry flows as well as the allowances for depreciation, we obtain the net material product, i.e., the *national income* as defined by Soviet economists.[4] This income equals wages and salaries plus profits and other means accruing to the state that are generated only in the sectors of material production. The flow of income from its *source* — the sphere of production — to the non-productive sphere of services is regarded as a set of transfers from primary to secondary and tertiary income receivers. Total consumption plus accumulation will, however, equal the income generated only in the sphere of material production, since purchases of consumers' goods by secondary, tertiary, etc., income receivers match outlays of primary income receivers on non-productive services, which are not accounted for in the national income totals. Total consumption equals roughly the net value of output of consumers' goods; it covers individual consumption and consumption of the armed forces as well as maintenance of non-productive capital. Accumulation includes capital formation, investment in process, addition to stocks, addition to state reserves in gold or foreign currency, and some outlays for defense. The decision about the division of income into consumption and investment is a political decision implemented by quantitative allocations of supplies and the pricing of each product.

The correlation between money flows and goods plus services in the economy as a whole is attempted through a set of balances; the balance of income and expenditures of 1] the state (budget), 2] banks (currency and credit plans), 3] enterprises (income, and

4. See *Chap. 8.*

sources and disposition of funds statements), and 4] households. The coordination and control of all money flows on current and capital account via a centralized operative financial plan have not appeared expedient in Soviet practice. The indicated financial balances are tied in specific ways to balances in kind and are kept flexible in their relation to the output plans. As we shall see later, each of these balances is constructed by different rules and each one is liable to different controls. In this situation, the state budget has been turned into the principal substitute for an over-all financial plan. The budget absorbs a large share of profits, along with revenues from sales taxes on consumers' goods and other taxes, and expends these funds for both capital investments and social overhead. If planners' expectations are fulfilled in the case of cost reduction, volume of output, and consumer demand at anticipated prices, the government receives its outlays on investment, defense, and services in the form of taxes and deductions from profits. If disequilibria arise between flow of consumers' goods and services and the monetary flows, the disturbances do not affect the initial division established by the natural balances. Equilibrium is reestablished by adjusting money flows through taxation, borrowing, price increases, monetary refunding, or some combination of these measures. Thus, the sum of retail prices is brought into line with the disposable income (minus the planned savings) of all groups of the population, including those employed in the production of capital goods and in the civil service.

Finally, a comprehensive balance of international payments is drawn up on the basis of the aggregate plan of foreign trade and of the export and import estimates of the main commodities entering foreign trade.

PLAN COORDINATION AND THE BALANCE OF THE NATIONAL ECONOMY

Soviet economists have not constructed a theory of planning that can unite all the physical balances into a single system and to fully integrate them with the financial balances. Building such a theory, a question hotly debated during the 1920's,[5] was finally circumvented by the adoption of the procedure just described, which, as we saw, implies shifting each plan from selected tasks to a

5. *See Chap. 12.*

more or less general program that tends to be inconsistent below the top priority levels. Since the balances cover the supply and allocation of a *selected* number of items and since they specify only the requirements of the *main* users, they combine ultimately into an unwieldy, overlapping system of targets and allocations built around a number of leading links selected by the policy makers. Diagrammatically, the basic balances may be broadly combined into the system of main plan indices shown in Figure 4.

Plan coordination between the *documented* plan figures (the figures that appear in the plan) and the "auxiliary" figures (data not appearing in the plan, such as the residuals between totals and the more detailed priority figures and data based on various aggregated coefficients) takes place in practice at a variety of levels and in a variety of forms. "Everybody [institution or person] who takes part in the coordination," writes the Hungarian economist J. Kornai, "is directly responsible for certain specified *variables* (documented and auxiliary plan figures) as well as for certain specified plan *equations* (also: for documented and auxiliary equations). Each of them bargains about his *own* figures and does so in such a way as to secure equality in his *own* equations. . . . When the plan coordination begins, in fact one cannot know for certain if there is a solution to this gigantic equation system or not; whether it has a single solution or several; and of course it is not proved whether this process of reconciliation converges toward some solution."

Since all indicated equations (*documented* and *auxiliary*), cannot be treated with equal priority, some plan interconnections are fully achieved in practice while others are not. At the top of the hierarchy of plan equations for which equilibrium must be reached are the product balances and the foreign-trade balances; all the other planned equations have only a secondary importance. Given this situation, J. Kornai rightly remarks: "The process actually tries to solve the immense equation system with a kind of guesswork, with repeated trials although we are well aware of the fact that equations systems with considerably fewer variables and equations cannot be solved by mere guessing."

The fact is that in practice no programming method using high-speed computers is available which could cope with such a gigantic equation system and could supersede the prevailing crude planning methods. The mathematical models now used must remain highly

FIGURE 4. *Diagram of Plan Indices in the Traditional Soviet Balance System*

		Supervisory Agencies (Addressees)					
					Trade		Other Uses (Investment & Changes in Inventories)
		1st Producer	. . .	nth Producer	Foreign	Domestic	
Product Balances							
	1st Product						
	.						
	.						
	.						
	nth Product						
Investment Balances							
	.						
	.						
	.						
Manpower Balances							
	.						
	.						
	.						
Cost and Profitability Figures							
	.						
	.						
	.						
Foreign Trade	Export Targets						
	Import Quotas						

After J. Kornai, Mathematical Planning of Structural Decisions, *Amsterdam: North Holland Publishing* Co., *1967.*

aggregated and must rest on numerous simplified assumptions. Input-output and linear programming techniques, however, provide the planners with useful tools for focusing, from a variety of angles, on the problems raised by the search for coordination in scheduled outputs and in their allocation among sectors, branches, ministries, and regions. Three basic types of input-output tabulations have been devised for planning purposes in the USSR and in various socialist economies, particularly since the beginning of the 1960's. In the first type, sectors (industry, agriculture, transport, and so on) are shown in rows, and the *administrative* authorities (ministries and other agencies) which actually handle output planning and allocation of the given resources are shown in columns. The table reflects, hence, *not* the technology employed but the actual organizational structure of the economy. In the second type of tabulation, rows show products, and columns show the specific agencies to which the products are directed. This is the traditional Soviet balance system consolidated in an orderly fashion. Finally, in the third type of tabulation, both rows and columns of the matrix are defined, as in the input-output tabulation in use in the West, by the customary criteria of industrial statistics; it hence shows interrelations between industries; e.g., machinery, textile, and others.[6] But no matter how detailed these tables become, they cannot be fully interconnected, and they cannot solve the entire system of plan equations. They remain an auxiliary tool of planning, superseding only partially the previous crude methods and only partially curing their traditional flaws.

This crude approach certainly implies that sometimes the economy will operate with larger reserves than needed, whereas, in other cases, it will run headlong into bottlenecks, which, let us not forget, do not imperil the execution of the top priorities. Soviet operational planning is molded by the interaction of two opposing forces — one at the level of the enterprise, tending to increase input requirements and inventories of raw materials in order to insure the fulfillment of output targets, and the other at the center, tending to push in the opposite direction, namely, toward the lowering of norms and the quickening of the technological pace. Since the central planners must operate with limited information about the real potentialities of the plants, their decisions are often arbitrary. Hence, in the absence of market pressures and in the framework of physical targets

6. *In 1961, the Central Statistical Administration published a matrix in value terms for the Soviet economy in 1959. The matrix comprises 73 sectors. Another matrix, in physical terms, comprised of 157 basic products, has also been constructed by the CSA but has not yet been released. Construction of larger intersector balances for 1966 were in progress in the late 1960's. The balances were said to contain approximately 110 sectors of material production, in value terms, and 247 basic products, as well as underlying balances for the union republics.*

and centralized controls, input norms will tend to be excessive in some cases and will lead to undue accumulation of inventories of raw materials and goods in process; in other cases, they may fall short of actual needs and lead to breakdowns in production, which, as a rule, are shifted toward the low-priority sectors.

In Soviet planning literature, the term *balance of the economy as a whole* is used ambiguously to designate both the idea of a consolidated balance capping all the other balances and what has become in practice a substitute for such a balance, namely, the simple presentation of various balances not directly integrated into a coherent system of social accounts. Thus, under the heading, "balance of the national economy," Soviet textbooks generally present diagrams of the balances of various product flows within the productive system and of money flows within both the productive and non-productive spheres, of the balance of manpower and of capital construction. There is no accepted system of consolidating the sector, branch, and product interconnections, the financial flows, and the changes in capital stock, although the need for such a balance has been repeatedly stressed and some precise proposals have been formulated for this purpose. One of the more debated proposals is that of the veteran Soviet planner, Academician S. G. Strumilin, who unifies into a matrix income and product by sector origin and end-uses. The rows present production (limited to material goods in accordance with the Marxian definition) and services, both by sectors of origin. The columns show first the so-called material cost of output (i.e., wear and tear of capital stock and utilization of raw materials) and the value added, followed by the end-uses of production and services for individual and collective consumption and for investment. Its principal difference from the Leontief matrix in value terms lies in the inclusion of the value of capital consumption as a production input, and the breakdown of end-uses by using sectors. The Strumilin proposal has been criticized because it does not use the indicators emerging directly from the plan itself (e.g., the planned relations between capital stock, manpower, and output) and does not reveal all the connections between allocation of physical resources and income flows. One of his critics, V. S. Novikov, would, for instance, record the indicators revealing changes in both stocks and flows in the following order:

1] Factors of production

A] Average value of capital stock
B] Average number of workers
C] Capital stock per worker

2] Gross value of output, total and per worker

3] Gross product and its end-uses.

The Soviet search, which is still going on, seeks to establish a balance encompassing a far broader macroeconomic field than that of either the physical balances or the income and related balances. As the Soviet economists put it, such a balance — a sort of yearly national balance sheet — should be consistent with the key indicators of the plan, should uncover all the concrete relations in the Soviet growth process, and should offer a truly dynamic view of each branch and of the economy as a whole. Actually, this master balance seems to elude the researchers, first, because the physical balances as they are now drawn are fully interconnected neither conceptually nor in practice and secondly, because the income and money flows are *inter alia* not clearly and specifically coordinated with the intersector outputs and distribution.

Although the underlying building blocks of the plans are distinct physical and financial balances, the published plans appear as combinations of data in both physical and monetary terms. Thus, for instance, the leading part of the national economic plan, the industrial program, consists of the following parts and data: production — gross value of total output and of commodity production as well as physical output targets for key commodities; technology — notably development of new branches and technical physical norms; labor — productivity indices, number of factory workers, average wage per worker, and total wage bill, number of white-collar and technical and engineering personnel, training of new skilled workers; costs — over-all volume of expenditures on production, cost of basic goods, targets for cost reduction; capital formation — volume and structure by sectors and branches; supply — procurement of equipment, fuels, materials; finances — income and expenditures by branches and territorial subdivisions.

Since 1929, the beginning of the all-embracing planning era, the Soviet Union has launched seven Five-Year Plans, four of which have been declared completed: the first (in four years), second, fourth, and fifth. Two plans have been discontinued: the third, interrupted by World War II, and the sixth, abandoned in 1958, followed by the first Seven-Year Plan, and then again by a Five-Year Plan, 1966–1970. The Soviet government has released an abundance of materials on the first and second Five-Year Plans, but not on the others. The data available for the latest plans give only key output targets and various growth rates by product, industries, and sectors. Release to the general public of complete data on the yearly plans was discontinued before the war.

For further examination of the problems of planning, we turn now to price formation, the role and utilization of the market mechanisms, incentives, and controls upon execution of planning goals.

3.

Pricing, Market Mechanisms, Controls

PLANNING AND PRICES

As we have seen in the preceding chapter, Soviet planning is founded on the transformation into quantitative physical balances of the policy makers' decisions relating to key outputs and growth. It is from these balances that the financial balances must be derived. The physical balances, however, are not exclusively engineering constructs created solely from technological materials. In certain respects, their formulation is dependent on economic calculations, i.e., on cost and price considerations. Prices thus influence the "physical" shape of the plan, although price considerations are never viewed as a determinant of this shape; yet even though the planner operates first and foremost with physical balances, prices are of crucial importance to producers' and consumers' goods alike for reasons which we are about to examine. Let us give brief consideration to the criteria by which prices are fixed in the Soviet economy. The Marxian definitions to which we now refer concern the capitalist system and as such are not fully applicable to the Soviet setting. They do, however, throw light on the Soviet approaches to value and pricing.

Marx affirms that *value* is directly proportional to the quantity of socially necessary labor expended to produce a given good. Thus, the relation between quantity of socially necessary labor plotted on an abscissa and value magnitude plotted along the ordinate is expressed by a perfectly straight line through the origin: total value grows proportionately to total supply, without any suggestion of decreasing marginal utilities as supply grows. Secondly, although prices, i.e., exchange ratios, may and do diverge under capitalist practice from values because of monopoly distortions, for instance, a "law of value" is deemed to operate throughout the capitalist economy in the sense that it *tends* to bring price relations into line with underlying value relations. Marx neglected, however, to formulate any specific rules as to the "deviations" of prices from values or as to the exact ranges in which the "law" operates to bring exchange ratios and value relations into line with each other. In his theoretical constructs, including his famous schema of reproduction, i.e., his growth model (to which we turn later), Marx completely disregards the problem of the transition from value (as defined) to price, since, for him, exchange value is merely the form behind which value hides itself and since he considers the forces set in motion by the capitalists as being unchanged whether the system be one of value calculation or of price calculation.[1] Thirdly, in the framework of the labor theory of value, since only labor is viewed as productive, one cannot speak of returns for the services of either capital or land. Further, the theory disregards the impact of demand except within specific limits and conditions,[2] and rejects the whole of the marginal calculus — i.e., the application of the theory of limits to value, supply and demand, etc. During the last century, non-Marxian economists have developed refined tools of the theory of pricing and of general equilibrium, whereas Soviet economists have approached the crucial problem of practical price fixing with the simple but blunted apparatus of the labor theory of value, to which various props have had to be added in day-to-day practice. Let us now examine some of the consequences of this fact.

Soviet wholesale prices are now based on industrial branch average *costs of current inputs* (i.e., depreciation, materials, and labor) *plus* a rate of return to *capital in use* (i.e., to both fixed assets and

1. *For a detailed discussion of this crucial point, see Paul M. Sweezy,* The Theory of Capitalist Development, Principles of Marxian Political Economy *(New York: Oxford University Press, 1942), "The Relation of the Quantitative to the Qualitative in Value Theory," pp. 32ff., and "The Significance of Price Calculation," pp. 125ff.*

2. *In his price theory, Marx treats casually the question of consumers' wants. For him wants condition only in part effective demand; the latter is determined primarily by income distribution and by society's technical and organizational development. Hence Marx affirms that "absolutely nothing can be explained by the relation of supply and demand unless the basis has first been ascertained on which this relation rests." Demand acquires a special significance only in the formation of "monopoly price." The monopolist's control over supply enables him to take advantage of "the eagerness of purchasers to buy and of their solvency"; monopoly price is thus rendered independent of the "value" of the product, alleged to be determined by the costs of production. (See Sweezy,* op. cit., *pp. 49ff.)*

circulating capital). Up to the mid-1960's, profitability was computed only in relation to current inputs, the idea of a return to capital being rejected as un-Marxian. Since then, however, certain intangible "opportunity costs" have been proclaimed as entering into the "socially necessary outlays" of production. The wholesale prices are centrally determined by price committees under the State Planning Committee of the USSR and of the republics and by the ministries. These prices are in principle submitted to periodic reviews in order to take account of changes in cost, product-quality, and technological progress. Actually, massive price reviews have taken place at long intervals only and have proven laborious in both formulation and implementation. After a comprehensive price reform in 1967, the rate of return on productive assets, which was designed to carry out the key division of the national product into consumption and investment and to ensure that each industrial branch could be run at a profit, was set at roughly 15 per cent for industry as a whole — 10–15 per cent for heavy industry and 30–35 per cent for most light industry, with wide variations within the branches of each. These rates of return do not, of course, demonstrate whether resources allocated to and within these branches have been efficient. (If anything, they may eventually reinforce the tendency of *using* capital, since a rate of return on any asset can be put into the profit rate — unless, of course, the enterprise is charged a rate as high as the allowable rate of return for the use of capital.)[3] In Soviet price planning, the set profit rates serve to ensure the profitability of *an industry* rather than that of all the *enterprises* within each industry. Within each branch, cost may vary substantially from one group of enterprises to another, and hence variations in profitability may be high. Actual profits are, up to a point, an index of the efficiency with which an enterprise is run, a source for the formation of certain incentive funds for the enterprise, and an instrument aiming at securing certain planned sector relationships (e.g., between industry and agriculture). However, the wholesale prices, determined on the basis of the previously indicated principles, of past and long-time distorted cost relationships, of past depreciation allowances, and of newly established

3. *As we shall see later, most of the enterprises must pay to the budget a "rental" for fixed assets and interest to the bank for part of the working capital.*

profit markups (not always consistently determined),[4] form in many respects an unwieldy structure. This structure, in principle, is correctible periodically by ministries and price committees on the basis of experience, improvement in management, and the action of supply and demand.

The function of producers' and consumers' prices is viewed as being, up to a point, qualitatively different. Policy makers and planners indeed regard producers' prices primarily as accounting devices and as message carriers to designers and operative managers; they see consumers' prices primarily as distributive devices intended to equate the volume of goods produced to the income distributed. As messengers, producers' prices may be adjusted so as to limit the use of given raw materials, encourage the use of substitutes, induce the spreading of given technological innovations, discourage or stimulate given outputs, or divert resources toward given industrial branches. Prices are thus to reinforce the provisions implicit in the physical balances and in the technical norms with respect to factor inputs and output mixes. In this way the policy makers try to confine the decisions of operative managers to narrow fields. Consum-

4. *Discussing the massive introduction of new wholesale prices in January–July, 1967, the chairman of the State Committee on Prices of the USSR State Planning Committee has pointed out that since prices of products are fixed uniformly for an industry, variations in profitability between enterprises cannot be eliminated "just by changing the technique of pricing." In some branches different internal accounting prices are used. Coal prices, for instance, are based on average production conditions in each coal basin; each basin may hence retain mines operating at a loss. In the oil and gas industry, prices are based on the exploitation of marginal deposits; rent will hence be paid to the budget for the exploitation of the better-than-marginal deposits. In the processing industries, special financial measures must be employed; fixed charges must be placed on enterprises with high rates of profitability — particularly in light industry where under the 1967 prices profit fluctuations continue to remain the highest. Further, whereas the profitability of an industry or enterprise may be determined on the basis of its use of productive capital, this approach fails in the case of each product. The profitability of each item is accordingly correlated with the average production cost and the uniform profitability rate. But even these principles cannot be applied consistently when outlays fluctuate significantly because of subcontractual work, for instance. In various cases, particularly in the light industries, where production costs are closely dependent on the cost of raw materials, the so-called processing cost is used as the basis for calculating profitability; it aims at discouraging enterprises from using "needlessly expensive raw materials." Further price differentials are established for machinery, for instance, by taking into account various technical indicators concerning precision, length of services between repairs, and other factors.* Ekonomicheskaia gazeta, No. 25 *(June 1967), pp. 10–11.*

ers' prices are fixed so as to achieve the crucial goals of striking a balance between effective demand and volume of goods in retail trade and between over-all scheduled savings and scheduled non-consumption expenditures. Although the central authorities rely primarily on a system of direct allocations of scarce non-labor resources, using producers' prices for accounting devices and as technological messengers, in the sphere of distribution of consumers' goods they rely on the consumer's liberty of choice. Even in a command economy, this liberty, though basically divorced from the right to decide on the kinds of output desired ("consumer sovereignty"), still appears to be the best way for implementing the plan, avoiding high distribution costs, and maximizing satisfactions within the limits of the volume of goods set aside for consumption. Though the Soviet economists state that the consumers' prices "equilibrate supply and demand," they are *not* equilibrium prices in the usual sense of the term. Indeed — except for the prices of the goods sold in the collective farm markets — these prices are not a result of market-determined supply-and-demand relationships, but a consequence of administrative decisions concerning the over-all volume of goods in retail trade and the purchasing power released. Most consumers' goods (and only a few producers' goods) carry a heavy tax burden over and above their cost plus profit markup. According to official Soviet data, the price patterns of capital goods and retail goods of popular consumption diverged as follows in the mid-1960's: prime costs accounted roughly for 81 per cent of the price of capital goods (as opposed to some 68 per cent for consumers' goods); profit and distribution markup amounted to 12 per cent on capital goods and 7 per cent on the retail goods; and sales taxes ("turnover tax") constituted 7 and 25 per cent, respectively. Tax plus profits — i.e., in the absence of property income, the difference between cost and price earmarked for savings — weighs heavily on consumers' goods. The turnover tax rests entirely on these (with only two minor exceptions) and for some key commodities reaches levels as high as, or higher than, 100 per cent of cost. In fact, some 15 to 20 groups of consumers' goods (grains, fibers, wines, fats, and meats) account for not less than 85 per cent of the total turnover tax. Soviet economists assert that the distinction between profits of enterprises and turnover tax (a tax actually included only once in price) is only a matter of expediency; both aim at placing savings at the disposal of the state. Profits are destined to remain, in part, in the hands of the (state) enterprises, whereas the turnover tax is to be entirely absorbed by the budget. Later, we shall give more detailed consideration to these problems, which have numerous implications. For the present, let us note that, since the planners want to make the sum of the prices of consumers' goods approximately equal to the purchasing power released, retail prices move with changes in the prices of producers' goods only to the extent that the costs of these goods would be changed.

Numerous types of prices are used in the Soviet Union. The prices at which the plans and projects are established are planning prices, i.e., planned average cost plus planned profit for each industrial branch. The planners and project makers may also take into account various "shadow prices," such as recoupment periods or coefficients of scarcity of various goods. Finally, the planners may use "unchangeable" prices and price indices for determining long trends, for aggregating or comparing various outputs, etc.

The planned prices may or may not diverge from the actual delivery prices of one industrial branch to another (the so-called wholesale price of the *enterprise*) [5] or from the "commodity" price (the wholesale price of the *industry*),[6] which is charged for deliveries to the retail network and to the collective farms. The wholesale prices are based on the industrial branch average cost plus average profit; the latter prices include the turnover tax over and above these items. Within industrial branches, accounting prices [7] at which goods are transferred to the branch may in their turn be differentiated as between enterprises.

In certain cases, the prices of specific producers' goods may not include profits, whereas certain new products may temporarily be priced below cost. Certain consumers' goods such as children's school uniforms may also be priced below cost. For almost all producers' goods and for some consumers' goods, a single set of prices prevails for the country as a whole. For most consumers' goods and for construction materials, prices are differentiated by zones.

In the case of agricultural produce, the following main categories of prices prevail, with zonal differentiations: prices at which the state farms deliver[8] to the state marketing organizations, prices, in theory comparable to the wholesale price of the enterprise; pro-

5. Optovye tseny predpriiatia.
6. Optovye tseny promyshlennosti.
7. Raschetnye tseny.
8. Sdatoch nye tseny.

curement prices[9] now higher than the state farm delivery prices — at which the collective farms make obligatory deliveries to the state; prices for voluntary deliveries above plan, which include a premium over the obligatory delivery prices; prices at which the marketing organizations transfer these products to industrial branches for further processing; prices at which retail deliveries are made to the retail network, which are gross of the turnover tax; and finally, the prices secured by collective farmers through sale to consumers, which are determined by supply and demand.

Thus, in the Soviet economy, prices are manipulated to conform to specific tasks; hence, we see not only a basic dichotomy between producers' and consumers' goods — the first free of the turnover tax, the latter burdened by it — but also significant variations within each group, though as a rule, prices tend to be based (since the mid-1960's) on variable costs plus a rate of return on capital in use. But distortions are in fact innumerable since they may occur for many reasons, ranging from encouraging the spread of the latest technology to keeping inefficient plants in production.

It is noteworthy that currently Soviet economists are divided about the basic dichotomy between producers' and consumers' goods prices. One school would like to continue the prevailing system, since it considers the system adequate for the goal of industrialization. Other schools would like to capture savings as either turnover tax or industry profits by pricing both producers' and consumers' goods in such a way that each price would be easily defined in terms of its components and would have a precise meaning for planners, project makers, managers, and consumers. The problems involved are quite numerous and will be examined later, in Chapter 13.

WAGE BILL AND WAGE DIFFERENTIALS

The wage scale is a key determinant both of income distribution — specifically of labor's share, including personal and social wages, in national income — and of the price structure, no matter how much each kind of price may afterwards be manipulated. Soviet wages are broadly differentiated in relation to scarcity and efficiency of labor, though other elements may be called into play in order to cope with exceptional difficulties, to break important bottlenecks in labor supply, etc. Labor is, however, free, in the sense

9. Zakupochnye tseny.

that people generally can work or not at the wage offered by the (operative) management. But labor does not have the right to enforce changes in wages through collective action; strikes are completely banned.[10] As we already know, the planner's basic objective is utilization of all available resources, which, in the case of labor, is to achieve full employment. But this objective may be pursued with various degrees of intensity in the economy as a whole as well as within each particular branch. While intensively developing certain techniques and processes within the key branches, the Soviets may rely, even within these branches, on less capital-intensive methods and may resort to far less intensive methods in certain low-priority branches, such as agriculture. The pattern of investment decided upon by the policy makers and planners, the employment and output targets within this framework, labor productivity, and labor market conditions will thus interact in various ways on the stated general objective of "full employment."

From the very beginning of the all-embracing planning era, wage differentials were established between skills, branches and regions in order to deploy labor according to planned output requirements and provide strong incentives for better work through increased skills and training. The rewards for skills were scheduled to make earnings represent fixed multiples of the basic wage of the unskilled laborer: the more important the skill, the higher the multiple. Emphasis on certain branches of heavy industry led to differentials that favored workers in mining, oil extraction, metallurgy, and machine construction. Emphasis on given regional projects gave rise to differentials in favor of the employed in "leading" areas, which were often remote, sparsely populated regions in the process of development. Additional social benefits and allocations of consumers' goods and housing were to reinforce these basic differentials.

The need to spur rapid increases of productivity in each trade led, however, to the interlacing of this primary wage pattern with a second system of incentives based on piecework. The pressure for rapid gains in productivity also led to the launching of various movements of "shock" workers, or *Stakhanovites* as they were

10. *Since the Soviet state is not only the "employer" but also the executive and legislative power and since classes are supposed to be abolished, any serious labor conflict in the USSR has been viewed as containing an element of revolt which cannot be tolerated. Given the specific position of the Soviet enterprise, the criminal law rather than the civil law or disciplinary statutes holds sway.*

called,[11] whose aim was to break the prevailing piecework norms. But under the new system, a semiskilled worker in any branch with low work norms soon earned more than a skilled worker in another. As more and more workers switched to either straight or progressive piece-rate pay (under which payment per unit increases at an accelerated pace once a given level of output is attained), the policy aims embodied in the primary wage system were thwarted. To add to the confusion, operating managers competing for given kinds of labor started to manipulate either grades or labor norms in various ways within the framework of their defined wage bills. Finally, incentive patterns and payments systems were mixed in various doses into each of the Soviet enterprises.

To establish new ways of centralized control over the wage bill and its distribution within each plant, a vast reorganization of the wage system has been in progress since the mid-1950's. The reorganization aims to establish more clearly defined work norms in industry as a whole and to stress *time* payments rather than *piecework* payments as the most appropriate system of pay. Although this reorganization tends to clear away the incredible silt accumulated throughout the all-embracing planning period in the officially established wage structure and to reassert the current planners' preferences, the new structure is unavoidably distorted by the interaction between the relatively inelastic demand of operative managers for certain kinds of skilled labor and the specific underlying conditions of labor supply and workers' preferences in each given area. As long as the system relies essentially on the labor market, market forces will assert themselves and "correct" any miscalculation by the planners about the wage rates needed to ensure allocation of labor among jobs in order to "reach and surpass" the output targets fixed by the plan itself.

Even though Soviet planners and policy makers rely primarily on the market mechanism, they have also resorted to a variety of administrative measures in order to ensure certain objectives in the recruitment of labor. The authorities have seriously restricted the mobility of labor; they have resorted to various schemes of recruitment and of transfer of people on a large scale and have indulged in compulsory assignment to jobs. Such practices are much more limited now than in the past; they are chiefly confined to mass

11. *This movement took its name from Alexander Stakhanov, a famous shock worker of the 1930's.*

mobilizations of non-skilled labor especially for launching the development of new areas. Except for such areas, compulsion and forced transfer are no longer viewed as instruments for allocating semiskilled or skilled labor among enterprises or branches of the economy.

Because utilization of the *mass* of labor is dominated by planners' (rather than consumers') decisions, because officially the emphasis is placed on productivity increases in each particular trade, and because there are apparent discrepancies in rewards as between related skills in different branches, a British economist, Peter Wiles, has suggested that there is no "rationality" whatever in the Soviet wage system. Wiles makes his argument hinge on the contention that the inequality of Soviet wages does not in any way reflect "the relative usefulness of the different products produced by workers in different trades." To this, another British economist, Mrs. Joan Robinson, has rightly retorted that in no industrial society are wages paid according to marginal social productivities, but that, given labor mobility, in the long run "the level of wages in any one line is determined by the level of wages in the economy as a whole." Reliance on the market mechanism for the supply of labor implies that in the Soviet Union also the level of wages in any one branch tends to be broadly determined by the level of wages in the economy as a whole; any central miscalculations as to wage rates and available labor supply are in practice corrected overtly or covertly in the implementation of the plan by the operative managers who are pressed by output targets and faced with the prospect of a high labor turnover due to poor pay.

The absence of complete wage statistics hampers detailed analysis of wage differences in the Soviet Union, but the available data point clearly toward an even broader wage dispersion in the USSR than in the West. Data on wages in the Soviet steel industry, which have been analyzed by Professor Gardner Clark, indicate that in this industry, with 10 rates on the wage scale for production workers in 1960, the ratio between the lowest and the highest rate was 1:3 as against 1:2 in a 31-grade structure in the United States. The higher Soviet dispersion illustrates, as H. M. Douty of the U.S. Bureau of Labor Statistics suggests, the impact of differences in stages of economic development and in labor market conditions, as well as differences in methods of wage payment. Douty underlines that even in the American South "the supply of workers at different levels of education and skill, as compared with the rest of the country, makes for a pattern of substantially wider differentials." Similarly, the market mechanism also operates within the indicated framework in the Soviet Union and affects the very foundation of the whole price structure.

CAPITAL BUDGET AND OPERATING DECISIONS

Aggregative decisions about allocation of resources have to be implemented in detail. Numerous alternatives confront, however, planners and policy makers who must formalize decisions for action. Choices must be made among competing industrial branches (coal versus oil, for instance), alternative processes (capital- or labor-intensive), present and postponable outlays, etc. In turn, the choices among these alternatives, as suggested by the project-making offices of the ministries and administrations, will influence planners and policy makers in their final choices of capital expenditures, though the projects will not set the ceiling for total investment, since that depends on what is considered politically feasible.

Although the theoretical solution to the "efficiency" — or productivity — of investments is, up to a point, complicated by a doctrinaire reluctance to recognize that capital is productive, and although special practical difficulties are added by the prevailing distortions in pricing and in costing, top management, like the project makers, engineers, and operative managers who have the task of preparing the projects, needs some objective standards of measuring the economic effectiveness of each investment proposal. The crux of the matter is the choice of an adequate yardstick. This is by no means simple. Soviet managers, like capitalist entrepreneurs, are plagued by the economics of capital budgeting: failure to measure the worth of each proposal, lack of adequate standards, and reliance on intuition, which often turns out to be a disregard for alternatives, are shortcomings that collectivist managers share with their counterparts in other systems.

After many years of soul searching, the Soviets have placed the stamp of official approval on two well-known types of indicators: the output to capital coefficient and the payoff period. The first concerns the relations between changes in output and capital investment. (Indicators of this type are rough guides for investment planning, particularly for the choice among branches of industry for the fulfillment of a given task – as, for example, a decision to increase fuel output by expanding either coal or oil production). The second indicator – the payoff period – is the number of years needed to recoup an original investment outlay. The form of the payoff depends on how both the initial investment and the revenues that "pay it back" are defined; its application consists then in making a choice among production alternatives. As defined in the Soviet Union by official "Recommendations" released in May, 1958, pairs of processes are to be evaluated by contrasting their respective operating expenses and capital outlays and by comparing the result with some given norm. Let K_1 and K_2 be the capital outlays, C_1 and C_2 the operating expenses, T the payoff period needed by the more expensive proposal of the pair to pay out, through savings in yearly operating expenses, the additional investment outlays it requires, and T_s the norm or standard payoff period. Then with $(K_1 - K_2)/(C_2 - C_1) = T$, if $T < T_s$, preference will be given to the expensive alternative; if $T > T_s$, to the cheaper one.[12] In practice, the reciprocal of the payoff period $(1/T)$ is the estimate of the proposal's rate of return; the Russians call it *coefficient of relative effectiveness* (CRE). If capital expenditures for the mutually exclusive alternatives are to be made at different periods, it has been suggested that the normative CRE might be used as a discounting factor; i.e., investment outlays at future dates can be discounted to the present by multiplying them by $1/(1 + \text{CRE})^t$.

Since the mid-1960's the USSR and various socialist countries have used widely an indicator of economic efficiency, e, equal to $Y/iI + C$. Y is the expected net yearly income of the new plant (calculated in certain countries at world market prices); i is the rate of return or "interest" on capital (expressed as a decimal frac-

12. *The following example – given by T. S. Khachaturov and quoted by Holland Hunter, "The Planning of Investments in the Soviet Union,"* The Review of Economics and Statistics, XXXI (1949), 55 – *illustrates the application of the formula. Let the capital investment* (K_1) *for constructing an electrified railroad be 90 billion rubles and the capital investment required for building the same line to operate with steam traction amount to 70 billion* (K_2). *The necessary operating expenses per year amount to 2.5* (C_1), *and 5.0 billion rubles* (C_2) *respectively. According to the formula* $[(90 - 70)/(5 - 2.5) = 8]$, *it would take eight years for the expensive alternative (the electrified railroad) to pay off the additional investment funds it requires. If this period is shorter than the norm* (T_s), *the electrified railroad will be constructed; if longer, the line will be operated by steam traction.*

tion); I is total investment (including working capital); and C is operating cost (including depreciation). An investment is considered favorable when $e > 1$ and unfavorable when $e < 1$.

Though these "coefficients" or "indicators" are carefully distinguished by Soviet economists, they are closely related. All concern an estimate of the investment's rate of return. The periods during which investments could be "recouped" under the form of output increases varied in 1958 from 16 to 17 years in the power industry, 10 years in transport, and 4 to 5 years in machine building and light industry. But it is extremely doubtful that these recoupment periods or their reciprocals (CRE) are very meaningful. The underlying prices are distorted by different rates of subsidies or taxes. Further, there is a lag between the period when investment takes place and when its effect (the product increase) occurs; often, the impact of capital investments in adjacent industries and other factors need to be taken into account. CRE's validity is equally in doubt, since the related computations are vitiated by price distortions and other factors. Soviet planning not only gives preference to certain branches in terms of investment, but within these branches, it gives preference to capital-intensive processes. Hence, for planning capital investments, the permissible CRE's are quite low for the priority branches and industries and high for the others (hence such branches as metallurgy, power and related industries, chemical, and petroleum industries have low normative CRE). The indicated coefficients take on one of the key roles played by interest rates in the West, namely, that of a screening device or a means of rationing investment funds. The official recognition of the need for such a device implies that the planners are forced to take into account both the services of nonlabor factors and, within each industry at least, the opportunity cost of investment outlays. It is clear that the opportunity cost does have a function in the allocation of resources within each branch — otherwise the CRE's would tend to be the same for all industries. It should be noted, moreover, that the design makers are warned that numerous elements other than the coefficients must be taken into account in formulating their proposals. These include the physical balances built around the basic priority output and investment choices, the need for "accelerating" the fulfillment of priority outputs, the existence of well-known supply shortages, the evaluation of the possible impacts of the introduction of new techniques into related branches, and a host of other elements. Consequently, in the end, the practical significance of the coefficients can scarcely be ascertained.

PLAN IMPLEMENTATION CONTROLS

After the approval of the plan, the appropriate economic organizations start combining the factors of production according to the planned schedules of their respective economic programs. Enterprises are provided with equipment and with working capital funds according to the plan; state farms are endowed with land and machines; credits are distributed throughout the economy according to the plan without the banks' taking into account possible returns of capital from other uses. Checking the performance seems simple: the assigned input norms, output targets, and weighted average cost of an industry should serve both as commands and as checking standards for managerial performance. In practice, a vast network of controls, reports, inspections, and cross checks is unavoidable in the implementation of the Soviet plans, because of the numerous and often contradictory instructions concerning the various operations of a plant — namely, two or three different indices for possible relation of inputs to outputs — and because of the lack of financial incentives attached to certain performances, and their importance in respect to other key indicators.

Furthermore, neither the accounting in kind nor the financial figures are readily usable in all circumstances. Accounting in kind is perforce restricted to a limited number of quantitative figures and is but a crude measure of a plant's performance when shifts in the output of amalgamated commodity groups are to be considered. This fact tends to enhance the importance of the monetary indicators and financial controls. Production values can, however, vary to a great extent according to the product mix. On the other hand, the financial controls, especially banking controls, are not very effective: they are pliable according to the degree of fulfillment both of the quantitative and qualitative aspects of the plan. Controls tend hence to be elaborate, since they imply the checking of each basic aspect of the activity of each enterprise. Controls involve, further, revisions of errors, shifting of certain targets, and breaking of impending bottlenecks. Although each plan is still handed down as a "law," in practice it is subjected during its implementation to numerous and often major adjustments. Thus, should any new important economic or political decisions be taken, the plans may be radically changed or simply discontinued. Within the span of a perspective plan — up to now at least, rigidly determined — pressures for upward revisions of various targets and continuous campaigns initiated by central authority usually lead to a zig-zag course of development, marked by sudden outbursts and irregular changes, which push the economy in various directions.

Notwithstanding the extensiveness of control mechanisms, numerous managerial practices, conditioned by conflicting pressures (for example, fulfill output but reduce cost), tend, as we shall see in detail in the next chapter, to divert to other channels the planned allocation of rationed raw materials, inflate the actual wage bill, distort the reports on the performance, and thwart the central decisions.

CONCLUDING COMMENTS

The basic economic problems — what to produce, in what ways, and for whom — that are solved through the operation of the market in capitalist economies, are solved through a combination of positive commands and market mechanisms in the Soviet economy. The Soviet approach to short-term (output) and long-term (expansion) planning is predominantly technical. It implies

1] Direct determination by the policy makers of both final outputs and some key intermediate products in physical terms

2] Quantitative exploration of the production functions and gradation of technical efficiency of the available plants

3] Direct allocation of scarce resources in relation to the selected output and expansion targets

4] Reliance on a whole set of commands concerning investment, outputs, procurement, wage levels, and use of variously adjusted prices in order to reinforce the physical technical provisions of the plan

5] Utilization of market mechanisms for deploying labor according to the plan and for the distribution of consumers' goods

6] Loose coordination between the set of physical balances concerning a variety of products and the monetary balances concerning certain macroeconomic magnitudes, such as investment and the income and expenditures of the population.

The emphasis on physical planning, on direct allocation of scarce supplies, and on a significant number of directives for both inputs and outputs should not, however, be taken to imply that planning of the Soviet type has no room for flexibility and offers no possibilities for large decentralization. Although planning in physical terms and formulation of key directives in quantitative terms are viewed as the *sine qua non* of planning of this type — since they guarantee that the decisions in respect to both basic division of national product and its allocation will be carried out — the extent of such physical planning, the range of direct allocations, and the scope of commands with respect to inputs and outputs should not be deemed fixed for all time. In the case of output, wide variations in both the volume and nature of direct allocations and of commands are possible and quite probable.

In practice, during each planning period, the Soviet plan aims at imposing a small number of selected tasks and not at drawing up, or carrying out, a necessarily fully consistent program. The Soviet strategy of development, which determines the size and pattern of investment and selection and ranking of objectives by policy makers, postulates a faster rate of development for industry than for agriculture, a faster rate for heavy industry than for light industry, and the fastest rates for machine tools and some key industries of the heavy industrial sector. The strategy has been followed inflexibly throughout the planning era, with shifts of emphasis among branches within the heavy industrial sector. Soviet prices of producers' or consumers' goods influence in only a limited way the drafting of the operational plans, the construction of specific physical balances, the choice among competing industrial branches, and the implementation and control of the plan. The sweeping price reform of 1967 does, however, pave the way in the Soviet economy for an increasingly significant role for *value* planning rather than for *quantity* fixation.

From an engineering point of view, a plan built around some "leading links" on the basis of technical data may be realistic, i.e., feasible as to targets selected and to means provided for their execution. The Soviet plans are realistic in this sense, though they exhibit glaring shortcomings — due *inter alia* to the poor quality of the information on which they are built, loose coordination among product balances, arbitrary adjustment of each of these balances (via random "pressures" on both the procurement and allocation end of each balance), faulty coordination between physical and monetary balances, conflicting impacts on operative management of instruction and incentives as to input and output mixes, etc. Later, in Chapter 8, we shall discuss in detail some problems posed by these shortcomings.

Although the plans are not optimal — i.e., certain outputs could be increased without diminishing other outputs — it should be noted that the plan, such as it is, does achieve its basic aim, namely, mobilizing the economy toward the fulfillment of the small number of tasks selected by the policy makers. Even in this respect, however, significant technical improvements are possible in the quality of the underlying data and their processing, the coordination among physical balances on the one hand and monetary balances on the other, the drafting of the plan, and the checking of its implementation. Broad utilization of input-output matrices for interbranch balance of production and for regional planning, wide application of linear programming for solving specific production and distribution tasks within the plant or a larger unit, and simplication of price-fixing rules and procedures may eventually eliminate many crudities of current Soviet planning. The State Planning Committee is experimenting with various interbranch balances of production and allocation. Operational input-output matrices are being drawn at the branch, sectoral, and regional levels in order to establish a foundation for the construction of balances in regional arrays for the elaboration of the national plan. The use of linear programming for tackling particular problems relating to choices and combination of processes is envisaged in various branches. Simplification and clarity in underlying methods of price formation make it now easier to ascertain the choices made in terms of these prices at all operative levels. Finally, even the basic emphasis postulated by the Soviet strategy of economic development may be attenuated — and hence the sacrificing of the low-priority branches may be avoided — as higher and higher output levels are reached in the key heavy industrial branches.

Notwithstanding all these important improvements which may reshape both the operational and the expansion plan, no optimum allocation is possible on a narrow technical-engineering base. Under a planned economy, as under a free economy, efficient allocation requires that factors which by definition are scarce be used in such fashion that maximum output is created with least expenditure of effort and resources and that, furthermore, the most urgent economic wants be satisfied first. The Soviet prices, even after the sweeping price reform of 1967, are not scarcity prices, prices which equate supply and demand; the planners cannot thus rely entirely on these prices to allocate scarce resources to achieve their goals. They are not "rational" prices in the usual sense in which the economist uses the term. But, as redefined, the interindustry prices do perform a number of other functions better than before: they allow a more effective control of certain managerial actions (concerning input and output mixes), provide for more appropriate uses of resources, and allow for a better evaluation of plan performance.

Part II

Sectoral Management and Planning

INTRODUCTION TO PART II

This part is concerned with the organizational principles and the operation of the component units of the main production sectors and of the distribution system and the ways in which their specific plans are connected to the national plan. Soviet industrial or commercial enterprises operate as autonomous units: they have certain obligations; they must normally balance their current accounts; and they must strive to achieve profits within the restraints set by the plan. But their autonomy resembles that of the technical divisions of large corporations: each technical unit operates within a centrally established framework, draws up its own profit and loss statement, and then routes it to the central office of its respective complex. The unit moreover, has a whole set of vertical connections from which it receives operative instructions and to which it must submit its accounts — these are not only the regional council or the local soviet, but also the State Bank and various state committees. On the other hand, the firm itself signs various contracts which set out its obligations concerning inputs, outputs, and their distribution in specific terms.

The following chapters consider, first, the connections between the national plan and a hierarchy of plans. These plans consist of the programs drawn up for varied time spans and for each type of activity within the enterprise, branch, region, or republic. Secondly, the section examines the role and limitations of the principle of the business accounting of each unit. The discussion indicates how the particular plans are drawn up and fitted into the existing and contemplated programs, how and why they differ in the spheres of industry, agriculture, and distribution, and finally how and to what extent central controls are respected or thwarted.

The state and cooperative enterprises, as well as the state or collective farms, are examined from the organizational point of view, with particular emphasis on scale, location, and operational regulations. The relations of industrial firms to output and capital construction plans are examined both with respect to allocation of supplies and control of production functions and with respect to cost and pricing policies. Since neither cooperative nor collective units participate in the system of centralized allocation of capital goods and raw materials and since their technical coefficients are not centrally determined, their connection to the plan is considered only in relation to output goals on the one hand and to costing and pricing on the other.

Operation and activity of the distribution system are examined here with respect to both domestic and foreign trade but only in connection with the output plan. The relation of foreign trade to international division of labor and to the problem of profitability of foreign trade transactions will be dealt with in Part V.

This part concludes (Chapter 7) with a discussion of the structure and organization of the Soviet labor force, the conflicting standards set up for operative managers, and the impact of various constraints on labor-management relations. This discussion furnishes some additional elements necessary for understanding the problems that arise during the implementation of the plan.

4.

Industry

FIRM'S TYPE, SIZE, LOCATION

Just as Soviet planning has a dual nature in which centralized decisions coexist with decentralized choices, so the organization of industry is the meeting ground of two conflicting tendencies. One pushes toward top-level centralization of decisions concerning investment and technological change as well as main aspects of current output; the other pulls toward decentralization in varying proportions at each level of the industrial structure. These tendencies have led to various shifts in the frontier between executive and operative management and in the over-all administrative setup of Soviet industry.

The state industry consists, as we have seen, of All-Union, republic, and local industries classified within these three groups according to size, economic importance, sources of supply, utilization of output, and the *supervisory agency* of their system. The basic unit of the industrial pyramid is the enterprise,[1] which may have one or a number of plants and may be vertically amalgamated into combines or horizontally into trusts. The enterprise is autonomous in the strict sense of the word in that it is deemed responsible for fulfilling the obligations of its contracts. But it does not determine either the rules of its operation or the scope of its activity. In this wider sense the enterprise is just a division of a higher managing institution (viz: a union ministry, a union-republic ministry, or any agency established by them). Many executive managerial functions are, in effect, discharged for All-Union industries by the All-Union industrial ministries, for republic industries by republic ministries and administrations, and for local industries by the appropriate mu-

1. *The Russian term is* predpriiatie.

nicipal authorities. Only a few executive managerial functions are discharged by the directors appointed by these authorities. Hence the Soviet literature somewhat inaccurately designates the enterprise as an autonomous *firm*.

The size of the enterprise is determined by a combination of centralized decisions and technical considerations. According to a Soviet textbook, expansion, integration, and combination among firms are determined principally by the need to balance the output and supply of branches and regions, to economize social labor, and to cut cost and transportation requirements. The emphasis on large- rather than small-scale production has, however, been systematic throughout the planning era even when performance of large-scale production appeared disadvantageous from the point of view of production technology or of prevailing consumers' demand. Industrial concentration is apparently now higher in the Soviet Union than anywhere else.[2] In the mid-1960's, for instance, there were hardly any small-scale industries operating in the form of *independent* enterprises. But as the Soviet economist Ya. Kvasha has pointed out, small-scale production has simply been absorbed into large industrial complexes or into institutions, where it subsists under the form of auxiliary, secondary, or collateral production not placed on a separate accounting footing. For instance, the apprehension of not receiving the planned machine spare parts or materials on time had made the large enterprises absorb or establish small-scale subsidiary and auxiliary production lines. However, the realization that the large enterprises must be freed from manufacturing their own spare parts, the desire to serve the consumer

2. *The distribution by size of Soviet industrial enterprises was, according to a Soviet source, as follows in the early 1960's:*

	Percentages of	
	Enterprises	Gainfully Employed
Total	100	100
up to 100 gainfully employed	29.8	2.7
101– 500	45.8	19.8
501–1000	12.7	15.7
over 1000	11.7	61.8
Total number in 1,000	41.2	23,302

SOURCE: Ya. Kvasha, *Vaprosy ekonomiki*, No. 15 (May, 1967).

more directly and promptly, and the more systematic application of linear programming to problems of efficiency and transportation may lead, in the not-too-distant future, to more meaningful solutions to these problems.

The Soviet system solves the question of location by taking into account a host of assorted considerations ranging from availability of raw materials and fuels and the regional utilization of the scheduled output, to industrialization of retarded areas, defense interests, and cooperation with the other socialist countries. In the past, the goal of industrializing retarded areas received top priority and was interpreted as implying the construction of a "heavy industrial base" in each and every national republic. Differences in endowment of factors have, however, asserted themselves so that disparities in the level of development between republics continue to be enormous.

Although Soviet planners still insist on the need of industrializing each republic, official awareness of differences in natural resources and of the need to develop the regional division of labor have finally led to the establishment of the following practical rules concerning the location of plants: Ferrous metallurgy is to be established close to sources of raw materials and fuels; heavy machinery close to metallurgy, but other machinery close to the places of distribution of output; food processing and light industries of all types are to be established in each republic, region, and locality, but key light industries are preferably to be built close to appropriate raw materials. Thus, in the location of industry too, technical engineering rules as well as political considerations are called upon to provide some guidance since the blunted pricing system is hardly adequate for this task.

BUSINESS ACCOUNTING

The state-owned enterprises are autonomous on the operational plane: they are juridical units participating in economic life on their own responsibility, as far as their specific obligations are concerned. The chief executive of the enterprise, who is responsible for carrying out the plan directives, is the director; he is appointed by a ministry or other supervisory authority according to the type of enterprise. His principal aides are the chief engineer, his usual deputy, who is responsible for the technical operation of the plant, and the chief accountant. Various departments, functional and operational, assist the director in his tasks. At each commanding echelon within each supervisory agency, or enterprise, the principle of having a single responsible authority is fully enforced. Below the director, in each production shop, the shop chief is the leader; he is assisted by a shop engineer, a shop accountant, and some other aides. Within each shop, a chief foreman leads a number of foremen; in turn, the latter supervise the workers, who are grouped in brigades, each one of which is headed by a brigade leader.

The enterprise is provided with fixed and circulating capital, for which it pays (since 1967) a yearly capital charge to the budget. Worn-out or surplus equipment may be liquidated after approval of the supervisory administration. A certain part of the funds earmarked for depreciation is left to the enterprise and may be used for updating the equipment or for repairs. Additional working capital may be borrowed from the State Bank at an officially established rate of interest. The enterprise carries all the accounts of its selling and purchasing operations with the State Bank: payments to the account of the seller are made upon acceptance of the goods by the buyer. Goods are transferred upon the basis of contracts of either a general or a local character. General contracts are drawn up between industrial branches; local contracts, between enterprises. The contracts establish the terms of delivery of products during a given plan period, the assortment of goods and their quality, and penalties for non-fulfillment. The contracts are concluded at established prices.

The state-owned enterprise is subject to a system of *business accounting*,[3] which allows it an assured profit margin within its total revenues (in an amount which allows for paying charges to the budget for the use of its assets, for paying interest to the bank for borrowed capital, and for the creation of certain incentive and expansion funds). The rules of business accounting are minimization of cost through the best possible utilization of inputs and maximization of income without infringing on any of the plan's provisions.

THE FIRM'S PLANS AND ITS ACTIVITY

The plans are executed in the enterprises. The major part

3. Khoziaistvennyi raschet, *abbreviated as* khozraschet.

of the industrial plans consists of the production and sales programs of the enterprises. About thirty to forty days after the adoption of the national control figures — though in practice this does not occur at the officially scheduled dates — each enterprise's management prepares its programs for the year preceding the actual execution of the plan. These programs are sent to the ministry or the supervisory agency whose task is to combine the *directives* of the SPC, which concern national targets and are based on scheduled relationships among sector and branches, and the *proposals* of each enterprise, which concern the development of the enterprise and are based on contracts with its customers. The supervisory administration corrects, finalizes, and authorizes the enterprise's plan. The enterprise's plan, called a *technical-industrial-financial plan*,[4] consists of a set of programs whose major component is the plan for output and sales in both physical and value terms. On the basis of these programs, the enterprise's production staff works out the operational calendar plans (the quarterly, monthly, and daily layouts for all shops, sections, and subsidiary services of the firm). The programs of the enterprise notably specify:

1] The indicators concerning over-all operation and management of the enterprise;

2] Scheduled gross production, sales (commodity output), and inventory changes;

3] Modernization, repairs, and scheduled efficiency increases in equipment utilization, quality improvement, and so on;

4] Norms of utilization of raw materials, fuels, and working capital;

5] Capital construction — "centralized" (funded from the state budget) and "decentralized" (funded from profits of the enterprise) — and the calendar for implementing the scheduled structures;

6] Procurement for essential and subsidiary materials (and the sources for covering these needs);

4. *Tekhpromfinplan. The standard model of tekhpromfinplan adopted for the NEM was issued in 1967.* Ekonomicheskaia gazeta, *No. 22 (June, 1967).*

7] Labor and wages — net of premia and other supplements from profits — productivity, labor-time utilization, and plans for labor training;

8] Scheduled cost reduction and various estimates concerning maintenance and operation, charges, depreciation, credits, and profits;

9] Formation (from specific profits shares) of: *a*] an incentive fund, *b*] a fund of sociocultural and housing measures, and *c*] a fund for the development of production and the estimated disbursements from these funds;

10] Over-all balance of income and outlay.

Thus, in theory, at the launching of the plan, the enterprise has a well-determined course drawn up for itself: it is supposed to know *what* it will produce (output plan), by what *means* (utilization of capacity, technical development, and capital construction programs), at what *cost* (procurement, payroll, and cost plans), for *whom*, and at *what prices* (sales plan).

Actually, there is a sizable gap between theory and practice, between the plans and their day-to-day execution. In order to visualize some of these problems, let us consider in succession the activity of the enterprise as it relates to output, procurement, and payroll programs.

The output plan of the enterprise is made up of the gross value of output and value of commodity production, as well as of a set of targets expressed in physical terms. In the composition of the industrial output, the enterprise's products, by-products, goods of subsidiary units serving basic production, and the shops' production are distinguished from the rejects of basic production and auxiliary services. Since it is not feasible to plan in kind all the diverse assortments of products according to types, brands, sizes, shape, power, etc., the basic forms of production are differentiated at the level of the enterprise, just as in the national plan, by devising conventional groupings through utilization of physical common denominators. Although, at the national level, this procedure represents a useful device for sketching the over-all programs of output, capital construction, utilization of productive capacities, and basic procurement needs, it has serious shortcomings when applied as a practical output guide at the level of the enterprise.

Before the mid-1960's, because of the priority of the gross value of output and the importance of certain specific physical indices, the activity of all Soviet enterprises has tended to be geared toward fulfilling the crucial aggregate target in value terms and the physical targets of each output according to planned specifications, such as number of pieces, sizes, weights, and total power. In attempting to meet and exceed the gross value target, enterprises have tended to produce an output mix, the bulk of which consisted of high-priced products or easy-to-manufacture items. In trying to meet and exceed the main physical indicators, enterprises have tended to stick literally to the given specifications: if the aggregative indices were expressed in tons, the enterprises tended to respond by providing unnecessarily heavy items; if expressed in some linear measure, by producing an output with reduced width and weight; if expressed in numbers, by producing only small items, and so on. Precisely because the enterprises were pressured to attain the specified *quantity* indices by all available means, they continued to produce obsolete models and therefore lowered the quality of their output. The output of defective goods — due in fact to a combination of deficiencies in the organization of production and in the flow of supplies — has been enormous, especially, as one would expect, in consumers' goods. In order to prevent at least some of these deleterious effects, *actual sales* and ensuing *profits*, rather than gross value of output and its related quantity indicators, have been proclaimed the "success indicators" of the enterprise. Sales and profits are to determine, in turn, the inflows into the incentive *funds* of the enterprise and stimulate the personnel to improve output and expand sales. Actually, the key objectives of the NEM — higher quality output and better product assortment tuned to the needs of the consumer — may still prove highly elusive. The changes in success indicators and in incentives, long advocated by Professor E. G. Liberman of Kharkov, may prove, at least in part, *formalistic* and serve only in a rather limited way as remedies for the prevailing ills. The output of unmarketable goods is due to a *combination of deficiencies* in planning, pricing, incentives, taxation, supply and distribution, quality control, and other factors. Changes in success indicators and in incentives are not sufficient for coping with these deficiencies. Consider the mechanics of the growth of the incentive funds. This growth depends on: *a*] the norms set for each percentage increase in the volume of "sales" and *b*] the percentage profitability set in the plan. Now, if the volume of "sales" does not *grow*, the incentive fund will be cut; the managers might hence prefer to plan only moderate increases in "sales" — to be able to secure "steady growth." Consider also the question of taxes. The turnover tax is still paid as soon as the enterprises "unload" their goods, rather than after the goods have actually been sold by the retail outlets. The plant manufacturing the unmarketable goods may not be at all incommoded by the situation and may even collect bonuses in accordance with its "internal" quantitative indices. Further, the bank automatically transfers the tax to the budget and does not wait until the goods are sold. Finally, the trade organizations pay their bills without really considering the quality and assortment of the goods brought to them. If the trading network would choose to reject previously ordered goods as unmarketable, it would find itself without any alternative supplies and would be unable to fulfill its own sales plans. As a Soviet source clearly puts it, "The enterprises have far more ways of training intransigent buyers; next time, for instance, they may deliver an order of genuinely scarce goods last of all."[5]

The volume of raw materials, fuels, and equipment needed for fulfilling the production and construction programs, for equipment repair, and for auxiliary services, as well as the volume of stock necessary for uninterrupted operation of the enterprise, is determined, as already stated, by the use of technical coefficients. The supply plan of each enterprise, based on All-Union, regional, and branch material balances and distribution plans, is spelled out in detail by commodities or groups of commodities, brands, sorts, sizes, and other specifications in the agreements with the distributors. Special authorizations, moreover, are provided for rationed commodities so that the enterprise is guaranteed continuous supplies while, at the

5. *The problem of "unmarketable" consumers goods is a perennial topic of discussion in the Soviet press. This thorny problem, as* Komsomolskaia pravda *of September 9, 1967, puts it, "abounds in paradoxes." A defective item may even be "unmarketable and in short supply at the same time." Some "complacent trade workers" resort apparently to the following "remedy." "If the goods don't sell in one place, we'll ship them miles away, where they will sell until the customers find out what they are really like."*

same time, a systematic check is kept on the flow of scarce materials. Again, however, in carrying out delivery programs wide discrepancies occur in assortment, quantity, quality, and timing. To start with, the claims of the enterprises are often viewed as exceeding their actual needs and hence are scaled down by the central authorities; for their part, the plants build stocks above the norm as insurance against expected and unavoidable bottlenecks in deliveries; finally, the synchronization of the various plans of production and supply is extremely poor. In order to cope with this involved situation, a whole class of intermediaries has sprung up. Called by various unsavory terms — "fixers," "ticks," "pushers," "speculators" — the intermediaries, hired on a permanent or temporary basis by the enterprises, spend their time at the central administrations or at delivery centers trying to expedite delivery of needed supplies to their firms and to correlate deliveries with their firms' output requirements.[6] The execution of the plan itself and the obtaining of timely and indispensable deliveries thus requires, paradoxically, an illicit mixture of traffic in influence, swapping authorizations for scarce products, and last but not least, extensive bribery. This unholy but customary combination — which the Russians call *blat*, "something rather stronger than 'pull,'" as Edward Crankshaw puts it, "and rather less than 'graft'" — cuts across the officially established channels, precisely in order that the plan itself may be carried out.

The plan for labor and wages in industry as a whole, the other key part of the national, regional, branch, and enterprise plans, consists of three main parts, dealing with productivity, number of workers, and payroll. Productivity is calculated and planned in monetary terms as gross output per worker; in certain limited cases, it is also measured in physical terms, notably in industries with highly homogeneous outputs, such as coal and wood. The planned number of factory workers per branch is derived, as already stated, from the movement of the output index and from the planned output norm per worker. At the national, regional, or branch levels, the computation of the planned payroll can then be derived from planned average wages times planned number of workers. At the

6. *According to* Izvestia *(Apr. 4, 1959), during eleven months of 1958, an automobile factory in the Urals sent no less than 2,762 "pushers" on business tours; a steel plant in Krivoi Rog sent 2,813. And these were priority plants!*

level of the enterprise, the computation is supposed to be based on the correct classification of workers, their planned numbers, and an official tariff or wage schedule.

In principle, workers are classified in each plant on the basis of an *ad hoc* classification manual detailing for each branch the required skills of each kind of labor, and its specific tasks in the operation and safekeeping of the respective equipment. The wage scale has from eight to twelve grades according to industry. A semi-skilled or a skilled worker has, in accordance with his skills, the right to a given wage coefficient, which is a multiple of the base pay of the unskilled worker. Hence, once the basic wage is set, total payroll is implicitly determined. Assume that a plant has eight wage categories and that the coefficients according to specific skills increase from 1 to 3; the total wage bill can then be computed as total wage coefficients times basic wage, as indicated in the following example:

TABLE 3. *Calculation of the Wage Bill in a Plant*

1. Wage categories	1	2	3	4	5	6	7	8
2. Wage coefficients	1.0	1.14	1.31	1.52	1.75	2.1	2.5	3.0
3. Number of workers	20	100	100	100	80	60	20	10
4. Total coefficients (2 × 3)	20	114	131	152	140	126	50	30
5. Total wage (4 × base)	763 × basic rate.							

Although the labor statutes specify that the wage of any skilled worker is a multiple of the basic hourly tariff rate of the unskilled worker of this plant, in practice the tariff rates of the first category of workers are also widely differentiated according to working conditions, prevailing forms of wages (time work or piece work), importance of any group of workers to production in the particular shop or section of the enterprise, and other criteria. The basic wage has thus been differentiated according to normal, dangerous, or particularly dangerous jobs (in chemical plants), surface and various types of underground assignments (in mining), jobs in cold or hot shops (in foundry, forge, and heat-treating work).

Differentiation between time rates and piece rates, arranged so as to stimulate piecework, utilization of special progressive piece rates (increasing faster than the rate at which the norms are surpassed), and finally, granting special bonuses to leading skilled workers vitiate strict planning of the wage bill.

After the launching of the wage reform of the 1950's, it was officially recognized that labor norms have been used not as aids to the organization of production, but as devious means for adjusting wages: thus, norms of output or of time were understated within enterprises so that they could easily be surpassed by the majority of workers, whereas the wage categories of workers were artificially overstated. In short, innumerable adjustments occurred within each combine, trust, and enterprise. Finally, the wage computed according to the plan's schedule covered only a small fraction of the actual pay, with the rest made up by various arbitrary, individual bonuses. Although labor norms are now better defined and the emphasis has been shifted from piecework to time payments, one can hardly see why the new labor norms and associated indices should not be manipulated at the operative level as extensively as in the recent past. In one respect, namely, bonuses, the new measures may be somewhat more effective because the emphasis is now on collective rather than on individual premiums, i.e., on the performance of the crew, shop, and plant as a whole.

To summarize, in the day-to-day activity of the enterprise, the various plans and programs, which, to start with, are based on numerous generalizations (e.g., amalgamated product groups, input and output norms, etc.), cannot be and are not fully synchronized. Wide discrepanices appear between the plans and each phase of their implementation. In laying the emphasis squarely on attaining certain so-called "success indicators," especially in the key industries, the central authorities force the managers to sacrifice various "secondary" programs and targets, such as controlling the size of the wage bill or introducing new technology. This emphasis has multiple consequences, as far as managerial behavior, aims, and aspirations are concerned. We shall return to these consequences, after a short discussion of cost, profits, and prices.

COST, PRICE, INCOME ACCOUNT

Prices are set on the basis of costs plus planned profits.

Up to the reforms of the 1960's, cost at the level of the enterprise consisted essentially of its "direct" or *prime costs*, i.e., the payments for wages and salaries, raw materials and fuels, depreciation allowances and some outlays for administration and marketing. Since the capital goods and the "normative" working capital were outright state grants, no payments for them (such as capital charges or interest) were necessary. Interest appeared on the book of the enterprise only for the additional funds needed as working capital.[7] Since the 1967 reforms, however, both interest payments for borrowed funds and certain *fixed costs* appear on the books of the enterprises. Thus, capital charges for the use of the fixed and circulating capital provided will now be included, and the enterprises are encouraged to compress their demands for capital. But, as already pointed out, in the centrally established prices, a rate of return on assets in use is included in the profit rate and may simply offset the payable capital charge.

Further, the depreciation allowances, which in Soviet accounting are supposed to provide funds both for replacement of the assets and for major repairs during their lifetime, are set at artificially low levels and inadequately reflect the costs of capital consumption. As noted by Professor Robert W. Campbell, the depreciation rates are not uniformly low but "differentially understated from branch to branch and from enterprise to enterprise." The inaccuracy of these charges may and does lead to unsound economic decisions concerning both the replacement of equipment and the choice among alternative processes. Finally, in joint product cases, no careful analysis of productivities is carried out.

Within any given industrial branch, the wholesale price of a product is set at the level of average cost, which consists of the defined elements plus a planned profit markup. For a branch, combine, or trust, this average is derived on the basis of 1] each firm's cost estimates, 2] a comparison between actual cost and some estimated "standard" cost, or 3] average "progressive norms" set for all the firms concerned. Serious shortcomings are acknowledged in all these methods, however; the first is unreliable, since firms tend to raise their planned costs in order to conceal possible productivity gains and thus increase profits; the second is unsatisfactory,

7. *The State Bank charges interest on the credits it extends to enterprises. The rates are differentiated according to the administration cost of each type of credit. The charge of an interest on the funds borrowed over and above estimated working-capital needs rations short-term credit.*

since the underlying cost data are not reliable; and the third method is inadequate, since such computations only imperfectly reflect the actual changes occurring in the economy.

Once the average is computed by one or a combination of the methods cited, a planned profit margin is added to it in order to establish the wholesale price of the product. Within an industrial branch, profits are carefully adjusted from enterprise to enterprise by taking into account each one's degree of mechanization and specific conditions of production. The ministry approves the prices and the rates for the output and services of each enterprise and organization belonging to the ministry's system. It guides their respective financial activities and opens clearing accounts in banks for redistribution within its entire system of working capital, profits, sums for the "mastery of new technology," and other funds.[8] Thus within any industry — at least in principle — a *perequation* (a redistribution) of the profits over and above the profits retained for the incentive funds of the successful enterprises is carried out, with the surplus profits of some plants used to subsidize other plants operating at cost levels above the average.

In transactions among state enterprises belonging to different industrial branches, the transfer prices are the "wholesale prices of the enterprise" net or gross of cost of the marketing organizations of the industry. In sale to *commercial* firms, prices also include the turnover tax. From the point of view of division of national income and of the state's total savings, it makes no difference whether the enterprises are allowed higher profits while, conversely, either subsidies and turnover tax or both are set at low levels. For planners and managers, such changes are meaningful, of course, since they imply changes within price structures and in respect to all transfer prices. The level of profits in any branch does not guide investment decisions: profits have been systematically set at lower levels in heavy industry and at higher levels in the light industries, which, moreover, carry the turnover tax on their consumers' goods. Savings in light industry are methodically turned into investments in heavy industry. For the enterprises themselves, however, any change in the size of profits is meaningful since many elements, such as the division of profits and the transfer prices, are linked to the level of profits.

8. Cf. *General Statute on USSR Ministries*, Ekonomicheskaia gazeta *No. 34 (August, 1967).*

Some of the problems related to cost, profits, and price calculations can be grasped only by looking closely at the situation within an industrial branch, i.e., a ministerial organization. (See Table 4.) Let the sales price of a given product of this industry be 100, and the average wholesale price net of turnover tax, 75. Among X, and Y, and Z, the three undertakings considered here, each of which has different planned unit costs owing to differences in their degree of mechanization, Z would be the most "efficient," according to Soviet accounting, since its actual cost is lower than the planned cost and since it has thus achieved above-plan profits.

TABLE 4. *Price Formation within an Industry*

	Firms		
	X	Y	Z
10. Sales price	100	100	100
9. Disposal and delivery charges	5	5	5
8. Wholesale gross of turnover tax	95	95	95
7. Turnover tax	20	20	20
6. Wholesale net of turnover tax	75	75	75
5. Actual profits (row 6 — 3)	8	0	—1
4. Above-plan profits (row 5 — 2)	0	—4	1
3. Actual costs	67	75	76
2. Planned profits (row 6 — 1)	8	4	—2
1. Planned costs	67	71	77

Thus, each enterprise, whatever its cost structure, is efficient in terms of Soviet economic accounting in relation to the planned standards established for it: X is less efficient than Z, since it has not realized above-plan profits, whereas Y appears to be the least efficient plant, since its actual costs have exceeded planned costs although in practice these costs are below those of Z. The plant in which costs are less than planned is therefore considered the most efficient.

The meaning of profits in the general framework of Soviet planning is clouded by the following facts: rates are set quite arbitrarily, varying between products in the same sector and between sectors. Within each broader unit (viz., ministry), a redistribution of profits is carried out, thus allowing certain enterprises to work with negative profits. Finally, the state first absorbs deductions from profits and then hands part of them back to the enterprise.

These procedures, which are a result of centralized control and expediency of administration, pose numerous problems for the Soviet national accounts, as we shall see later. Let us note at this point that, in these conditions, any income account of a Soviet enterprise normally reflects not only a given relation between sales and charges against sales, but also other elements, such as relations between non-operating incomes and non-operating expenses, and transfers between the enterprise as such, the broader unit to which it belongs (trust, combine, and industrial branch), and the state. The income and expenditure balance of an enterprise thus is a combination of an income and sources and disposition of funds statement, in which there appear both branch and budget allotments and transfers to the branch and to the budget. If, for simplification, we omit the dealings within a branch, trust, etc., the income statement of an enterprise can be presented as follows:

TABLE 5. *Income Statement of Enterprise X **
(in thousands of rubles)

I

Incomes			*Expenses*		
A. Incomes from operations:			A. Operational expenses:		
Sales	10,600		Cost of goods sold	8,710	
Profits		700	Excluding non-cash expenses	300	
Turnover tax		1,000	Net operating expenses	8,410	
B. Non-operating incomes	180		B. Non-operating expenses	2,040	
Rentals		100	Capital investment and capital repair		1,150
Total income	10,780		Total expenses	10,450	

Income balance 330

II

Budget allotments:		Transfers to budget:	
Capital construction	725	Turnover tax	1,000
Other	25	Capital charge and profit tax	80
Total allotments	750	Total transfers	1,080

Transfer balance 330

* *The Balance discloses not only the position of the enterprise as far as its production operations are concerned, but also its activities as a channel for the state budget.*

SOURCE: *Based on* Ekonomika promyshlenosti SSSR [*The Economics of Soviet Industry*]. *Moscow: Gospolitizdat, 1956.*

Thus, the accounts involved actually fall into three broad groups: (1) sales and cost of goods sold, net (in our example 10,600 — 8,410); (2) funds provided from operation plus other income (2,190 + 180) versus total funds applied (2,040); (3) net transfer to the state (330).

OPERATIVE DECISIONS AND INCENTIVES

If all the plans could be perfectly defined and synchronized, the manager of the enterprise would need little authority. As we have seen, however, the plans are far from being either uniquely defined or perfectly timed, and as a result, discrepancies among programs as well as among their various parts are bound to arise as they are carried out. Hence, the manager must be empowered to make a wide variety of choices at the operational level. The director must and does make the day-to-day operating decisions as to what materials are to be used and when, which materials or spare parts may be produced within the enterprise, with which local suppliers he should deal, etc. The planners employ various methods in order to make the manager and his subordinates carry out their tasks in as close agreement as possible with the main centralized decisions. The most notable of the material stimuli are the sharing of the enterprise's profits and above-plan profits (i.e., economies resulting from reduction of cost) and the award of bonuses for fulfillment and overfulfillment of the sales and profit target and of the physical indicators of the plan.

The importance of profit sharing and of cost reduction are heavily stressed in the Soviet textbooks. Profit sharing, however, has not proved to be a very useful device. Managers have, furthermore, shown only slight interest in reducing costs — since each cost reduction is integrated into the subsequent plan and leads to reductions in the (scarce) planned supplies of the enterprise. Accordingly, cost reductions within the plant or within a broader unit have tended to be limited at best to cuts in "unproductive expenditures" related to administration and marketing expenses. It is precisely because cost reduction by way of profit sharing has not proved effective that the central authorities have always relied on centrally planned decreases in input norms, on centrally launched campaigns of mechanization and rationalization, on contrived "socialist emulations," and on various kinds of "competitions" between enterprises, shops, and units for breaking the actual norms. The stimuli introduced after the NEM reforms — namely, increases in the allowable share of retained profits for the incentive funds of the enterprise, are seriously hampered by the authority of *perequating* profits vested in the supervisory agencies of the enterprises. The ministry (or any other agency it may establish) may indeed divest the profits of the successful enterprises in order to ensure the *over-all* financial balance of the supervisory agency. Here too the theoretical emphasis on incentives at the level of operational management conflicts with the practical emphasis on centralization at the level of the supervisory agency.

COOPERATIVE INDUSTRY

The official Soviet statistics concerning size of industrial plants and structure of industrial employment convey a distorted image of small-scale production. Since 1960, small-scale "producers' cooperatives," were absorbed by the state industry, and the number of small-scale enterprises became officially insignificant. Actually small-scale *production* and hundreds of thousands of small-scale handicraft units and workshops (limestone quarries, lumber enterprises, print shops, tailor shops, bakeries, even illegal private production, and others) are "hidden" within the industrial and non-industrial enterprises and institutions, where they continue to provide gainful employment for over one million people.

In 1929, at the beginning of the thoroughgoing planning era, the main aims of the producers' cooperatives were stated to be: (i) production to satisfy consumer demand especially in the rural areas; (ii) provision of equipment to cooperatives and to local industries in cooperation with the state plan; (iii) utilization of local raw materials and/or of waste materials which the state industry cannot efficiently utilize. The producers' cooperatives encompassed artisans' workshops and cottage industries, disabled persons' cooperatives, and auxiliary industries serving the consumers' cooperatives. In some remote regions, instead of the regular type of handicraftmen's cooperative entirely devoted to repair work, some artisan collectives combined handicraft organization and farming. Since 1946 the handicraft cooperatives have been turned primarily toward the production of consumer goods — e.g., leather goods of all kinds, household and artistic items, pottery and furniture, transportation carts used by the peasants, and other similar products. The disabled persons' cooperatives have offered the traditional products and services of handicapped labor — e.g., watches, radios, photography, and repair work. Finally, the industries serving the consumers' cooperatives have been engaged in shoemaking, tailoring, soft-drink production, and similar goods.

Serious pressures are now building up for re-establishing the former cooperatives on an autonomous accounting basis and for reviving the framework in which they developed before their absorption by the state industries and institutions. In this framework:

1. Each cooperative has a charter establishing its organizational rules and sphere of activity. As a rule, a cooperative consists of not one but a series of enterprises and institutions. The production capital of the cooperative comes from share payments and dues of the members. The workers in the cooperatives are paid according to their specific skills; as members, they also receive additional earnings in the form of a share in profits. In principle, the highest authority of a cooperative is the general assembly of the members and, between its meetings, the administrative organs elected by it. (In practice, not only was the organization of any cooperative dependent on the immediate aims and whims of the local authorities, but all the phases of its activities were strongly controlled by various echelons of the state administration. Thus, the cooperatives were linked into local, territorial, and regional unions. In the case of producers' cooperatives and of disabled persons' associations, their organizational and planning direction was established for a region or territory

by the appropriate administration for producers' cooperatives under the council of ministers of a union republic.) The industries of the consumers' associations are dependent on the central and regional administrations controlling these associations.
2. The development and the production of the cooperatives are determined by the state, republic, and regional plans. Their supply of materials, their types of output, and the distribution of their goods are closely scrutinized. The plan provides that state industries manufacture machines, appliances, and tools for the cooperatives. The cooperatives may obtain the surplus or obsolete machines of the state industry, trucks, and other equipment. The cooperatives get raw materials from state-controlled stocks, waste, and rejects of the state industry, as well as from local resources, their own products, and contractual raw materials (i.e., materials provided directly by the respective customers). Credit control and taxes keep the expansion of the cooperatives within the desired limits. Credits are extended to them through the State Banks. Taxes are adjusted so as to maintain uniformity in the prices of manufactured goods; account is thus taken in the fixing of the turnover tax of their higher costs as compared to some corresponding state industries.

As pointed out by some Soviet economists such as Ya. Kvasha, a revival of the independence of the producers' cooperatives would simplify the cumbersome structural organization of the big state industry and would allow the freed small-scale enterprises — with their simpler equipment and organization, smaller fixed assets, and higher operational flexibility — to adjust their output to the needs of both the consumers and the large industry itself. Even in the most developed Western economies, large firms act as the "modernized distribution offices" of constellations of small firms tied permanently as subcontractors to large companies. One must not forget, however, that many of these arguments were already known in the USSR before the liquidation of the cooperatives. Yet, big state industry finally absorbed the small companies because it has an inexhaustible appetite for skilled labor, and secondly, because the large firms try all means to keep their own supplies free from the vagaries of the official supply system and its often uncertain deliveries.

5.

Agriculture

INDUSTRIALIZING AGRICULTURE

A cardinal communist objective is the complete "restructuring" of agriculture so that its multiple and deeply intertwined socio-economic characteristics — the producing-consuming nature of the agricultural enterprise, its wide seasonal fluctuations in labor-intake requirements, the weak connection of the peasantry with the market, and the particularism and isolation of the villages — will be profoundly altered. Agricultural enterprises should be turned into fully mechanized, state-owned grain and meat factories in the fields; their output should be appropriated and distributed through state outlets. The peasant would then become a proto-industrial wage earner; and traditional rural communities would be superseded by new and modern "farm cities."

The complete transformation of agriculture has always been regarded as a touchstone for the success or failure of communism. In the early phase of Soviet power, this transformation seemed to be within easy reach, as a result of forced collectivization and the injection of a good dose of tractors into the countryside. As L. E. Hubbard once put it: "The tractor is to the Russian Communist something more than a machine; in his heart of hearts, he regards it in some way a mystical symbol of the new faith." But enormous investment is required for complete mechanization of all agricultural work — plowing, seeding, cultivation, harvesting, and storing — for the more complex and costly mechanization of livestock husbandry — breeding, feeding, milking, refrigeration, and shed construction — for the fusion of agriculture, livestock husbandry, and food processing industries into an integrated whole so as to eliminate fluctuation in labor-intake, and finally, for an ambitious program of relocation and large-scale urbanization, with its requirements for buildings, electrification, and extension of transportation networks. Since the Communist Party was primarily bent on the reconstruction and expansion of the industrial-military machine, however, it decided to squeeze out of agriculture the investments needed for industry; therefore agriculture was assigned the lowest priority level in the development of the Soviet system.

Because industrialization and urbanization demanded an increasing amount of agricultural produce for the expanding towns and because, on the other hand, adequate increments in agricultural output could not be secured either from the state-owned farms or through sufficient investments, the agricultural setup finally had to be adjusted so as to allow the largest possible increase in the *marketed* share of agricultural produce, notably of grains, even if output remained stationary or was decreasing. This paradoxical result was secured by putting agriculture into a different mold from that suggested by the basic communist blueprints. Private property was ruthlessly liquidated, but on its ruins were established not highly mechanized *state* farms, which proved often inefficient and primarily remained heavily dependent on state subsidies,[1] but *group*-owned collective farms, which continued to use many of the old-fashioned farming methods and distributed the output of the farms to the members only after deliveries to the state were met. Inefficient units, with low productivity per capita, still abound within the agricultural sector; mechanization is still unevenly spread; and the impact of natural calamities may still be severe. The Soviet policy makers have inconsistently attempted to implement a series of complex measures aimed at eradicating the difference between *state*-owned and *group*-owned farms, leading ultimately to the merger of the two.[2]

Since the mid-1950's the collective-farm sector has increasingly been drawn into monetary relations with both the state complex and its own collective members. In the early 1950's roughly one half of the transactions between the state and the collectives were conducted in products, as was about 75 per cent of the transactions between the collectives and their members. By the late 1950's all payments in kind, as well as taxation in kind, were replaced by a

1. *In 1964, 62 per cent of the state farms were operating at a loss; in 1965, 48 per cent.* Kommunist, *No. 15 (Oct. 1966), pp. 75–85.*

2. *State farms are called* sovkhozy; *group-owned farms,* kolkhozy.

system of sales; in the early 1960's over 75 per cent of the total payments to the collective farmers were made in money.

While over the years the state farms have systematically increased their share in marketed agricultural produce (thanks to the absorption of the least efficient collective farms and to mechanization and increases in yields), the collective farms and the collective farmers' private plots continue to play a decisive role in the output and marketing of agricultural produce. By the mid-1960's the state farms had become the *main* suppliers of meat, eggs, and vegetables. But, even though the role of the collective farms and the private plots has been decreasing, in the mid-1960's the collective farms were still supplying the *largest* shares of the marketed outputs of grain, cotton, sugar beets, milk, and wool, and the private plots accounted for the *largest* share of the marketed output of potatoes and for significant shares of the marketed outputs of vegetables, meat, milk, eggs, and wool.[3] Despite the almost trebling in the investment per sown area in the late 1950's, Soviet agriculture still has low priority for receiving investments, and despite progress in Soviet agriculture, this sector still trails far behind the agriculture of the United States or of the advanced countries of Western Europe.

3. *The following changes in the relative shares of marketed output in agriculture were registered in 1965, as compared to 1950 and 1940.*

Changing Patterns of Marketed Outputs in Agriculture
(Percentage Shares by Suppliers, 1940, 1950, 1965)

	State Sector			Collective Farm			Private		
Output Marketed	1940	1950	1965	1940	1950	1965	1940	1950	1965
Total	12	14	36	61	62	51	27	26	13
Grain	10	11	37	87	87	63	3	2	0
Cotton, raw	6	4	20	94	96	80	0	0	0
Sugar beet	4	3	9	90	97	91	6	0	0
Potatoes	5	8	26	41	31	30	54	61	44
Vegetables	10	21	53	66	55	35	18	24	12
Meat	16	20	42	29	33	41	55	47	17
Milk	15	15	41	34	35	52	51	50	17
Eggs	3	7	39	4	21	24	93	74	37
Wool	15	15	42	59	69	44	26	16	14

Shaded box: highest relative share.

SOURCE: Narodnoe khoziaistvo SSSR v 1965 g. (National Economy of the USSR in 1965) pp. 267ff.

THE STATE FARM: SIZE, ORGANIZATION, OPERATION

The state farm — the agricultural homologue of the industrial enterprise — has a status and organization similar to that of the industrial firm. It too is to be managed, according to the principles of business accounting, by a director appointed by a higher authority — in this case, the republic agricultural ministry. But from inception most of the state farms have been poor economic propositions: they have been unable to meet their expenses and provide for expanding their capital. Since 1967, however, in line with the reorganization introduced in industry and with the price reforms, a number of state farms have been shifted to "full business accounting," i.e., have been placed on their own as far as income and expenditures are concerned. Since large variations in output occur in agriculture from year to year, various schemes have been considered in order to find ways of preserving the solvency of the farms (e.g., special profit provisions, short-term bank credits, and insurance) during bad crop years.

As of 1965, about 11,500 state farms were in operation, many of which specialized in one or two types of crops (such as grain and/or cotton), in livestock breeding, dairy products, or vegetable growing. The location and type of output of the state farms are reciprocally determined: grain-producing farms are in the black earth and virgin land areas; dairy and vegetable units are close to the towns which they are assigned to serve; and the state livestock farms are scattered in almost all regions.

The size of these state farms is determined partly by specialization and location, and partly by a combination of extraneous factors in which the old preference for giantism and the bureaucratic confusion of bigness with optimum size still play a key role. As of 1965, the state farms were large-scale units averaging some 60,000 acres, with an annual average of over 660 workers. The state grain farms averaged over 100,000 acres with some 55,000 acres of sown area; the largest state farms, those for caracul raising, averaged 330,000 acres.[4]

4. *It is interesting to note that in the United States, the total crop land harvested in 1954 was divided equally among the following three groups of commercial farms: farms with less than 180 acres; farms with 180–500 acres; farms with over 500 acres. Although large corporate farming now accounts for only 1 per cent of the total farm acreage in the country, both incorporation and consolidation are gaining ground owing to the increased investment required in modern farming. The* average *unit in the large-farm class is now about* 4,000 *acres.*

The director of each state farm carries the full responsibility for performance. He hires the personnel, except for his deputy and other main agricultural specialists, who are appointed by his higher authorities upon his recommendation. As in industrial enterprises, he discharges his tasks with the help of appropriate functional and operational departments. State farms engaged in the same type of production may be grouped into trusts acting under the authority of a ministerial administration. Each state farm is divided into a number of basic production units, such as tractor brigades and livestock brigades, as its particular specialty requires. The units in this sector correspond to the shops into which the industrial firm is organized. The leaders of the basic unit are assisted by mechanics and various other skilled workers, as well as by unskilled laborers, a number of whom are only seasonally employed. In accordance with state and regional planning directives and on the basis of its contracts with procurement, trade, and marketing organizations, the state farm establishes its preliminary targets for sales, costs, profits, and capital construction. The higher administrative organs henceforth modify and adjust only the indices concerning sales, wage fund, and profits for the farms on so-called "full" business accounting and set limits in the budget for the financing of working capital and capital construction. Just as in the case of the industrial enterprise, the state farm operates on the basis of "full" cost (i.e., including fixed costs), pays capital charges, and is authorized to retain various shares in profits for the material incentive funds, the socio-cultural fund, insurance, and farm expansion. On the basis of these decisions, the state farms draw up their own output financial plans, which need no further approval by higher authorities.

The farm's own plan consists of a set of programs; the leading part, which concerns output, indicates the scheduled volume of gross production, the pattern of sowing, the availability of cattle per 100 acres, the productivity of labor, machinery, and cattle, and some other indicators. The plan of sales details the schedule of delivery for basic produce (milk, meat, wool, eggs, and similar products) and indicates the magnitude of the marketed shares. The cost plan specifies the labor expenditure per type of crop, farm, brigade, etc. The labor and wage plan specifies the number of workers by skills and production units and makes various breakdowns of the scheduled wage bill. The financial program details capital investments and repairs and expenses for "non-productive" needs and presents in conclusion a consolidated income and sources and disposition of funds statement which shows the relations between income, outlays, and the state budget. Gross production is computed at the established prices f.o.b. or c.i.f., net of turnover tax for deliveries to industries and gross of turnover tax for deliveries to the retail network. Costs are divided into variable and fixed — the latter includes insurance, interest, and other capital charges for capital in use.

Workers' wages are determined by means of a trades scale and the established work norms based on an eight-hour workday. Specialists are paid on a monthly basis, with salaries varying according to the scale of the enterprise. If the plan of sales is overfulfilled, from 5 to 12 per cent of profits above those planned are distributed as premiums among the personnel. Thus, like his colleague in industry, the director of the state farm has a very high stake in attaining and surpassing the total sales target and a relatively mild interest in cost reduction. Workers are paid some 70 to 80 per cent of their wages according to output, the rest according to assorted norms depending on the quality of their work, number of cattle tended, etc.

In order to check the large turnover of workers in the state farms, each permanent worker is provided with a plot of land slightly larger than an acre and with credits for the construction of a house. The produce raised by the workers on these plots may not be marketed.

THE COLLECTIVE FARM: SIZE, ORGANIZATION, OPERATION

The collective farm, or "artel," the other form of organization of Soviet agriculture, has a dual character: it combines in a strange symbiosis collective work with private farming, giantism with dwarfism. The vast mass of the peasantry of the USSR, still living on 15.4 million homesteads, is grouped within 36,000 collectives that are very unequal in size and income. In the mid-1960's about 42 per cent of these collectives combined less than 300 households each; 28 per cent had 300–500 homesteads each; and close to 30 per cent had over 500 homesteads each. As for income, one third of all farms had an income of less than 10,000 rubles per 100 hectares; another third, an income of from 10,000 to 20,000 rubles per 100 hectares; and the last third, an income of over 20,000 rubles per 100 hectares. Since the mid-1950's, a vast movement of mergers and amalgamations of all sorts, along with massive injections of agricultural specialists, has been carried out in the collectives, and the number of these farms has been drastically reduced from 123,000 to 36,000. Various collective farm associations of a local or regional character have been created for carrying out joint projects of electrification and irrigation, for establishing auxiliary agricultural enterprises, and for other specific purposes. It is argued that these consolidations will allow the artels to hire skilled personnel, purchase adequate machinery, construct needed agricultural buildings, and raise their productivity. In some cases, the work of collective farms and of state farms has been combined. It is doubtful, however, that the mergers are due to economic considerations alone. By Western criteria, some collective farms are very large; the push toward even larger-scale units is puzzling, to say the least. In fact, as in the case of giantism in industry, the Soviets may later decide to reverse this trend and pay more attention to the problems of size. One basic purpose of consolidating the artels, forming interfarm associations, and injecting large numbers of specialized workers into these collectives is the progressive elimination of the individuality of the collective farm and of the characteristics that distinguish it from the state farm.

Within each artel, whatever its size, each peasant family, or the family of each permanently engaged specialist, is assigned a small house and garden plot of not over 2.5 acres. The private plots vary in size according to the labor which able-bodied members of each household contribute to the collective. Families with able-bodied members who do not work on the collective farm are allotted smaller plots. The household is allowed to raise various crops, other than those cultivated on the collective land, and to possess a small number of livestock (such as one cow, two calves, one hog, ten sheep, and a certain number of poultry). The permissible number of privately owned cattle varies according to local conditions and the participation of the household in the collective work. Although private possession of livestock still represents the mainstay of private ownership in agriculture, the regime has repeatedly warned that it considers this situation as transitory. No deadline, however, has yet been fixed for banning all private ownership of livestock.

Up to the late 1960's the operation of each collective farm was governed by a charter based on a "Model Statute" adopted in the mid-1930's, completed by various subsequent regulations. The statute emphasized from the outset the principle that the collective is a "voluntary" organization. In practice, the collectivization of all the peasantry was carried out by force during a few years in the 1930's. According to regulations, the highest authority of the collective is the general assembly of its members. With the increase in the size of the collectives, however, the general assembly has been replaced by an assembly of elected delegates. The latter, in principle, elect the chairman and the executive board of the collectives; in practice, the party "recommends" the chairmen, dismisses or transfers them, and places whom it wishes in the key administrative posts.[5]

According to its charter, each collective farm holds its land in perpetuity. This land cannot be sold or leased; it may be taken by the state, but only if proper compensation is made. In the past few years, new state farms have been established on land previously occupied by "economically weak" artels. Illegal sales or leases to individuals or institutions have also occurred from time to time and have been reported and severely censured officially. The capital assets of the collective, called *indivisible funds,* are composed of the original contribution of the members, augmented by annual deductions from current income. In addition to their own "indivisible funds" and current deductions, the collective farms may obtain long-term state credits.

A collective farmer may be expelled from the collective for slack work. He may leave the artel on his own accord, but only with the authorization of the management. If his departure is authorized, he may obtain a cash payment for what is considered his invested share as a member.

Until a few years ago, the collectives had no right to acquire agricultural machinery. Such important means of production could not, according to the prevailing theory, belong to anyone other than the state enterprises. All agricultural equipment other than that

5. *The "Decision of the Communist Party of the Soviet Union on N. S. Khrushchev's Report," adopted on February 26, 1958, states explicitly: "The party has directed to administrative posts at collective farms several thousand communists – party and administrative workers – engineers from industrial enterprises, agronomists, veterinarians, and other specialists."*

owned by state farms was concentrated in special organizations, called *Machine and Tractor Stations* (MTS), which exercised wide political, administrative, and planning powers in the countryside. But although the MTS embodied some obvious technical advantages, such as the capacity of each organization to service a number of collective farms — an important consideration because agricultural equipment was relatively scarce — generally speaking, they were inefficient and costly. They tended systematically to prolong work time; they often lacked adequate personnel, and in numerous instances, they hampered rather than helped the fulfillment of the agricultural plans. In 1958, without much concern for past theoretical contentions, it was successfully suggested that the MTS be disbanded and their machinery sold to the collective farms.[6] After the liquidation of the cumbersome MTS organizations, *ad hoc* All-Union and republic associations, organized with the status of State Committees of the USSR and of the republic councils of ministers, were established for handling the sale of machinery, spare parts, and fuels to the collectives. In principle, the collective farms themselves have the right to order, purchase, and own the necessary machinery. This is supposed to have great impact on patterns of production and distribution of agricultural equipment and on agricultural output. In practice, it is largely up to the state association to assess the needs of the collectives and to guide their choices. Two factors limit the freedom of the collectives with respect to planning patterns of cultivation and of livestock breeding. First, the central authorities — the State Planning Committee and the ministries of agriculture — determine the quotas for farm products to be delivered to the state, and meeting these quotas is compulsory.[7] Secondly, groups of inspectors attached to the regional executive committees are entrusted with the task of providing guidance to the collective farms on planning patterns and investment, and their influence is decisive at the establishment of the output program.

A collective may establish both long- and short-term plans. Long-term plans deal with such problems as soil improvement, livestock breeding and fodder supply, labor force and productivity, and

6. *Most of the MTS personnel — about 3 million individuals in 1955 — were simultaneously "injected" into the collective farms so as to broaden their "technical base."*

7. *The collective farms were informed by September 1 of the minimum delivery quotas and then left to draw their output plans. In the mid-1960's, it was determined that the quotas were to remain unchange for a quinquennium.*

capital formation. The yearly plans usually cover in detail the following matters:

1] Patterns of sowing, harvesting, and threshing (so as to meet the obligations toward the state concerning marketed output)

2] Technical improvements

3] Planning of livestock breeding (gross value in physical terms, improvement of stock, sale of meat, fodder plans, construction of shelter, etc.)[8]

4] Planning of capital construction of subsidiary enterprises and of transportation as well as of capital repairs, spare parts, fertilizers, and other materials purchased

5] Cost plan, detailing labor inputs per type of crop, farm, brigade, etc., and plans for cost reduction

6] Financial plan, with monetary incomes and their distribution (scheduled means for capital investment, working capital, non-productive expenses, etc.).

From the inception of collectives until the mid-1950's, the government had three principal ways of ensuring the fulfillment of its procurement plans: through purchase at very low prices of obligatory deliveries assessed according to the land area of the collectives; through the collectives' payment in kind for services obtained from the MTS; through special purchases of certain crops (over and above obligatory deliveries) at higher than the obligatory delivery prices. These procurement methods have been replaced since 1958 by a single system of state purchase at prices substantially higher than those prevailing previously for the obligatory deliveries. Although for the basic produce — grain, potatoes, milk, meat, wool, and eggs — delivery quotas are still assessed according to area, norms are set by product for each collective farm according to its specialization.

From the creation of the collectives until the late 1960's, the

8. *Norms are established for productivity per head of livestock (milk per cow, meat per type of cattle) or per unit of land (milk and meat per 100 hectares of pasture land, eggs per 100 hectares of agricultural land).*

system made the collective farmer the *last* claimant to his output. After all financial obligations of the farm were met, the net proceeds of the farm were distributed among its members on the basis of work performed as evaluated according to three factors: 1] the *rate of workday units* credited to each member of the collective according to the job he has performed; 2] the *total* number of units accumulated by him; 3] the total output of the collective, net of statutory deductions. The workdays, or fraction thereof to be credited per job, were established following a scale resembling that used in industry for the computation of wages. All farm jobs were classified into a number of categories, each of which was rewarded according to a graduated scale. Let us assume that there are nine job categories, each one credited as follows in workday units:

Job categories	1	2	3	4	5	6	7	8	9
Workday units per job	0.5	0.75	1	1.25	1.5	1.75	2	2.25	2.5

A full day's work for lower types of jobs, such as cleaning, may have accounted for only half a workday unit; a mechanical or managerial job may have been credited with several units. Since mid-1966 the collective farms have been advised to guarantee a *monthly wage in money* and a yearly share in the net output or income of the collective for each of its members. The monthly wage is to be based on the rates of pay of corresponding categories of state farm workers and on the volume of work performed. In the disbursement of earnings by the collective farms, the means for paying for the collective farmers' labor are to be allocated *first*; when collective farms lack funds for earning the guaranteed wage payments, the State Bank is obligated to grant them a credit, which must be repaid by the third year after its receipt.

Because of lack of specialization among the peasants, fluctuating needs for labor intake on the farm, and various other factors, the managerial staff has wide powers in assigning each member's volume of work and type of task, and therefore exercises a strong influence on each member's total workdays and, hence, his income. The collective farmers supplement the incomes earned in the collective by taking work in forestry, road construction, or temporarily on the state farms, either independently or on the basis of contracts entered into by their collective. But first and foremost, the peasants supplement their incomes by working intensively on their own small plots and selling their own produce at free market prices in the collective-farm market. Thus, the tiny, private subsidiary farms, with a small fraction of the cultivated area but with a still significant livestock population, continue to be not only the peasant's last stand in the struggle for what is left of his independence but also a source of income for the peasantry and of supplies for the towns.[9] In order to ensure that collective work is not neglected, each member must devote a minimum number of workdays annually to the collective farm. Those who do not complete the minimum required without acceptable reason are expelled from the collective and may be punished by law.

Almost 80 per cent of the labor resources of Soviet agriculture are still concentrated in the collective farms.[10] In the mid-1960's

9. *The collective farms produce the largest share of the country's output of grains, cotton, sugar beets, and wool; the private plots produce the largest share of country's outputs of potatoes, vegetables, meat, milk, and eggs.*

Percentage Shares in Total Agriculture Output, 1965

	State Farm	Collective Farm	Private Plots
Grain	37	61*	2
Cotton	20	80	0
Sugar beet	9	91	0
Potatoes	15	22	63
Vegetables	34	25	41
Meat	30	30	40
Milk	26	35	39
Eggs	20	13	67
Wool	39	41	20

* *Shaded box: highest relative share.*

SOURCE: Naradnoe khoziaistvo SSSR v 1965g, *op. cit.*, pp. 257ff.

10. *A variety of associations with respect to work and to the ownership of land, implements, and draft animals has been devised in the socialist economies of Eastern Europe in order to make the recalcitrant peasantry advance toward the "superior type" of Soviet collective farming organization. Some of these associations left untouched the principle of private ownership of land, but provided for joint ownership of draft animals and joint tillage. Other cooperatives grouped all the land into collective compounds, but left livestock and implements under private ownership; these cooperatives paid rent to the members according to the size of the land they contributed to the association.*

In China, in the 1950's, the Soviet artel was considered an inferior type of association, the superior one being the commune *in which all land, livestock, and implements were taken over by the collectives, while personal property was reduced to a minimum of articles of personal use.*

every collective farmer taking part in the collective-farm operations has been occupied in the communal operations less than 200 days a year, or less than 75 per cent of what the Soviets call the "annual fund of working time" (roughly 270 days per year). The extensive conversion of collective farms into state farms has reduced the level of use of labor resources in the communal economy, for not all the collective farmers were accepted on the newly formed state farms. Surplus farm labor exists in nearly all regions and is particularly conspicuous in the least developed ones, where up to 65 per cent of the potential labor force is unused in the communal economy.[11] Moreover, the seasonal nature of agricultural work swells unused labor time to very high levels during the winter months when, for example, in the early 1960's, about 9.5 million fewer collective farmers were engaged in communal work than in the summer months. Given both the declining growth of labor requirements in industry (because of the development of automated production) and the increase in labor supply in the cities, the number of workers which could be released eventually from agriculture could considerably exceed the number that industry could use.

PRICES, INCENTIVES, AND LEVEL OF SAVINGS

The differences between the prices the state pays for agricultural products and the prices it charges consumers have represented a key source of the state's capital accumulation. The prices for most compulsory deliveries remained virtually unchanged from 1928 to 1955, while consumer retail prices rose approximately eight times during the same period. As stated officially, "the prices for the major agricultural produce existing before 1953 were low and did not cover the labor and resources involved in their production and did not provide the minimum conditions for the development of the economy of the collective farms.[11] After 1953, delivery quotas were reduced for several commodities and prices of some products were increased; finally, in 1958, new unified prices were set at a level corresponding approximately to average cost plus a small markup. Regional differences were established, however, so as to eliminate the effect of differential rent. The new prices were said to be stable under normal harvesting conditions but at the same time

11. Kommunist, *No. 18 (1965), pp. 65–74.*

sufficiently flexible to take into account output variations, production expenses, and the collectives' needs for further growth. The data available suggest that the prices of compulsory deliveries before the introduction of the new unified prices were only 5 to 20 per cent of those paid by consumers in the free farm markets where prices fluctuate in response to supply and demand. After the reform, most procurement prices, though far higher than previously, still diverged significantly from those paid in the farm markets.[12] Finally, a number of further price revisions increased state prices significantly and narrowed the differentials.

The increase in procurement prices and hence in farm incomes raises the problem of increasing the supply of goods delivered to the peasants. If the new prices are to be as effective as intended in stimulating increased output, a serious beginning must be made toward increasing supplies of manufactured goods to the villages. On the other hand, the state can avail itself of at least three measures for keeping its capital accumulation at the desired levels. Admittedly, past state procurement prices were only a small fraction of the retail price net of distribution costs; the indirect tax levied through the retail price (which includes the substantial turnover tax) burdened both the producer and the consumer. Following the increase in the prices paid to producers, a larger part of the former tax burden may eventually be shifted to the consumer. Secondly, with the sale of the machinery previously owned by the MTS to the farms, their electric current, fuel, and spare parts requirements have increased tremendously. Prices of these goods and services may eventually be raised so as to offset some of the increase in procurement prices. Thirdly, with increased output and with better management of procurement — in which loss and deterioration of goods, poor transportation, and inadequate storing facilities have been chronic — the state may build its agricultural stocks to the point where it can deliberately choose among suppliers and buy only from the collective

12. *For instance, in 1953–54 the compulsory delivery price for potatoes was 10 rubles per quintal, as against 194 rubles per quintal in the Moscow free market. The unified price per quintal was increased in 1958 to 40 rubles (as against a free market price of 118 rubles per quintal in 1957). For milk, the 1953–54 compulsory delivery price was 55 rubles per quintal, the free market price 394, the new unified price 115 (as against a free market price of 307 rubles in 1957). For eggs, the 1953–54 compulsory price was 20 rubles per quintal, the free market price 239, the unified price 60 (as against a free market price of 226 rubles in 1957). (These data are from United Nations,* World Economic Survey, 1958, *New York, 1959, chap. 4.)*

selling at the lowest price. Unified procurement prices thus may serve not only as stimuli to output, but also as powerful levers for restructuring agriculture. As monopsonist and price fixer, the state would ultimately be able to favor the development of specialization and competition among collectives, with the expectation of reaping advantages in the form of price reductions.

If and when this stage is reached, the subsidiary farms of the individual collective farmers will be the first to suffer, since the price of their output would be too low to encourage intensive individual work and to justify the expenses and time needed for marketing their commodities. By connecting the collectives directly to the state industry (by allowing them to own and operate agricultural machinery) and by offering new incentives for them to increase their output and their capital formation (via increased prices), the state has opened new ways not only for breaking the stagnation in agriculture but also for liquidating its old enemy, the tiny subsidiary farm of the collectivized peasant.

PRODUCTIVITY AND LONG-RUN SOLUTIONS IN AGRICULTURE

Soviet data on output and labor force engaged in agriculture are not sufficiently detailed and not always fully consistent. They do, however, point clearly toward wide disparities in labor inputs required in the collectives as compared to the state farms. Data released by Khrushchev in 1958 point, furthermore, toward striking differences in productivity between both the state and collective farms and farms in the United States. According to these data, the number of man-hours expended per centner (100 kg.) of grain, for example, was 1.8 times higher in the state farms and 7.3 times higher in the collective farms than in the United States; for potatoes, 4.2 and 5.1 times higher than in the United States; for sugar beets, 4.2 and 6.2 times higher.[13] The very high labor inputs required by the collective farms can be further illustrated by direct comparisons between similar Soviet and American farms. In a careful study of a Soviet and an American dairy farm of equal size and similar livestock population, Professor Gardner Clark of Cornell University has shown that the Soviet farm was outproducing its American counter-

13. *Report by N. S. Khrushchev to the Plenum of the Central Committee of the C.P.S.U., Dec. 15, 1958.*

part by 50 per cent with respect to their primary product, milk. This discrepancy was substantially narrowed, however, when comparing the marketed shares of the output of the two farms: a much larger share of the Soviet output was consumed on the farm. Furthermore, the Soviet farm was operated with a labor force *thirty-one times* larger than that of the American farm.

Commenting upon the low productivity of Soviet agriculture, Khrushchev contended that under capitalist farming "what is economically unprofitable has no right to live," whereas under the collective farm system the number of people employed "does not actually represent the bare minimum needed to cope with soil cultivation, the tending of crops, and breeding of livestock and poultry, but is rather determined by the number of able-bodied persons united by that particular cooperative." [14] In fact, the collectives serve as a mechanism for transforming potential emigration to the towns or visible agricultural unemployment into *under*employment concentrated in the collectives. The state farms are more productive than the collectives simply because they need not put up with excess labor. There is nothing inherently more efficient about the state farms. It is the collectives which have had to absorb the numerous employees of the disbanded and inefficient MTS. This, incidentally, has helped improve them technologically but, at the same time, has also inflated their already oversized bureaucracy.

In the Soviet Union as well as in Eastern Europe, industrialization has only slowly reduced the *absolute* number of people engaged in agriculture. In the USSR in 1959, 33.9 million persons were engaged in manual work in agriculture, as compared to 34.7 million in 1939.[15] After the exodus from the villages to urban concentrations in the first phases of the industrialization drive (in the Soviet Union in the 1930's, in Eastern Europe in the early 1950's), the rate of labor intake into industry from agriculture has slowed down appreciably. Many factors have contributed to this slowing down — lack of urban housing, and competition between urban female labor and job-seekers from the countryside, on the one hand, and, on the other, the ability of the collectives to absorb surplus labor. The collectives have thus been forced to support low-productivity marginal

14. *N. S. Khrushchev's speech at Des Moines, Iowa,* New York Times, *Sept. 24, 1959.*

15. *"Distribution of USSR Population According to Social Groups, Branches of Economy and Occupation and Education Level of Manual and Brain Workers," Report of Central Statistical Administration, Feb. 10, 1961.*

workers for whom no other job opportunities exist. The counterpart of this has been an appalling situation in many villages. As stated by Gale Johnson: "There is no question that the changes in agricultural policy since 1953 have increased farm incomes, but compared to the American farmer, the rewards received by the Russian peasant are meager indeed. The Russian peasant has a small house and sufficient food to eat, and that is about all." [16]

In the 1960's, a reorganization of former collective farms into state farms, forced "freeing" of a large part of the collective farmers, and an outflow of the rural youth from the villages far "in excess of objectively allowable norms" — as a Soviet source significantly puts it — have finally reduced the officially employed population in agriculture and have substantially changed its structure. According to the same source, 25.6 million people were directly employed in agriculture at the beginning of the second half of the 1960's. Of this total, 17.6 million were employed in the collective farms and 8.0 million in the state farms and state agricultural institutions; in addition, an estimated total of over 12 million persons — chiefly women and the elderly — spent all of their time working on the personal plots. The conversion of certain rural communities into urban-type settlements and the departure of young rural residents for study and work in the cities are now outstripping the natural population growth and the influx of city-trained agricultural technicians into the country. The new exodus of the rural young, prompted by an increasing gap in living conditions between the villages and the towns, is not viewed with equanimity by the officialdom, which is beset by unemployment problems in the towns and on construction sites. However, only a significant increase in both productivity and living conditions in the countryside could stave off this migration.

What could the Soviet government do about the poverty prevailing in most of these collectives? As we have noted, the government might increase the prices paid to farmers and further reduce its prevailing indirect tax on them. The point is illustrated in Figure 5. With supply *SS*, demand *DD*, the prices for obligatory deliveries at P_1 and the prices charged to urban consumers at P_3, the government could reduce the differential represented by the shaded area and increase the price of obligatory deliveries to, say, P_2. This would raise the revenue of the collectives while still leaving a differential be-

16. Time, *Sept. 12, 1955, p. 31.*

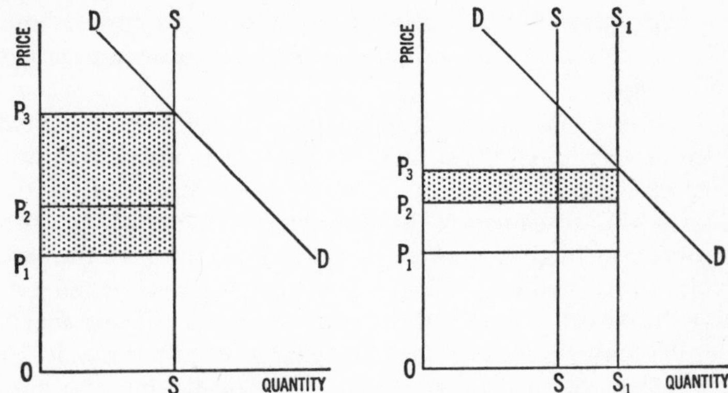

FIGURE 5. *Price Changes and Increases in Farm Income*

tween prices paid to farmers and prices charged to consumers. The government could, furthermore, reduce its prices for fertilizers, machinery, fuels, etc. This would facilitate an increase in farm output — from *OS* to OS_1 — thus further raising, under certain conditions, farm total revenue.

These measures would ease the pressure of marginal labor by raising living standards. Promotion of small-scale industry and construction in rural areas could further help to absorb surplus agricultural workers and, at the same time, increase living standards. In the long run, however, another aspect of this same problem is reducing the number of people who share this increased revenue. This is a key problem involving creation of new job opportunities in the towns, an increase in urban housing, and an increase in the physical mobility of labor. Here, Soviet policy makers are faced with a fundamental dilemma. Increases in job opportunities and in labor mobility require not only more investment in housing, but also higher investment in an area even less attractive to Soviet policy makers, namely, the "non-productive" expansion of services. In the West, a large part of the agricultural surplus population has been absorbed, not by industry but by services, most of which even now are labor-intensive. The systematic Soviet deemphasis of consumers' goods and of services — the latter the companion of highly diversified personal consumption — has caused disguised unemployment in agriculture to rise and has shut the door on a progressive solution to this problem. In so far as the maintenance of underemployment in agriculture is reinforced by lack of urban facilities and consumer services, however, investment in these facilities and services would, of course, result in an extremely high yield and in a high increase in aggregate physical output.

After a long period of stagnation, marked by very limited progress in output and little change in yields, the prospects for improving efficiency in agriculture have increased, as a result of the transfer of MTS machinery to the collectives, the increase in procurement prices, and decentralization measures in planning. In the past, in contrast to a fixed wage bill — the inelastic overhead of the state farm — the collective farm had the great advantage of being able to reduce the consumption of its members whenever output was declining or the state requirements were rising. This "heroic" measure, most dramatically pressed during the 1930's, when the marketed share of grain out of a declining output was continuously raised, may no longer be used by the Soviet leaders, as output expands and the marketed volume grows to more comfortable levels (see Figure 6).

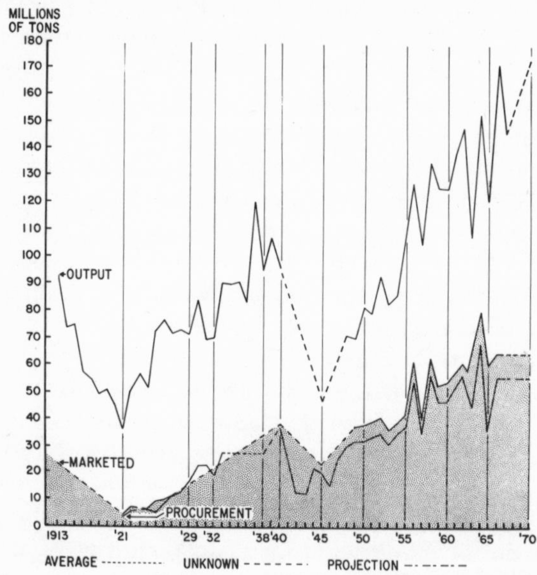

FIGURE 6. *Fluctuations in Grain Output and Marketed Share in Russia and the Soviet Union, 1913–70*

SOURCE: *Narodnoe khoziaistvo* SSSR [The National Economy of the USSR] (for 1958 and 1960), Moscow: Gosstatizdat, 1959, pp. 350, 351; 1961, pp. 365, 368, and Five Year Plan data, 1966–1970.

With the introduction and the extension of fixed labor rewards and of economic accounting, the collective farms may come to diverge less and less from the state farms, notwithstanding the maintenance of the fiction that the first embody group or cooperative ownership and the second constitute state property.

By changing the pattern of investment earmarked for agriculture (as, for example, from mechanization of field activities to mechanization of livestock feeding), by shifting the pattern of cultivation from low-yield crops to corn, by trying to bring under the plan the fallow land of the collectives on which the collective farmers graze their cattle,[17] by shifting labor from the private plots to the collective farm itself (where its marginal productivity would be higher), by linking the rich collective farms to the poor ones, Soviet leadership expects to boost yields and to increase the return from its investments without increasing the amount invested. Although this approach is far more imaginative than the one followed until the disbanding of the MTS, it remains to be seen whether systematic increases in yields per person and sustained technological changes can actually be secured without larger investments in agriculture and in urban facilities than the Soviet leadership seems prepared to undertake.

In the early 1960's, although industry had approximately 5,000 rubles' worth of fixed assets per worker, agriculture had less than 2,000 rubles. The USSR had only one third as much farm machinery per hectare of sown area as did the United States, and less than one fourth as much capital (excluding land) per agricultural worker.

17. *This would bring under cultivation an estimated total of 6 million hectares situated in the zones of high humidity. In 1959, N. S. Khrushchev labeled these areas the "new Soviet virgin lands."*

6.

Supply and Distribution

CENTRALIZED SUPPLY AND TRADE NETWORKS

In the USSR, goods are distributed through two distinct networks: material-technical supply and trade. The bulk of producers' goods are supplied through the former. All consumers' goods, as well as some producers' goods (e.g., construction materials for the collective farms), are sold through the latter. As we have mentioned, scarce supplies and the principal producers' goods are not marketed but allocated centrally. Even though each material transfer takes place against a money payment, the right and ability of each enterprise to obtain the goods involved and to pay for them depend in only a limited way on the enterprise itself. For example, an enterprise called, for this purpose, the *investor*, may buy plant and machinery. These purchases may be made only from appropriate funds, deposited with a special bank, for specific goods at predetermined prices and times of delivery, from suppliers who have been ordered to comply with the "investor's" requests. In Soviet economic theory, the goods transferred through this network were long considered to be only "quasi-commodities," since no real change of ownership occurs when they are transferred among state-owned firms. We shall turn later — principally in the discussions on money and banking — to some of the implications of this contention. For the present, let us note that in the sphere of material-technical supply, goods move on the basis of centralized orders directed to both suppliers and recipients. In the sphere of trade, goods move on the basis of buyers' being able to pay the price asked for the goods available.

At the apex of the single, unified program of supply and sales of capital goods and materials is the USSR State Committee for Material Technical Supply (Gossnab). Under its jurisdiction are placed various all-union interbranch, interrepublic, and territorial administrations, which market the most important producers' goods through their regional warehouses. In principle, the State Committee and its administrations work in close cooperation with the ministers and enterprises, survey the implementation of the details of the supply plan, control the prompt and specific fulfillment of the plan, smooth out wholesale distribution, and avoid stockpiling and bottlenecks. In practice, the ministries tend to maintain parallel supply and distribution organs of their own; the large suppliers fulfill their assignments only in large lots in accordance with their own plan norms, while the receivers need only small shipments for carrying out their specific assignments. Unwanted inventories thus accumulate at certain points, while chronic shortages persist at others; in addition, low technical standards prevail in the handling of supplies from the enterprise, to the warehouses and storage centers, to the receivers. The lack of *autonomous* territorial supply and procurement agencies that sell and buy materials and manufactured products *directly* to and from the enterprises renders the operation of the supply system cumbersome, rigid, and wasteful — notwithstanding the increasing help of some of the best-known Soviet economists (such as L. V. Kantorovich, V. A. Trapeznikov, N. P. Fedorenko) and the use of electronic computers for mapping the optimum links between tens of thousands of consumer plants and suppliers. The Soviet officials still view this gigantic centralized system as the best instrument they have for ensuring the execution of the plan in accordance with its key priorities.

The sphere of trade comprises, along with all sales of goods for personal consumption, sales of some producers' goods and state and cooperative purchases of agricultural produce from the collective farms. Trade, thus defined, is carried out through an "organized" and an "unorganized" market. The organized market is composed of state and cooperative commerce — the first primarily urban, the second primarily rural — both directly planned by the state. The unorganized market consists of the collective-farm trade.

State commerce occupies, of course, the prominent place in both wholesale and retail operations. Interrepublic planning of trade, coordination, and allocation of main consumers' goods supplies are carried out by the USSR ministry of trade. Within each republic, the republic ministry of trade is responsible for all consumer trade carried on therein. Each ministry of trade is organized into functional departments and operational administrations and maintains, moreover, various specialized agencies and warehouses. The ministerial departments deal with planning, pricing, labor and wages, etc. The administrations supervise and control the sales of manufactured goods, foodstuffs, and other commodities within the republic as a whole. All the wholesale offices and warehouses are under the operational direction of the ministry. Department stores may also be placed directly under a ministerial administration. City stores and public catering establishments are placed under the control of both the ministry of trade and the respective city trade organization. Workers' canteens and similar facilities in state enterprises are under republic control (see Figure 7).

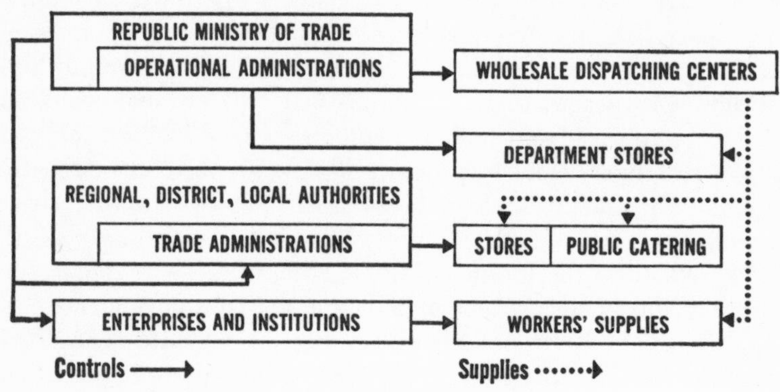

FIGURE 7. *State Trading Network*

The second component of the organized market, cooperative commerce, consists primarily of the trade of consumers' cooperatives. Consumers' cooperatives are formed mostly of peasants and represent the basic trading organization in the village. Although each consumers' cooperative is autonomous, they all, as already indicated, are organized into a regional, a republic, and a central union of cooperatives. The union carries on the wholesale operations of the entire system through its wholesale warehouses at the republic, regional, and district levels. Besides their main purpose of supplying their members with manufactured consumers' goods, some cooperatives also retail collective-farm produce on a commission basis in the cities. The sales on commission have been devised in order to allow poorly located farms to sell their produce in the towns.

The unorganized market is represented by the collective-farm trade. This trade is carried out under the direction and control of the trade departments of regional and local authorities, in year-round sheltered or open stalls in places assigned *ad hoc*. There are no intermediaries in these markets: the salesmen of the collective farms or of the cooperatives must be members of the collective whose produce they sell. The peasants sell homemade dairy products, fruits, vegetables, and poultry. The state retail organizations also participate in these markets: sometimes they unload their supplies in order to influence the market price; more often they sell special types of products, mostly those suited to the peasant clientele.

PLANNING OF TRADE

Operational and long-range plans, republic or regional, are worked out for trade, just as for any other branch of the economy. The balances are drawn up in both physical and monetary terms by the State Planning Committee in accord with the All-Union ministry of trade, and the republic ministries of trade. The financial balances evidently play a key role, since they involve the problems of price setting, turnover tax, and markups, as well as the problems of currency circulation and of the income and expenditure of the population. As for other branches of the economy, the draft plans for trade are based on the directives concerning output and its division into a market and non-market supply. The market supply is the part earmarked for sale to the public; the non-market supply encompasses the raw materials, intermediate products, and manufactured goods destined for industry, defense, public health institutions, and exports. The final state trading plan, which is subdivided into plans of turnover, employment and wage procurement, and finances, consolidates the trade and financial plans [1] of each of the trading enterprises (warehouses, stores, and shops). These plans are the counterpart of the output-financial plans of each producing enterprise.

During the elaboration of the plans, the main administrations of the ministries of trade submit to the producing organizations preliminary requests for certain commodities and definite orders for others. These requests and orders seek to convey the desires of the

1. Torgovofinansovyiplan, *abbreviated as* torgfinplan.

consumers to the producers and thus help in setting the plan ratios between branches and types of products. The production plans, however, must first take into account the basic decisions concerning the allocations between investment and consumption, so that in practice the actual impact of the trade requests and orders may be felt in only limited measure.

Once the plans are adopted, contracts are signed between trading and producing organizations specifying value, volume, assortment, quality, method of payment, and terms of delivery of the goods to be supplied. The main administrations of the ministries of trade conclude trade agreements with the suppliers, and in turn, the wholesale organizations sign contracts with the retail enterprises. Often the latter also sign contracts directly with local producers. Since the plan is further modified during its implementation (e.g., by managers who may vary the product mix) and since supplies are not channeled as rapidly as needed from plants to warehouses and from warehouses to retail outlets, wide discrepancies arise between the original requests and the actual goods received for sale. The superficial consideration given to consumers' demand, the shoddy quality of some commodities, the limited selection of goods actually offered for sale, the poor synchronization between the supply and delivery of seasonal goods, and the prevalence of inattentive and rude salesmen victimize consumers in innumerable ways.

Following the usual Soviet remuneration pattern, managers, cashiers, inspectors, and staff receive bonuses when actual sales for their department store or shop exceed planned sales. Sales personnel are usually rewarded on the incentive basis of piece-rate wages (starting from a given level of planned sales) and thus are stimulated to increase sales. On the other hand, part of their remuneration is withheld if the sales plan is not carried out. But notwithstanding these usual Soviet incentives, trade employees — like their colleagues of the material-technical supply system — are accustomed to rely on operating in a sellers' market rather than on direct initiative for stimulating consumers' demand. "Progressive sales methods," such as open display of goods, trade by samples in department stores, installment buying, and other modern marketing methods, are used only on a limited scale in the Soviet Union.[2] Defective as is this

2. *Consumer credit was introduced in the late 1950's for purchases of consumer durables, such as phonographs, radios, cameras, scooters, motorcycles, and some other goods. Customers make an initial down payment of 20 per cent and*

trade apparatus from the consumer's point of view, it serves two functions for the state: it distributes the earmarked commodities (if possible on schedule), and it raises tax revenues to the levels prescribed. If the market is cleared at the established relative prices, a number of key planned balances concerning taxes, retail sales, volume and pattern of expenditure of the population, and so on will be realized. If discrepancies arise between the planned pattern of supply and the pattern of consumers' demand, a chain of reactions is provoked. The retail plans remain unfulfilled; excess demand for some goods and surpluses of other goods appear; and unplanned increases in liquidity in the hands of the population take place. If the disturbances prove to be perennial – as they did in the early 1960's – they can ultimately force substantive revisions in planning approaches and management.

CONSUMERS' GOODS PRICING AND SUPPLY AND DEMAND

Soviet economists reject both the underlying assumptions and the tools of "subjective" supply and demand analysis. Soviet textbooks do not attack the problems of pricing in terms of demand and elasticity, substitution effects, and so on. They attack each problem pragmatically and try to solve it on its own merits within the constraints established by the plan. In really obvious cases, they cannot fail to notice the impacts on the quantity of a given commodity that is in demand when its price changes, when the price of competing or complementary goods changes, or when shifts in income distribution occur. But the determination of certain prices centrally and of others regionally or locally, the application in certain cases of arbitrary political decisions, and the seriatim approach to each problem lead finally to the establishment of bizarre price constellations which may bear little or no relation to planned and actual supplies.

In the mid-1960's, roughly half the total domestic retail trade turnover was carried in commodities whose prices were fixed centrally. The prices of other commodities were established either at the republic or at the regional and local levels. Prices may be uniform

---

pay off the balance at 2 per cent interest over a period of 6 to 12 months. It is difficult to know whether this procedure has been very effective in eliminating the accumulation of stocks.

for the Soviet Union as a whole, or differentiated zonally, by urban-rural areas, by sectors, or by regions and localities. Uniform prices are established by the State Planning Committee on the basis of the average All-Union cost of production of the given item, including the cost of transportation to all distributing points. The commodities included in this group are mostly standard manufactured consumers' goods, such as fabrics, knitted goods, shoes, cameras, bicycles, as well as some foodstuffs and related products of mass consumption like vodka, tea, coffee, and tobacco products. Zonally differentiated prices — called *uniform zonal prices* in the USSR — are also established centrally and are typical for most foodstuffs — bread, meat, fish products, salt, canned goods, and some other commodities. Zonal differences are also established for merchandise whose transportation cost is high, namely, furniture, wood products, and glass. For most products, three price zones are established. For certain products, however, the number of zones may be reduced to two or increased to as many as seven. Zone I is usually the zone with the lowest price and includes the districts where the given commodity is mass-produced; Zone II comprises the districts into which the given products are imported; Zone III usually encompasses the remote districts, i.e., the far North and the far East. Incidentally, it cannot be ascertained how much this sort of differentiation offsets the wage differentiations which are meant to stimulate the movement of the labor force toward certain districts included in Zone III. A complicating factor in setting these prices is the fact that some of the products, such as fish, meat, and butter, are traded also in the collective-farm markets. The rural-urban differentiation also affects the price of certain products. For such commodities as sugar, confectionery, clothing, shoes, soap, and kerosene, rural prices tend to be between 7 and 10 per cent higher than the prices prevailing in the town stores. Often the differential may stimulate the peasants to buy in the town stores, to the detriment of the village shops.

There are also temporary price variations, established either centrally or locally, in the case of new commodities, or in order to cope with seasonal shifts in supply. In the case of commodities produced by small local industry, there are substantial differences from region to region and from locality to locality.

Centrally, as well as locally, the established prices may be manipulated in various ways for certain established reasons. Thus the price of bread does not exceed the price of the flour it contains, and prices of clothing are set relatively lower than those of fabrics in order to achieve, as an official textbook puts it, "a better utilization of raw materials and an economy of domestic labor." Some consumers' goods are usually underpriced: this is the case for children's apparel, books, and even private cars, although the price of cars may appear extremely high by Western standards. The underpricing of certain goods, i.e., pricing them below the market equilibrium level, leads to shortages and queuing, deflection of purchases to other goods and services, including luxury consumption, as well as to black marketing. On the other hand, many goods have been typically overpriced in the past, i.e., their price was above the market equilibrium level. This has been true principally in the case of phonographs, radios, cameras, and other consumer durables.

In the collective-farm market, prices are set through the interaction of supply and demand. For a number of commodities, the government stores and the collective farms as a whole may be likened to two competing firms, one of which operates with rigid prices and fixed supplies in the short run, and the other under market-determined prices, with a relatively elastic supply schedule. Some of the consequences arising from this situation may be illustrated with the usual supply-demand apparatus. Let S_gS_g be the inelastic supply schedule of the state stores, S_kS_k, the supply schedule of the peasant markets; S_tS_t, total supply; and DD, the demand curve. If the state shops retail at price P_o a commodity also available in the collective farm market, the entire market will be cleared at that price (see Figure 8*a*). The demand as seen by the collective-farm market is total demand less the (inelastic) portion supplied by the state. In the event that the state supplies are sold at any price below P_o, then the new equilibrium price for the produce of the collective farms will in general differ from P_o. This price, P_2, will tend to be higher, since more purchasing power remains in the hands of consumers after obtaining the state produce at P_1. Hence, the demand curve for the collective market supplies will tend to shift to the right as compared to its position if the state price were P_o — that is, from D_1D_1 to $D'_1D'_1$ (Figure 8*b*).

Alternatively, it is possible to regard the problem from the viewpoint of interaction between total demand and total supply. If the state shops overprice the commodity, total supply becomes in fact S_kS_k with the market clear at P_1 (Figure 8*c*). This price will be higher than that which would have prevailed if the state shops had

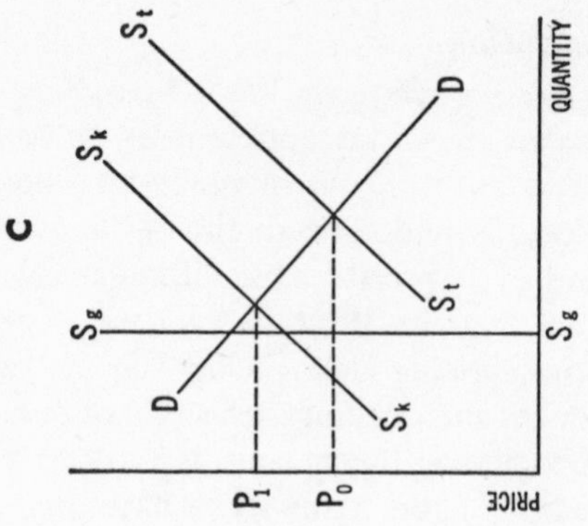

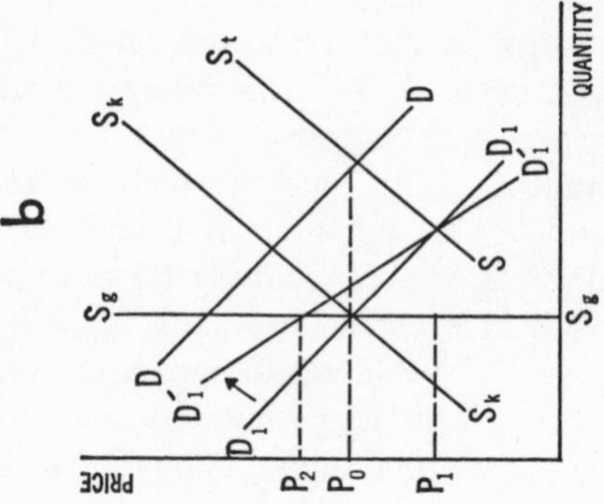

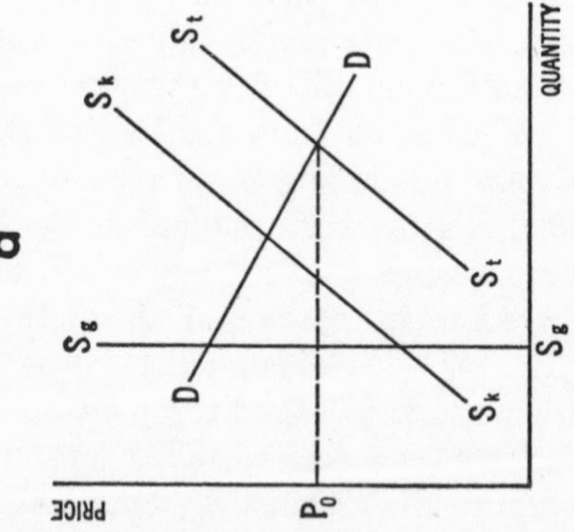

FIGURE 8. *Demand and Supply in State Shops and Peasant Markets*

not priced themselves out of the market. To unload their supplies, the state shops would now have to cut their price below P_1 (Figure 8*c*). Thus, it is possible to have two prices for the same commodity if the state price is lower than that prevailing in the collective-farm market; two prices cannot, however, prevail for the same commodity when the state price is higher. In this case, these shops simply price their commodity out of the market.

In special circumstances the state can, however, play a decisive role in the collective-farm markets, since it alone channels the bulk of food products from one part of the country to another and since private intermediaries in wholesale foodstuffs are eliminated. In a competitive market, prices of goods in one locality cannot in the long run differ from those in another locality, except for the cost of transportation. In the Soviet Union, prices may differ from one local market to another, for the consumer buys directly from the farmer on territorially limited markets. But the prices prevailing on all these markets can be brought into line if and when the state so chooses; state trading thus may affect market equilibrium in most of the foodstuff trade at any chosen moment.

In summary, consumers' goods reach the Soviet consumer through three networks: state, cooperative, and collective-farm market. Owing to limited investments in stores, buildings, and equipment, a large share of retail trading is carried out in small shops often wrongly located and poorly equipped. Unsanitary premises, poor storage facilities, lack of refrigeration, and lack of packaging of goods were common in the mid-1960's. At that time, a limited number of retail stores were officially recorded as using "progressive" methods of sale, namely, packaged goods and self-service.[3] The use of automatic selling machines was still in its infancy; even so, the ratio of personnel employed in both retail trading and public dining to total population was roughly one-fourth that in the United States. By volume of sales, the three networks ranked as follows: state trading accounted for some 68 per cent of the total, cooperative trade for 29 per cent, and the collective-farm markets for 3 per cent. In the sale of foodstuffs, however, the collective-farm markets accounted for more than 10 per cent.

3. *In the mid-1960's the Soviet domestic trade was carried on in 640,000 stores (470,000 of which were department stores) and 170,000 one-counter shops, half of which were located in urban and half in rural areas. In addition there were some 7,200 collective-farm markets and a total of some 192,000 public dining enterprises.*

Under free-market conditions, the consumer gets what he thinks he wants from where he wants it, even though, admittedly, his will is strongly swayed by advertising and by various other factors. Under Soviet conditions, the consumer is left free to choose what to buy; but he may do so only within the arbitrary limits arising from policy makers' decisions as to what he as a consumer should want, the haphazard implementation of the plans of output and deliveries, and the manipulations of the salesmen themselves, operating as far as many products are concerned in a comfortable sellers' market.

FOREIGN TRADE ORGANIZATION

Soviet foreign trade is a state monopoly. It encompasses not only the export and import operations carried on exclusively by state-chartered or designated agencies, but all the country's economic transactions with the rest of the world and all the ensuing international accounts. Consequently, the monopoly of foreign exchange is an organic component of the monopoly of foreign trade. The stated tasks of the monopoly are "warding off" capitalist economic penetration, providing maximum assistance to domestic capital formation, and facilitating the eventual coordination of the economic plans of the socialist countries.

The underlying assumptions of the Marxian theory of economic growth [4] and the Soviet corollary of methodical emphasis on the development of heavy industry only partially supplant the assumptions and implications of the comparative-cost chain of reasoning, as we shall see subsequently. For the USSR (and the other socialist countries) the volume of foreign trade is dependent, first and foremost, on the domestic output plan and on its emphases. Even under conditions of expanding socialist foreign trade, the emphases placed on domestic outputs determine primarily the dynamics of imports, which in their turn determine the dynamics of exports. The government's decisions concerning the volume, value, structure, and direction of its trade, however, are also influenced by various policy considerations and existing commitments. Since the monopoly of foreign trade implies the control of each foreign trade operation, tariffs, the key factor in the foreign trade of Western countries, play only a secondary role in the USSR.

The foreign trade system is headed by the All-Union Ministry of

4. *See Chap.* 8.

Foreign Trade. This ministry plans the relevant elements concerning foreign transactions in connection with scheduled outputs, policy considerations, and commitments. It prepares and participates in the negotiation of foreign trade agreements and controls and directs the trading organizations. Following the familiar pattern, the ministry is organized into functional and operational departments. The former comprise planning, foreign exchange and finance, contracts, bookkeeping and auditing, arbitration, personnel, and capital construction; the latter, import, export, tariffs, transport, and international forwarding.

Working closely with the State Planning Committee, the key planning department drafts a plan of foreign trade within the framework of the party directives. The draft takes into account the output plans and the prevailing commitments and requirements. It specifies volume, prices, and transport, cost structure, and direction of foreign trade. The relevant parts of the draft are routed to the importing and exporting corporations, which in turn draw their specific plans on the basis of the physical balances submitted to them by the producing organizations and their selling and purchasing departments. The foreign trade corporations complete the basic blueprint, which they present to the planning department of the ministry. The coordinated yearly or long-term (five to seven years) plan can then be established by the ministry and submitted for final approval to the SPC and the Council of Ministers.

Among the other functional departments, an outstanding role is played by the foreign exchange and finance department, which, in close contact with the State Bank, concerns itself with balance of payments problems. The contracts department studies market trends abroad, prepares the projects for negotiations with other states, and drafts instructions for the foreign trade organizations concerning the execution of contracts after they are signed. The other departments prepare the budget of the ministry, survey the expenditure of the foreign trade organs and the financial accounts of the ministry as a whole, and perform some other administrative functions.

Schematically, the departments for import and export are subdivided into sections for planning and finance, and into operational sections corresponding to the basic industrial branches (metallurgy, chemicals, textiles, leather, food and agricultural products, etc.). The other operational departments — tariffs, transport, and forwarding — are each subdivided into sections for planning, finance, accounting, and personnel.

The ministry conducts its domestic activities through foreign trade commissioners and through some twenty chartered monopolistic corporations. The commissioners are members of the regional or republic central bodies. They supervise the facilities connected with foreign trade, propose measures for trade expansion, and oversee the application of the instructions and regulations of the ministry. Like other state enterprises, the state-owned monopolistic corporations are organized on a business accounting basis. Each foreign trade corporation is an independent legal entity organized under its own charter, which specifies its endowment by the state for the pursuit of its assigned business. In carrying out the tasks assigned by the plan and in transacting purchases and sales at the prices established by the government, each corporation is expected to produce planned profits, or profits higher than planned, in accordance with planned costs and planned profit margins. The state does not guarantee their obligations, since they are independent legal entities. Their relation to the production enterprises is that of customer and supplier, regulated by special contracts. Once the over-all economic plan has been approved, contracts specifying prices for types of products and terms of delivery are concluded by the foreign trade corporations with the domestic suppliers or customers, within the framework of the plan.

Each importing, exporting, or forwarding corporation has its own functional and operational offices organized along the same lines as the Ministry of Foreign Trade. Basically, the importing and exporting corporations specialize according to the main industrial branches and their needs, whereas their offices specialize in one type of commodity. Thus, the main importing corporations are established for capital goods, basic raw materials, metals, and "goods of mass consumption" (household appliances, textiles, food, etc.). The main exporting corporations are diversified according to the principal exports which the country has to offer, namely, grain (Eksportkhleb), coal (Soiuzugleeksport), oil (Soiuznefteksport), lumber (Eksportles), fibers (Eksportlen), machines, equipment, and finished articles (Tekhnoeksport). A chamber of commerce, which is not directly included in the system of the Ministry of Foreign Trade, assists foreign customers in all matters connected with trade, sends delegations [5] abroad, arranges participation in foreign trade fairs,

5. *The Soviets call their trade delegates "representatives" and their dele-*

obtains patents for its citizens, etc.

The Ministry of Foreign Trade conducts its operations abroad through trade delegations or through commercial agencies. In Soviet law, the commercial delegates represent the state; they therefore enjoy full diplomatic immunity wherever foreign trade is accepted as a state function. The trade delegations control the commercial activity carried on abroad by their national foreign trade corporations, ensure that it conforms to the laws of the foreign trade monopoly, grant the documents needed for the agreed commercial operations, and also study general business trends in each country with respect to trade possibilities. In the United States, where these delegations are not accepted as state delegations, the Soviet Union maintains a commercial agency.

TECHNIQUES OF INTERNATIONAL PAYMENTS

In foreign trade, Soviet economists make no special distinction between the producers' and the consumers' goods traded with socialist or capitalist countries; all are "commodities," since all involve a change of ownership. But the very existence of a group of economies of the Soviet type has led to the appearance of a particular market with distinctive characteristics. In this market, the prevailing commercial treaties are based on preliminary agreements of friendship and mutual aid and have both a political and a commercial character. The stated political aim is to help the signatory countries to construct a "communist society" in the USSR and a "socialist society" in all the other countries; the commercial aim is to provide a clearly defined framework for trade relations. The commercial treaties include provisions for most-favored-nation treatment, export–import operations, transport of freight or passengers, and customs duties. They contain further provisions concerning arbitrage competence, exchange of specialists, organization of trade fairs, and other points of secondary importance.

Within the general framework established by their commercial treaties, the socialist governments sign trade agreements for a specified period of one, two, or five years. These agreements state the

gations "trade missions": Torgovoe predstavitel'stvo SSSR, *abbreviated as* Torgpredstva.

value of the envisaged trade in rubles and specify that the prices of the goods will be fixed "on the basis of world prices." Quota lists attached to these agreements indicate, in quantity or value terms, the broad categories of the commodities to be exchanged. The quinquennial trade agreements are meant to ensure the basic *minimum* supplies needed for the output scheduled by the long-term plans. The yearly agreements are meant to adjust the flows of trade to the precise needs of the yearly operational plan.

Payments other than those concerning merchandise trade – i.e., payments for service transactions – are expressed in the currency of the country where the services are rendered. Until 1964 both commercial and noncommercial payments were cleared through bilateral accounts maintained by the respective State Banks (or by the Foreign Trade Banks, which are dependent on the State Banks). Since 1964, after the formation of an *International Bank for Economic Cooperation* (IBEC)[6] by the Soviet Union and its East European socialist associates in the Council of Economic Mutual Assistance (CEMA),[7] all such accounts are cleared through IBEC. Schematically, omitting the IBEC route, the clearing arrangements consist in the following operations:

When a trade agreement is signed, the state banks of the two trading countries open special non-interest-bearing credit accounts, recording the value of transactions. The bank of, say, country A debits the account of country B for B's imports from A, and also credits B's account for its exports to A, up to the limit set in the trade agreement. On the other hand, the appropriate foreign trade corporations of the two countries negotiate and sign contracts which stipulate the quality, assortment price, and delivery date for each item, the amount of which is specified, either in quantity or in value terms, in the quota lists.

A foreign trade operation is carried in practice as follows: On the basis of the plan, contracts are concluded between the exporting corporations and the appropriate domestic organizations selling commodities earmarked for export. The exporting corporations pay factory price f.o.b., net of turnover tax. For certain scarce commodities, a special purchase authorization may also be needed. Payment to the producer is made by the "acceptance" form, i.e., in this case,

6. *In Russian* Mezhdunarodnyi bank ekonomicheskogo sotrudnichestva (MBES).

7. *For a discussion of* CEMA, CMEA *or* COMECON, *see Chap.* 14.

acceptance by the purchasing exporting corporation of the documents indicating that the goods have been sent to it by the producer. Once received, the shipment is forwarded by the exporting agency to the foreign importing agency via the appropriate channels. Each foreign trade organization has an established profit norm, a markup ranging from 1 to 50 per cent of the domestic wholesale price of the item traded. The markup on exported goods is calculated on the domestic wholesale price, net of turnover tax, at which a good is usually sold by a domestic producer to a wholesale organization. For an imported good, the markup is computed on the basis of the domestic wholesale price at which the good is sold to an industry.

Although each Soviet agency tries to maximize profit on individual transactions, the Ministry of Foreign Trade considers the relation of the total values of exports and imports traded with any given partner and attempts to maximize the difference between them in internal Soviet wholesale prices. In order to obtain an import that is particularly sought after, the ministry will readily enjoin the trading agency to sell below cost. The difference between the price obtained and the domestic price, including the profit of the exporting organization, is covered in the agency's account by the state budget. If some exports are sold below cost, the loss may be more than balanced by the high internal prices of some imports. There are, however, some severe restraints on this maximizing of gains; first, the plan often decrees what is to be imported and exported not in value terms but in specific physical terms; secondly, trade must be bilaterally rather than multilaterally balanced.

Transactions with socialist partners are settled by the system of direct "encashment." The export organization is paid by its central bank from the account of the importing country upon receipt of the export documents. The bank then sends the documents to the central bank of the importing country which in turn immediately credits the account of the exporter's country and then presents the documents to the importing organization for collection. Should the buyer refuse to accept the goods, the banks rapidly notify one another and adjust their accounts accordingly. Trade agreements with capitalist countries are concluded in the same way, but the values involved are variously expressed, in the currency of the capitalist partner, in dollars, or in rubles. These, too, are bilateral agreements. with clearing arrangements, as in the trade with the socialist countries. The balance of such accounts can be covered either by gold or foreign exchange, or by shipment of additional commodities, as with the socialist partners. In countries with which no clearing accounts are established, the payments are made through the foreign accounts kept by the central banks with various foreign banks. Whatever the case, trade settlements with Western countries are made via the usual letter of credit (and not through direct encashment). The exporter receives his payment from a designated bank upon presentation, under specified conditions, of the export documents.

Some limited triangular arrangements involving socialist and capitalist countries have been established. Thus under one arrangement, specific Finnish exports to the Soviet Union were offset by certain Polish exports to Finland in exchange for Soviet exports to Poland. In another case, Burmese exports to the Soviet Union were offset by Czechoslovakian exports to Burma counterbalancing Soviet exports to Czechoslovakia.

Until June, 1957, no multilateral compensation arrangements involving clearing rubles existed. After that date the State Bank of the Soviet Union acted as a clearinghouse for certain socialist multilateral compensations. Finally, since January, 1964, the IBEC has become the clearinghouse of multilateral settlements conducted in so-called "transferable rubles" – a unit defined in terms of gold but not freely convertible either into the Soviet ruble (which is its equivalent) or into any other monetary unit. The transferable ruble is simply a conventional internal accounting unit of the socialist countries cooperating in CEMA by which all claims and payments in national currencies are expressed on the basis of fixed exchange rates. The clearing agreements are based on the principle of maintenance of continuous balance with all CEMA (and IBEC) countries, without necessarily balancing payments between each pair of partners. As pointed out by Dr. George Garvy of the Federal Reserve Bank of New York, the nonconvertibility of the transferable ruble creates a dilemma whenever there is a possibility of increasing exports outside the inter-socialist market "and thereby earn convertible currency rather than accepting the less desirable goods (in terms of kind, quality, or price) that the other members can offer in exchange."

PRICES AND RATES OF EXCHANGE

Prices of Soviet goods and services traded with CEMA or

with other countries, as specified in the contracts with the Soviet exporting or importing companies, are the prices prevailing in the world markets for that particular item or type of service. In the case of non-CEMA nations, the agreed-upon price also depends on the time at which the contract is signed, the total volume of transactions involved, and the bargaining power of the signatories. Within the CEMA, various rules commonly agreed upon aim at counteracting precisely such factors as price fluctuations, preferential treatment, differences in bargaining strength, and other unsettling elements. Thus, the Soviet Union and each CEMA member are supposed to charge any CEMA partner the same price for the same commodity, except for differences in transportation cost. The prices at which goods are traded are supposed to be "the international prices as they prevail in the capitalist markets in usual conditions of supply and demand." These prices are to be "kept unchanged for at least one year, and for the overwhelming majority of commodities for a number of years" in order to avoid unsettling the plans of the signatories.

It is difficult to ascertain the full scope of each of these rules. There is evidence of price discrimination in the CEMA, though in certain respects a tendency toward price uniformity exists, given the mobility of buyers and sellers. It is impossible for an outsider to know where and when the international prices used by the Soviet companies have been or are prevailing, and how the Soviet Union and its CEMA partners ascertain the "usual conditions of supply and demand in the capitalist markets." Presumably, this rule implies that the agreed-upon prices are based on an "average" world market price, purged of short-term fluctuations. Since these prices may be kept unchanged for a year or more, it follows, finally, that the price constellation within the CEMA diverges in each planning period from the price constellation in the world market, although the former is always derived from the latter.

The Soviet importing or exporting corporation pays or receives payment for the respective goods from the State Bank in rubles at the prevailing rate of exchange. The ruble and all the other CEMA currencies are defined in terms of gold so that each currency can be expressed in terms of the other. With full state control over all import and export operations, these rates can be established only in a more or less arbitrary fashion. Changes in domestic wholesale and retail prices or changes in the world market prices of the goods exported or imported do not necessarily affect their "planned" levels. On the other hand, within each CEMA country, these official rates are used in computing the profitability of each foreign trade operation, though with doubtful success, as we shall see. At the moment, let us note that, as far as intra-CEMA accounts are concerned, the rates are unimportant since, as we have stated, the bookkeeping operations are carried out in a commonly agreed-upon unit, which happens to be the ruble — as defined in gold and hence in any international currency — but which could be any other clearly defined accounting unit. We shall turn in detail to the crucial question of economic calculation in foreign trade and to its impact on the division of labor among CEMA countries in Part V when we discuss the problems of socialist cooperation and the competition with capitalism.

7.

Labor

LABOR FORCE: DEFINITIONS, STRUCTURE, GROWTH

Following a basic distinction made by Adam Smith, Marx classifies labor as productive and non-productive. In Marxian terminology, productive labor is engaged in material production, where it creates "surplus value" (i.e., profit, rent, and interest) for its employer. The criteria set forth in this definition — namely, production of physical commodities and creation of surplus value for an employer — do not necessarily coexist. Artisans and small land owners produce physical commodities but do not work for an employer. They are, however, included by Marx in the productive sphere — for a reason extraneous to the given definition; namely, that this sphere is dominated by the prevailing capitalist methods of production. Marx defines as non-productive the labor engaged in any branch of endeavor other than that of material production, since only the latter is assumed to create value. The activity of the doctor, teacher, or lawyer, is non-productive, therefore, even though Marx himself explicitly states that the occupations of at least the first two are eminently useful.

This distinction should not be taken to mean that productive labor is synonymous with physical labor and non-productive labor with either services or all non-manual work. In their interpretation of Marx, Soviet economists treat the same type of work — that of a clerk, bookkeeper, or technician, for instance — as productive when it enters into a combination of activities aiming at the creation, storage, transportation, and delivery of physical goods, and as non-productive when it has nothing to do with the manufacture or distribution of material goods. In the current Soviet interpretation, the productive sphere thus combines all the activities related to the production and manipulation of physical goods. This interpretation is apparently not entirely consistent with Marx's own definitions and has at intervals been subjected to various criticisms within the Soviet Union itself. It remains, however, the foundation of certain basic Soviet formulae concerning cost, gross value of output, and income, and of certain statistical classifications, such as those concerning labor statistics and the classification of the gainfully employed. Considered as productive then, are all persons gainfully employed in industry, agriculture, freight transport, trade, and some related activities. Soviet statistics group the gainfully employed in industry, for instance, into 1] manual workers; 2] trainees and apprentices; 3] engineering and technical personnel; 4] salaried employees (higher administrative personnel); and finally 5] junior (lower) service personnel. On the other hand, treated as non-productive are all those gainfully employed in civil service, education, and public health. Given these definitions, the official ratios of productive to non-productive labor express only imperfectly the true ratio of employment in production to employment in services, since some services are included in the production category.

According to a detailed study by Murray S. Weitzman and Andrew Elias, in 1959 the total Soviet civilian labor force amounted to more than 96 million persons, i.e., over 65 per cent of the total population. The administrative managerial-technical elites numbered some 7.3 million persons; the professionals (scientists, teachers, economists, doctors, lawyers, and their auxiliary personnel), some 5.3 million. The *intelligentsia* as a whole, i.e., managerial-technical elites, professionals, and related groups, reached a total of 12.5 million gainfully employed, as against only 2.6 million in 1928, at the beginning of the all-embracing planning era. Its share in total manpower has risen in three decades (1929–59) from 3.5 to 13 per cent.

The whole pattern of employment has changed radically under the plans. The gainfully employed in all non-farm occupations reached close to 52 million in 1959, as against 15 million thirty years earlier. In industry, workers and employees numbered over 20.2 million, compared with 5.2 million in 1928. Characteristically, the increases in non-farm occupations were not matched by appreciable decreases in total agricultural employment. As already indicated, in 1959 there were almost the same number of collective-farm households as twenty years earlier (18.5 and 18.1 million within the geographical boundaries of the USSR for those years).

In 1959, farm work occupied 44.6 million persons, still over 46 per cent of the labor force. According to the estimates and projections of Ritchie H. Reed of the U.S. Bureau of the Census, total Soviet civilian employment should amount to close to 117 million by the end of the fourth planning decade in 1969 and to 133 million by 1975 – i.e., some 66 and 62 per cent of the total population respectively. The non-agricultural labor force should rise from close to 78 million in 1969 to over 96 million in 1975, while agricultural employment should fall from close to 39 million in 1969 to less than 37 million in 1975 (a decline in the expanding total employment of 32 per cent and close to 28 per cent, respectively).

Some basic contrasts readily emerge when one compares Soviet and American patterns of employment in the mid-1960's. First, the size of total non-farm employment and the size of employment in industry diverged significantly in the two countries. In the USSR, 67.7 million persons were employed in non-farm jobs – close to one half of whom worked in industry and construction – as opposed to 60.7 million in the United States – only one third of whom worked in industry and construction. But the more impressive Soviet totals reflected only the lower productivity of the Soviet labor force; indeed, according to various estimates, the Soviet industrial output fluctuated between 45 and 65 per cent of the United States output. Second, Soviet employment in trade, credit, insurance, and other services was far smaller than the American – a fact reflecting the long-time neglect of services in the USSR. Finally, an estimated total of 40.1 million persons were employed in Soviet agriculture (12 million in the private sector), as opposed to 4.4 million in the United States (37 per cent and about 7 per cent of total civilian employment, respectively). Even though in industrial employment the Soviets moved between 1928 and 1965 from a level corresponding to that of the United States in 1890 to one exceeding the United States employment level in 1965, in rural employment, the Soviets lag significantly. In relative terms, in the mid-1960's the share of gainfully employed in agriculture in total Soviet manpower still stood at the United States level of 1899.

Under favorable conditions and with appropriate training, vast human resources could be shifted from agriculture to certain industrial and other non-farm occupations. It is doubtful, however, whether the planners would change their present strategy of development in this respect. As has been shown, the policy makers wish to employ the surplus agricultural workers on the farm and hold migration to the cities from the rural areas to a minimum. The improvement of living standards in the countryside and the easing of the pressure of marginal labor to some extent deter emigration to the towns. Under these conditions, the number of persons on farms may be expected to remain still very large in the 1970's.

World War II deeply affected both the magnitude and the structure of the population of the Soviet Union. According to Soviet estimates, in 1939 there were 190.7 million people in the present Soviet territory. If there had been no war, this population would have grown to some 223.2 million by 1952, instead of only returning to the 190.7 million mark in that year. In other words, losses may be estimated at the staggering figure of over 32 million persons. Data on age and sex distribution further underline the devastating consequences of the war. According to the 1959 census, there were some 34 million persons aged thirty-five to forty-nine years in the Soviet Union in 1959, as against 50 million people aged fifteen to twenty-nine years in 1939; the former are the survivors of the latter group which bore the brunt of the war. Undoubtedly, the male losses in the same group were even higher than this total suggests. In the late 1950's, the young people reaching maturity numbered some 4 million annually; this total dropped for the next few years to 3 million or less. In 1939 there were 7 million more women than men; in 1959, women outnumbered men by some 20 million.

War and industrialization brought about dramatic changes in urban-rural ratios, regional distribution of the population, birth and death rates, and in other demographic respects. Between 1939 and 1959, the number of city dwellers grew from 60 to 100 million, while rural population fell from 130.3 to 109 million. Population east of the Urals grew from some 47 to 63 million, or in relative terms, from less than 25 to over 30 per cent of the total population. Over the longer span, 1913–59, birth rates fell from 47 to 25 per thousand, death rates from 30.2 to 7.5 per thousand. According to estimates made by Western statisticians, the crude growth rate of the Soviet population may decline to 1.7 per cent in 1960–65 and to 1.3 per cent in 1965–75, so that the projected Soviet population would amount to from 259 to 263 million persons by 1975.

The relative shortage of adult males — due first to internal strife and later to the war — reinforced the systematic resort to female labor. As the era of thoroughgoing planning gained momentum, job opportunities for women increased at a rate unknown in other countries.[1] Low real wages of the chief family breadwinners forced women to compete vigorously with workers coming from agriculture and to accept all kinds of work, including the dirtiest and the hardest. This helped maintain urban housing investments and various urban social overheads at a minimum, in conformity with the policy makers' decisions concerning the investment pattern. On the other hand, systematic training of female labor made it possible to put certain occupations almost entirely in the hands of women. In 1965, female labor accounted for 30 per cent of the gainfully employed in construction, 46 per cent in industry, 55 per cent in administration staffs, 71 per cent in education, and 86 per cent in public health. Seventy-five per cent of physicians were women, and women accounted for over 90 per cent of the nurses and laboratory workers.

The pressures resulting from an unfavorable population structure are now offset in part by the appearance of technological unemployment in certain industrial agglomerations. Because of this danger, or for various other considerations, since the late 1950's the Soviets have tended to reduce the participation in the labor force of both young people and the aged by lengthening obligatory schooling for youth and by increasing the pensions of the old. In accord with changes in military techniques, the Soviets have also cut their military forces significantly, including their officer corps,[2] and have retrained some of the "cadres" for civil jobs.

Both demographic and income factors suggest that the share of female employment in the total labor force may tend to decline in the years ahead. As the proportion of married women to all women increases, as sex ratios at marriageable ages become normal, and as income increases, the female activity rate should tend to fall from

1. *Eastern European countries followed the same policy from the beginning of their all-out industrialization drive in the late 1940's, so that the share of female labor in total non-agricultural employment has been systematically rising in the area. This share now compares with that of the developed Western European countries – namely, from 30 to 35 per cent – but nowhere is it close to the Soviet level, where women constitute over 50 per cent of the labor force.*

2. *According to official data, Soviet military forces increased from 1.4 million in 1937 to 4.2 million in 1941 and then to 11.3 million by the end of World War II. By 1948, the total was reduced to 2.8 million and then increased again by 1955, to 5.7 million. The planned figure for 1961 was 2.4 million. Various western estimates place the total of all Soviet armed forces – including security forces – at 4.6 million persons in 1960.*

its present high levels. On the other hand, the vast development plans for Siberia require large inputs of labor for which only limited local human resources are available; the demand for women's labor should, therefore, remain strong in the years to come.

DEMAND AND SUPPLY OF LABOR

Planned employment is a derived figure from planned output targets and planned productivity per person.[3] In Soviet practice, the employment plan outside agriculture has often been overfulfilled — in certain periods, by wide margins.[4] The effective demand for labor has exceeded the plan figures and pressure for doing so is still felt because of the need for enterprises to meet the set plan goals even though productivity may lag compared with planned norms. The possibility of enterprises' allocating their planned wage fund among their workers as they see fit, the linking

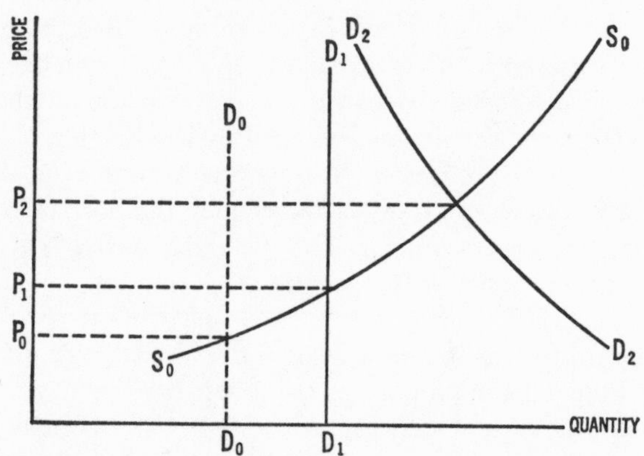

FIGURE 9. *Supply of Labor and Shifts in Planned and Above-Planned Demand*

of total wage bill to output fulfillment, and finally, the incentive of premiums awarded for overfulfillment of the plan targets have all pushed in the same direction. The supply of labor, moreover, has

3. *See Chap. 2 and Chap. 4.*

4. *The planned increase in non-agricultural employment for the first Five-Year Plan (1928–32) was 3.7 million, the actual increase, 9.8 million; the planned increase for the fourth Five-Year Plan (1945–50) was 5.7 million, the actual increase, 11.1 million.*

been sufficiently flexible so that these demands could be met.

Since goals must be fulfilled and since demand for labor in each branch or enterprise is determined by technological requirements, this demand is, for all practical purposes, inelastic. Neither planners nor enterprises take the productivity of the marginal worker into close account; hiring is carried out up to the point where the total labor secured can produce what the plan requires. Assume, as in Figure 9, that for a given planned output, the planned demand for labor is set at D_0D_0. But actual demand, D_1D_1, exceeds the planned level if productivity lags, and it continues to remain inelastic for the labor actually needed to meet the given output target. Since enterprises do attempt to exceed planned goals, total demand moves further, say to D_2D_2, though the demand generated for outputs above plan is relatively elastic. With S_oS_o as the supply curve, the market price of labor tends to rise to P_2 as against the planned wage P_o. The fact that enterprises are in the market both for a fixed quantity of labor (D_1D_1), more likely than not in excess of plan, and for an additional quantity certainly in excess of plan, is a key factor in widening the discrepancy between planned and actual wages.

It should be recalled here, however, that in the rapidly developing process of Soviet industrialization the problems of obtaining the kinds and amounts of labor needed and of deploying them by enterprises, branches, and regions have not been regarded as entirely soluble through a well-balanced system of wage differentials.[5] Instead of seeking to facilitate labor mobility between branches, sectors, and regions, the Soviet authorities have been inclined to check the tendency toward high labor turnover as much as possible and to rely not only on the market mechanism but also on administrative measures for solving the problems of labor recruitment and direction.

Currently, the system of recruitment involves the following basic channels: the Organized Recruitment of Workers (ORW),[6] various resettlement schemes of farmers or non-farmers, and finally, vocational training for the young and compulsory assignment of jobs to them. The ORW recruits unskilled workers in towns or the countryside for the benefit of contracting ministries, for seasonal work, or for permanent settlement in remote areas. Massive, more or less

5. *See. Chap. 3.*
6. *The Russian name is* Organizovannyi nabor, *abbreviated as* Orgnabor.

voluntary resettlements of farm population[7] from the densely populated areas of the European part of the USSR to the regions of Siberia, now in the process of industrialization, are spurred through land grants, tax exemptions, free transportation, and the like. Other schemes provide special opportunities for demobilized servicemen. Finally, "corrective" or prison labor is apparently still a significant source of labor supply. Although all available indications show that the number of prison camps has decreased sharply since 1953, a large number of persons recruited among former camp inmates or from other sources are kept in forced residence in the far North and in other inclement regions.

Vocational training and compulsory assignment of the young to production affect young people from fifteen to sixteen years of age and older, in either intermediate or in higher technical schools. After completing work in the compulsory eight-year elementary schools, youngsters not registered in higher educational establishments — i.e., those ready to enter production — are directed toward the so-called labor-technical establishments. These young people come mostly from the countryside and from families in the lower income brackets. The three-year training program they undergo includes participation in production in the appropriate enterprises, construction sites, workshops, or collective and state farms. Since 1959, municipally organized labor-technical schools have tended to absorb the previously highly centralized system of labor reserve schools (mostly training rural youth for mechanized tasks in agriculture) as well as various other schools for factory training. Students pursuing a secondary education may enter the higher educational establishments intended to train specialists. At the completion of either of these courses of study, the graduates of both labor-technical training and the higher educational establishments are subject to compulsory assignment to jobs for between two and four years. In 1965 the labor training schools alone graduated over 1 million workers, a third of whom were directed toward agriculture.

Large-scale on-the-job training programs are carried out in all Soviet enterprises so that both apprentices and workers may acquire new skills. This training is undertaken by skilled workers and foremen and, in the big enterprises, by a permanent staff of specialized teachers. In the mid-1960's no fewer than 7.2 million workers

7. *The old-fashioned term for this sort of migration within Russia is* pereselenie.

and apprentices participated in these programs each year and qualified for better jobs. The qualification examinations were given by *ad hoc* commissions composed of the chief engineer of the given workshop or department and a specialized teacher of the enterprise. Since 1959, some of these programs, notably those for young workers, have been put under municipal supervision, apparently in order that a centralized control outside the enterprises may be established for the training and deployment of new workers.

Recruitment through the market and assignment through schools and training on the job tend to overlap, so that at certain times supply may exceed demand for certain types of workers in given areas, whereas the reverse situation may occur in other regions. Because of the higher wage level in heavy industry, one would expect that, in times of labor shortage, the difficulty of securing enough workers would generally affect the non-priority branches most.

There are no organized employment agencies in the USSR. A worker who has lost his job or who wishes to change his employment is on his own in his search for another job. Reentry into the labor market presents no particular problem for the skilled worker living in a large and expanding community, but for the skilled worker living in a small place inability to get the same type of job may imply either unemployment or the need to shift to a lower-paying occupation. Official doctrine stresses the "impossibility" of unemployment under socialism, but there is increasing awareness in the Soviet Union that powerful forces tend to build unemployment pockets in any highly industrialized society, planned or unplanned. Such factors as automation and technological changes of various kinds, failure of some plans to mesh, and the difficulties which certain organizations meet in their attempts to integrate the new entrants in the labor market, all contribute to creating various types of unemployment, particularly in the small cities and among the youth.

UNIONS: COLLECTIVE LABOR AGREEMENTS AND STATUTES

The majority of Soviet workers and employees are grouped in trade unions.[8] A trade union is composed of the gainfully em-

8. *Called* professional *trade unions:* professionalnye soiuzy, *abbreviated as* profsoiuzy.

ployed of any given branch of the national economy. The number of these trade unions varies according to changes in the administrative setup; currently there are twenty-three trade unions. In 1965, trade-union membership represented some 95 per cent of the labor force, excluding collective farmers, i.e., a total of some 73 million persons, 25 million of whom were stated to be active members. In principle, the unions are proclaimed to be "voluntary" associations, since in theory at least, union membership is not compulsory. The unions are not independent organizations; their work must be carried out under the express guidance of the Communist party. Their main role consists in checking on the observance of labor legislation and the state of safety in the plants. Their behavior is determined by the postulate that the Soviet Union is a workers' state and consequently the interests and objectives of the employees and of the state establishments as such are supposed to be identical.

The basic unit of the Soviet trade-union pyramid is the enterprise or factory union; it incorporates all the workers and employees of an enterprise, including the higher administrative personnel. Entrance fees and monthly membership dues are both set at 1 per cent of net earnings. To coordinate the activities of unions in towns, provinces, and republics, union councils are established in each of these geographic areas. The supreme controlling organs of the unions are the general meeting for the basic organizations; the conference for town, provincial, area, and republic organizations; and the congress for the national trade union. The supreme organ of the trade unions is the All-Union congress. The latter elects the All-Union central council, which in turn elects two smaller bodies, the presidium and the secretariat, to act as its executives. In theory, all the directing bodies are elected; in practice, the statutory provisions are disregarded and the central power is unlimited.[9]

As the recognized representative of the workers and employees, the trade-union committee of an enterprise signs a collective labor agreement with the management representing the enterprise as a juridical person. This agreement is drawn up on the basis both of a standard model and of the specific provisions of the plan concerning the given enterprise. The standard model is prepared by

9. *No less than seventeen years passed between the ninth and the tenth Congress of the Trade Unions, which took place in 1932 and 1949 respectively. The eleventh and twelfth congresses met in 1954 and 1959, i.e., with a five-year interval instead of the four-year interval set by the statutes. The thirteenth congress met in 1963, and the fourteenth in 1968.*

the central committee of the national union of the respective industrial branch. The basic question of wages is dealt with only in general terms, repeating governmental regulations concerning methods of compensation of piecework and time work, changes in workers' skills, promotions, etc. The agreement then stresses the specific obligations of the personnel, trade-union committee, and management. The workers pledge to utilize their workday fully, fulfill the norms, and handle equipment and materials with care. The union committee pledges to promote socialist emulation, guide production conferences, and check management's adherence to regulations concerning wages, norms, safety, housing, and related measures. Finally, management pledges to establish suitable conditions for workers' competition, to carry out methods of production recommended by production leaders, to improve the training and skills of the personnel, and to maintain adequate sanitary conditions. Certain clauses specify the utilization of the sums allocated for health, living conditions, cultural services, and the like, and set a timetable for fulfillment of the given programs. Soviet collective labor agreements look more like summaries of the labor code than living documents born from the initiative of the signatories and reflecting actual local conditions. Only 53,000 such documents were signed in 1958 instead of a total of 400,000. This means that many agreements were signed not by single enterprises but by the trusts, without any consideration of local problems or participation of the personnel in the elaboration of the document.

Such as they are, the labor agreements, together with the decrees concerning the statute on union rights, determine the framework within which the trade-union committees carry their activity. Following these provisions, the union committee exercises consultative, controlling, guiding, and administrative functions in the enterprise. The management consults the committee concerning grades allocated to workers under the wage schedule and qualification rules in force, the amount and distribution of premiums, the hiring of young people between fifteen and sixteen years of age, and dismissals. Dismissals may be made only for such reasons as reduction in personnel, negligence, absence from work due to imprisonment for more than two months, or sickness lasting more than two to four months (excepting pregnancy).

Each enterprise has a commission for the arbitration of labor disputes. Management and the union have equal representation on the commissions which are empowered to deal with all conflicts related to the application of the collective agreements. Decisions must be unanimous; they may, moreover, be appealed to the popular tribunal.

The union is further authorized to control the adherence of management to all regulations concerning wages and to all welfare measures relating to personnel. As the guiding organization of the employees, the union must bring the negligent or undisciplined worker into line, stimulate workers' competition for higher output, and guide production conferences (in undertakings with more than 100 workers) with the aim of improving plan fulfillment. Finally, the union is charged with the determination of social insurance benefits; it participates in the fixing of pensions, sends workers to sanatoria and health resorts, and manages the cultural, educational, and athletic establishments provided by the enterprise. Thus, unions in the USSR are the administrative agency of the social security system, a position which puts enormous resources into their hands and helps them consolidate their control over the mass of the gainfully employed. They may combine their attempts toward enforcing labor discipline and promoting plan fulfillment with their activities directed toward improvement in workers' welfare and security benefits.

The unions do not enter into conflict with the managers or with the state over the fixing of wages. In fact, even in areas where they are supposed to control the management, they avoid conflicts and, as stated by one official publication, are rather inclined to compromise the interests of the workers. Actually, the bureaucracy of the unions does little to differentiate itself from the rest of the state machine, even though unions are independent organizations. For many decades, the unions have been trained to behave as company unions, and they act accordingly; their efforts are always oriented toward developing production first and increasing workers' welfare second.

WORKING CONDITIONS AND REAL WAGES

Since the Soviet system combines executive and legislative power with state ownership and management of the economy, any serious conflict has been and is treated as containing an element of revolt which cannot be tolerated. Strikes, for instance, are and always have been prohibited in the Soviet Union. But not only conflicts of such magnitude have been viewed as potential insurrections. In fact, any petty conflict, any implied lack of subjection and of absolute cooperation with the plan hierarchies (management, party, and also trade-union) has at times been treated as a seed of revolt. Significant changes in this respect, however, have occurred since the war and particularly since the late 1950's. Within the plant, the criminal law has given way to the civil law. Although union pressure restricts managerial authority probably less in the USSR than in most other countries,[10] now — at least on the statute books — workers have certain guarantees against arbitrary discharge, arbitrary changes in wages and bonuses, and arbitrary rules within the plant. Furthermore, the worker is now free to quit his job after giving management two weeks' notice.

A large share of the increasing productivity gains is now passed on to workers in the form of shorter hours rather than in the form of benefits to consumers. In 1958, most gainfully employed persons in the USSR still worked 46 hours a week: eight hours daily Monday through Friday, six hours on Saturday. During the next two years, the workweek was cut to 41 hours (seven hours a day plus six on Saturday), with 35 hours for hard underground work. By the late 1960's the switch to a standard five-day week was in process of completion throughout the economy. Young people under sixteen may work only four hours a day; those between sixteen and eighteen not more than six hours. Overtime is permitted only in extraordinary cases and is limited to four hours on consecutive days and ten hours a month. Since 1959, six paid holidays are granted per year as against no paid holidays previously. As for vacations, after a year's work each worker is entitled to a minimum leave of one day for each month on the job. In certain enterprises, for each three-year period of employment, the worker is given three extra days up to a maximum of 24 working days. Young workers are entitled to one month's vacation each year.

A substantial number of services provided free by the state and by enterprises represent a significant addition to real incomes. These social wages are made up of free health and education facilities, a varied and well-maintained system of public recreational facilities, subsidized crèches, kindergartens, vacations, and housing. Further-

10. *The management's range of discretion is in fact extremely broad in* any *type of dictatorial society.*

more, social insurance covers almost all categories of workers and employees and is more comprehensive than anywhere else, perhaps, with respect to insurance during pregnancy and childbirth, disability, sickness, pensions to families of deceased persons, etc. On the other hand, one should note that safety conditions on the job are far less satisfactory in the Soviet Union than in the West. Some Soviet plants set up under pioneering conditions have poor safety and sanitary facilities and have a far higher accident rate than in the older industrial countries.[11]

Real wages are rising in the USSR, but slowly and from very low levels. In this respect, three periods can be distinguished since the start of the thoroughgoing planning era. In the first phase, during the late 1930's, prices of consumers' goods and wages both increased, the former faster than the latter, notwithstanding productivity gains in certain years. Although average real wages decreased, sharp differentials were established in favor of the more productive and of highly skilled workers. The wage span was thus increased systematically throughout these years. The second phase began after World War II. This time, some of the benefits of increased productivity were passed on to consumers in the form of retail price reductions. Average real wages began to climb, but the internal structure of wages and wage differentials was left unaffected. The third phase began in the late 1950's. First, as in the preceding period, some productivity gains continued to be passed on to the consumers. Then, the whole system of workers' classification and rewards — time versus piece rates, basic wages versus bonuses, etc. — was brought under scrutiny. Although revisions did not, as officially claimed, reduce the wage dispersion, which continues to remain

11. *In M. Gardner Clark (ed.),* Steel in the Soviet Union, *a very detailed report published by the American Iron and Steel Institute, an American delegation of steel experts thus summarizes the situation in Soviet steel mills in 1958:*

"Based on information received, it appears that the Soviet steel mills have far more accidents than those in the United States. For example, at Magnitogorsk it was said that they had approximately 720 lost-time accidents last year, including six cases of severe disability, and four fatalities. This is several times as many lost-time accidents as occur today in a plant of comparable size in the United States.

"Safety apparel was conspicuous by its absence. Safety shoes were seldom seen, and protective clothing (including hard hats) was not observed in any steel plant. The use of goggles appeared to be limited to welding and burning. The workers in general seemed to take a great many chances that would be forbidden in this country. Sanitary facilities, including toilets and drinking water facilities were few and considerably below American standards" (p. 290).

greater than in the United States in certain branches, they did establish some more appropriate controls on the movement of the wage bill in each plant and in the economy as a whole.

It should be noted that the increases in real wages initiated in the early postwar years followed a period of attrition extending over about two decades, from 1928 to 1948. The increases in real wages after 1948 caught up with the pre-plan wage level by 1952 or perhaps a few years later. According to a detailed study by Mrs. Janet G. Chapman, real earnings computed at 1937 prices fell in the USSR from 100 in 1928 to 82 in 1937 and 62 in 1948, and rose by 1952 to 103. Computed at 1928 prices, the index for 1952 would stand at only 72, still below the 1928 level.[12] By and large, it is only since the mid-1950's that the personal lot of the average Soviet worker has started to improve as compared to the pre-plan period. There has also been a continuous, parallel improvement in all consumer fields in the past few years. Nevertheless, although food is adequate (even if not very varied), clothing remains drab and expensive, and housing and various types of services (such as repairs, cleaning, shopping facilities) are far from satisfactory. Construction in towns is proceeding rapidly, as compared with the past, but it will take many years to cope with the existing backlog and provide decent and adequate living space for the population.

In the USSR, as anywhere else, material incentives are the predominant factors in motivating workers. One must note, however, that a quite significant function is assigned to an intricate system of honorific distinctions and prestige symbols, adroitly manipulated by the state and party propaganda machines. All possible media — press, radio, television, party congresses, literary works — are systematically used in order to spur the leaders of labor, chide laggards, and push workers ahead on the road to higher and higher productivity achievements. The systematic emphasis on respect for work; the glorification of the shock worker, the scientist, and the engineer; the indefatigable spurring of the production race with the United States — all help to create the appropriate climate for technological change.

OPERATIVE MANAGEMENT, TECHNOLOGY, AND PRODUCTIVITY

The principle officially stressed in the administration of the

12. *These computations, however, do not include the social benefits mentioned previously.*

Soviet enterprise is, as has been stated, unity of management, i.e., subordination of all the employed to the single will and decisions of the leader of the firm, the director.[13] The Soviet managerial elite represents a competent, highly trained, and ambitious group of people. Roughly two-thirds of this elite — namely, the heads of establishments and their assisting engineers and technicians — are now graduates of the higher engineering technical schools. Although the director himself wields considerable power in his establishment, his activities are, as we have seen, determined from above by executive managerial decisions and scrutinized from below by both the party's and trade union's committees within the plant. One would expect this second element to create a *de facto* three-way division of power in each plant among the director, the secretary of the party, and the secretary of the trade union. Such a division did occur in the pre-plan period, but it has since been discarded as far as the immediate day-to-day operations of the plant are concerned.

Since the launching of the thoroughgoing planning era, the operative manager has increasingly become the direct leader of the activity of his enterprise. Notwithstanding the cardinal Soviet postulate that the party is always and in all circumstances the unique leading force of the economy, in the day-to-day activity of each plant the party organization plays a completely subordinate role. This paradox has emerged from the need to rely in operational activities on the personnel selected for the job and placed in the command positions by the party itself. The plant manager's only guarantee for keeping his job is his continued success in fulfilling the assigned tasks. The path leading to top management is open only to the ambitious and the successful. The party-state hierarchy is impatient with what it considers failures, and consequently the turnover at various levels of management is rather high. In the post-Stalin period, the weight of the party plant organization has been somewhat increased as the scope and activity of the trade-union committee within the plant have been broadened. Now, perhaps more than in the past, the manager feels the need to consult with the party secretary and, when necessary, to act through him on the trade-union hierarchy. But now, as before, the manager's authority is unchallenged in matters concerning the day-to-day operations of the plant: neither the party cell nor the trade-union organs can give orders or interfere with the functions and activities of the managerial hierarchy. A

13. *See Chap. 4.*

character in a Soviet novel makes the following quip about the role of the director in the plant's "troika" (director, party, and trade-union secretaries): "There may be three persons to the Trinity, but there is only one God Almighty." [14]

The scrutiny of the plant party cell may, however, force the operative manager to pay attention to certain basic orientations heavily stressed by the party machine, notably in such matters as revision of obsolete methods of production, changes in output mix, and introduction of technological improvements. It should be noted here that, although Soviet executive management is very receptive to new technological ideas, the operative manager is very reluctant to apply them. The top planners may easily decree the scrapping of some more or less obsolete plants, but enforcing the spread of technological improvements throughout the existing industrial structure is more difficult. The operative manager has multiple reasons for resisting shifts in technology, and this situation is hard to correct through the use of centralized controls. Resistance occurs because the plant as a whole, as well as its personnel from engineers down to workers, may be worse off when shifting to new methods than the gainfully employed of comparable enterprise which stick to outdated, well-worn methods which ensure rapid fulfillment of output goals. Precisely for this reason, the authorities attempt both to break the tacit solidarity which exists between management and personnel in this respect and to use the party cell as the spearhead of the drives for technological improvement. But resistance to new techniques is deep-seated and widespread, and the revision of prevailing incentives is still insufficient for ensuring the rapid and systematic introduction of improved technological methods.

As new techniques are introduced in the key branches and new industries are developed, significant increases in Soviet output and productivity are certain to result. On the other hand, even if high positive rates of productivity are built into the new industries, progress in numerous backward consumers' goods industries may continue to remain slow for many years to come. According to the estimates of Professor Walter Galenson, labor productivity in Soviet industries, varying probably between 44 and 59 per cent of United States productivity in 1960, should reach the 49 to 86 per cent level (depending on branches) by 1970. In agriculture, where the base is

14. *See George Gibian, "The Factory Manager in Soviet Fiction,"* Problems of Communism, *VIII, No. 2 (March–April, 1959), 44.*

very low — some 20 to 25 per cent of United States farm productivity — the Soviet performance will undoubtedly also improve throughout the next decade, though far less than in industry. Further increases in the technological level of the managerial and engineering-technical personnel portend improvements in the economy as a whole; the exact scope of such improvements, however, is difficult to assess.

Part III

Social Accounting and Finance

INTRODUCTION TO PART III

From our discussion of the connection of the sector's component units to the plan, we turn now to intersector relations and their interaction in the economy. Intersector relations may be viewed through 1] input-output constructs, 2] national income tabulations, or 3] flow of funds accounts. The first reveal interindustry dependence for final and intermediate goods. The second present the money measure of the yearly flow of goods and services, and the utilization of final or net product for current consumption or capital formation. The third disclose the activity of the financial transactors in the production field and make explicit the financial processes connected with production. How do Soviet economists view the relation between the so-called productive and non-productive spheres; how do they plan and account for money and income flows; how do they ascertain the sectoral and the over-all performance of their economy? To what extent are the concepts and measurements they propose acceptable and on what grounds?

We have already referred to input-output techniques in relation to the plan. As previously indicated, Soviet economists and statisticians are adapting in various ways these new tools to their planning needs. As far as income and product accounting is concerned, the Soviet conceptual framework differs substantially from the concepts and methods in use in the West. In order to understand Soviet rationale and accounting procedures, we begin this section by considering the implications for Soviet income theory of the Marxian definitions of production, productive labor, and net output and of the Marxian schema of simple and enlarged reproduction. Conceptual differences with the West, as well as certain biased statistical theories and practices, render Soviet data on national income and the related measurements of sectoral values of output both difficult to handle and of dubious quality. This has led Western economists to make remarkable attempts to recompute Soviet national income and to reconstruct Soviet income and industrial output series. In this section, we discuss these attempts only so far as they clarify income concepts and income accounting. We shall turn to the broader implications of the data in Part V when we shall examine Soviet performance and the Soviet race with the United States.

From the study of product and sector accounts, we move to the fields of money and finance. What are the functions of money and of financial programs in a system which, as we know, relies heavily on positive commands, direct quantitative controls, and extensive manipulations of prices? In Soviet economic theory, maximum production, full employment, and full utilization of capacity are considered the characteristic achievements of planning; the existence of any idle resource is regarded as evidence of wrongly planned allocation. Thus, the economy must be provided with the financial means needed to achieve full utilization of factors; expansionist credit policies are a built-in feature of the system. On the other hand, various checks and controls, such as economic accounting in each enterprise, control of the banks over volume and kind of expenditures made by enterprises and over plan fulfillment, balancing the price-sum of consumers' goods with disposable income, balancing investment expenditure with excess of price-sum over planned cost of consumers' goods output, maintaining a budget surplus — all attempt to check inflationary pressures. In order to follow the interactions between expansionist credit policies and anti-inflationary checks, this section examines in turn the process and implications of the division of money according to various uses, the organization and functions of Soviet banks, the interconnections between supply of money by the banks (currency and credit plans) and the budget (financing of certain investments and of social overhead). As already indicated, in Soviet practice, financial planning is not carried out on the basis of a unified administrative financial plan. Although the Soviets have developed sectoral balances of income and expenditures — of consumers, firms, banking system, government, and foreign trade — these balances are not integrated into a well-established flow of funds system of accounts. The connections between these sectors (consumers, firms, bank, etc.) may be examined only within the framework of a model, which we present in Chapter 10. This section, then, opens with an examination of Soviet concepts and measurement of income, followed by Western critiques and suggested revaluations (Chapter 8), turns to the banking system and its operation (Chapter 9), and finally examines the government accounts and sets up a general flow of funds model (Chapter 10).

8.

Income and Product Accounts

THE MARXIAN TWO-SECTOR ECONOMIC MODEL

Perhaps more than anything else in Marx's writing, the schema of simple and enlarged reproduction published in his *Capital* has served to color Soviet thinking and action on matters of economic development. Soviet social accounting, pricing, strategy of development, growth theories, and planning techniques may be understood more easily if one refers to Marx's famous two-sector economic model. On the basis of its destination, Marx divides the physical output of the economy into two categories: producers' goods (i_g), and consumers' goods (c_g), produced respectively by producers' goods industries — or industries of Sector I — and consumers' goods industries — or industries of Sector II. Producers' goods embrace both raw materials and capital goods. Each output is in turn equated to depreciation plus raw materials used (c), wage bill (v), and surplus value (m), that is, property income, although Marx does not define it in this way. The two-sector model seeks to portray the mutual relations between the components of each output and the demand and supply of producers' and consumers' goods in either "simple reproduction," i.e., in conditions of zero net investment, or "enlarged reproduction," i.e., in conditions of positive net investment. Total output under the schema is equal to

$$\begin{array}{l} c_1 + v_1 + m_1 = i_g \\ \underline{c_2 + v_2 + m_2 = c_g} \\ c \ + v \ + m \ = i_g + c_g \end{array} \qquad (1)$$

Under repetitive stationary conditions, the output of sector I must match the capital consumption and raw materials used up in both sectors, that is, $c_1 + c_2$, whereas consumers' goods output must equal the grand total of wages and of all the surplus. From this, it follows that the necessary and sufficient condition for simple reproduction is that the demand for investment goods of the second sector should equal the demand for consumers' goods of the first sector. Effectively, this can be shown either from

$$c_1 + c_2 = c_1 + v_1 + m_1$$

or from $$v_1 + m_1 + v_2 + m_2 = c_2 + v_2 + m_2$$

which gives $$c_2 = v_1 + m_1 \qquad (2)$$

To achieve growth, the output of sector I must be larger than replacements — that is, than $c_1 + c_2$ by, say, Δc. As the Soviet Academician Nemchinov points out, Marx assumes in all his numerical examples elaborating the schema that in the second (expanded) cycle of production, the total demand for producers' goods, say, c' (that is, $c_1 + c_2 + \Delta c_1 + \Delta c_2$) must equal the output produced by sector I during the first cycle, that is,

$$\Delta c = c_1 + v_1 + m_1 - (c_1 + c_2) \quad \text{or} \quad \Delta c = v_1 + m_1 - c_2$$

$$\text{or} \quad c'_1 + c'_2 = c_1 + v_1 + m_1 = i_g \qquad (3)$$

Further, the surplus, m (that is, $m_1 + m_2$) must be split three ways: m_c is set aside for the purchase of additional capital goods and raw materials (Δc); m_v is set aside for the wages (Δv) of the additional workers needed to produce the extra producers' goods; whereas only the remainder, m_r, is to be spent on consumption by the capitalists (that is, the consumption of the non-productive sphere). The demand for consumers' goods in the second cycle — represented by the wage bill v' (that is, $v_1 + v_2 + \Delta v_1 + \Delta v_2$) and the consumption outlays of the non-productive sphere, m_r — must equal the output of consumers' goods produced during the first cycle, that is,

$$v'_1 + v'_2 + m_{r1} + m_{r2} = c_2 + v_2 + m_2 = c_g \qquad (4)$$

Since $m_2 - m_{r2} = m_{c2} + m_{v2} = \Delta c_2 + \Delta v_2$ Equation (4) may be rewritten as

$$v_1 + \Delta_{v1} + v_2 + \Delta v_2 + m_{r1} = c_2 + v_2 + \Delta c_2 + \Delta v_2 = c_g$$

From which, we obtain, after making the proper cancellations and replacements, the basic Marxian equation for balanced growth, namely:

$$c'_2 = v'_1 + m_{r1} \qquad (5)$$

This same equality may also be obtained from equation (3):

since $\Delta c_1 + \Delta c_2 = v_1 + m_1 - c_2$ and $c_2 + \Delta c_2 = v_1 + m_1 - \Delta c_1$
replacing $m_1 - \Delta c_1$ by $m_{v1} + m_{r1}$
we may note that $c'_2 = v'_1 + m_{r1}$.

Simple and enlarged reproduction can be effected smoothly only if certain mutual relationships between the components of the national (physical) product and of the outputs of the two sectors are realized. In actual economic life, m_c may exceed or fall short of the potential growth $[i_g - (c_1 + c_2)]$, so that we may see either overinvestment or underinvestment. Given the expansion of c and v by Δc and Δv, total output at the second round (i'_g and c'_g) will in turn increase automatically in the fixed proportion required by a so-called surplus norm m/v, so that expanded output at the second round will finally equal

$$c' + v' + m' = i'_g + c'_g$$

in which $c' = c + \Delta c$, $v' = v + \Delta v$, and $m' = m + \Delta m$.

Thus, the model is based on constant returns to scale. In Marx's numerical examples of the model, the organic composition of capital (the ratio of c to v) remains unchanged, and the output of the two sectors develops at an unchanged rate. The proportions in which new investment is distributed between the two sectors may, however, be easily varied and, following the shifts in the ratio of Δc_1 to Δc_2, the growth rate of total output may be increased, kept constant, or decreased.

These are the core equations of the Marxian growth theory. In Chapter 12, we shall deal in more detail with some implications of this model during the discussion of the Soviet strategy of development. Here in the study of Soviet national accounts let us stress that, in the model discussed, production is confined to the sphere of physical goods. The activity of sectors I and II is ascertained from the end-use of their products. In keeping with the labor theory of value, the aggregate net product is equated to $v + m$ in material production excluding services; incomes outside this sphere are treated as transfers from the "primary" fund $v + m$, since, in accordance with Marx's basic assumption, no new value may be created outside the defined boundary of material production. Finally, m — that is, profits, rent, and interest charges — is assumed to be engendered exclusively by labor (engaged in material production); it is a "surplus value" consisting of the difference between the product of labor and the cost of labor.

Numerous Western economists have questioned the general validity of Marx's schema because of its confusion of stocks (i.e., of c) and flows $(v + m)$, its abstraction with respect to internal interchanges in the two sectors, and the vagueness of the dividing line between investment and consumers' goods industries according to the destination of their products.[1] Furthermore, the theoretical foundation of the schema has been shown to have fatal flaws when one moves from "values" (in the Marxian sense of materialized labor) to prices, which diverge from "values," and when one drops the unrealistic assumption concerning the identity of the organic composition of capital in all the branches of industry.[2] It is, however, not the theoretical neatness of the schema but its broad implications which have attracted the Soviet policy makers and planners and which must concern us here. Joan Robinson — who, incidentally, has also formulated some of the very criticisms just cited — notes that the schema provides after all "a simple and indispensable approach to the problem of saving and investment and the balances between production of capital goods and demand for consumer goods." In practice, the schema has furnished Soviet policy makers with a rough guide for dealing with precisely these basic macroeconomic problems. Although the Marxian tool is obviously crude compared to flexible input-output and linear programming models, which reveal not only gross balances between sectors but also the flows, in each sector, of the intermediate products, it tackles certain key problems simply and directly. Whatever its merits and deficiencies, the schema has served as the foundation for both the Soviet conceptual framework and Soviet accounting procedures for dealing with product and income.

SOVIET INCOME CONCEPTS AND ACCOUNTING PROCEDURES

Following Marx, Soviet economists start the accounting of the national product from cost of production and gross value of out-

1. *Western classifications of product by end-use are similar to the Marxian classification of producers' and consumers' goods. But in the West, this definition is not carried into the sphere of industrial activity; consumers' goods industries, for instance, include yarn manufacturing, which Marx includes in his sector I.*

2. *See Paul M. Sweezy,* The Theory of Capitalist Development, *New York: Oxford University Press, 1942, pp. 109ff.*

put of physical products. Hence, they exclude completely from their aggregate product all personal and domestic services, government (including defense), health, education, scientific research, welfare, as well as housing and municipal services. But they adjust the boundaries of the sphere of material production in various ways. They include in it not only "the acquiring of the products of nature and their processing" but also their *distribution* and *transportation*. Product, *genus sovieticus*, thus includes certain services, namely, those directly connected with production and its distribution.

In Soviet social accounting, net product is computed from gross output by either the enterprise or the sector method. *Gross output* is defined as production of each enterprise at its selling prices; it excludes internal turnover of the enterprise so that the total depends on the organizational structure of the given industry. This computation method is used for industry and agriculture. For construction, transportation, and trade, the so-called sector method of computation is used; this method excludes the internal turnover in the given sector as a whole. Material production is divided into the following branches: industry, agriculture, forestry, building, transport of commodities, communications serving production, material-technical supply, agricultural procurement, trade, and other material services. Industry includes both mining and manufacturing. Agriculture covers only production of non-processed goods, any processing being included directly in industry. Agriculture includes both crop and livestock output, and its total output is computed at the respective selling prices, the non-marketed share being estimated at average prices of all agricultural sales. Forestry is accounted for separately and includes various subbranches (culture of trees, grafting, etc.). Building covers construction work, installation of equipment, and designing connected with construction. Transport includes all types of freight, but excludes passenger transportation. Material-technical supply, agricultural procurement, and trade are all computed at selling prices — trade therefore includes the turnover tax. Foreign trade surplus in foreign currency converted at domestic prices or the deficit is added to, or subtracted from, total trade.

Gross value of output, of each enterprise or branch, consolidated for the economy as a whole [3] reveals the broad interenterprise and

3. *In Russian, the gross value of output of each enterprise or sector is called* valovaia produktsia; *the aggregate product of the economy as a whole is called* sovokupnyi obshchestvennyi produkt.

interbranch connections. From the same data, value added is obtainable by deduction of depreciation and interfirm transactions (c) for each unit or for an industrial branch as a whole, i.e., the total of raw materials, fuels, electricity, and other materials used, and the capital consumption. Similarly, for agriculture value added may be obtained after deduction of value of seed, animal feed, fertilizers, insecticides, etc.

Income generated in material production may also be computed by factor payments through summation of the incomes of workers and employees in enterprises of material production (including state farms), the incomes of peasants (in money and kind) from collective farms and from their own plots, the incomes of workers and employees of producers' cooperatives, profits retained by enterprises, deductions from profits, transfers to the budget, and turnover tax.

The net product can be either consumed or invested. Consumption is divided into personal and collective consumption. Personal consumption consists of goods and services consumed by individuals plus depreciation of dwellings, but excluding actual and imputed rent. Collective consumption is equated to value of raw materials and fuels and of material services used up in institutions and organizations in the non-productive sphere, as well as the depreciation of fixed assets other than dwellings. Accumulation is income minus consumption and consists of net investment and increases in stocks and reserves. The value of net investment is derived from the sum of gross investment plus capital repairs minus depreciation charges fixed according to given rules. Changes in reserves probably include strategic stocks and gold. (See the illustrative data for 1959 in Table 6.)

The flow of income from its generation in the sphere of material production to the sphere of services may be visualized as a set of transfers from primary to secondary income receivers through purchases of goods and services and through tax payments. Total consumption plus accumulation match the income generated in material production only, since the outlays of primary income receivers on services not accounted for in the income tabulations are matched by the outlays of secondary income receivers on goods and services which do enter the income totals. (See Figure 10.) The final division between consumption and accumulation corresponds broadly to the division of total output into production of consumers' and producers' goods; the flow of goods is actually accounted for, starting from the

TABLE 6. *Soviet Income and Product (Soviet Definitions) Illustrative Data (billion rubles and percentage, 1959)*

Product by Sector and Industrial Origin	Billion Rubles	Per Cent
Sector I		
Inputs incl. depreciation (c)	81.8	51.1
Wages and salaries (*v*)	46.3	29.5
Surplus (*m*)	29.0	18.4
Total	157.1	100.0
Sector II		
Inputs incl. depreciation (c)	55.8	49.0
Wages and salaries (*v*)	24.4	21.5
Surplus (*m*)	33.6	29.5
Total	113.8	100.0
Aggregate product ($c+v+m$)	270.9	100.0
Inputs incl. depreciation (c)	—137.6	—50.8
Net Product ($v+m$)	133.3	49.2
Net Product Produced in:		
Industry	70.1	52.6
Construction	13.2	9.9
Agriculture	28.3	21.2
Transp. and Communication	6.4	4.8
Trade and other	15.3	11.5
Net Product	133.3	100.0

Product by Use	Billion Rubles	Per Cent
A. Individual Consumption (productive sphere)	70.7	53.0
B. Public Funds Consumption (nonproductive sphere)	26.5	19.9
Accumulation	36.1	27.1
Net Product (A+B)	133.3	100.0
A. Consumption		
Population	88.0	66.0
Institutions	9.2	6.9
Total	97.2	72.9
B. Accumulation		
Investment	22.5	16.9
Addition to working capital and reserves	13.6	10.2
Total	36.1	27.1
Net Product (A+B)	133.3	100.0

SOURCE: Ia. G. Liberman, Gosudarstvenyi biudzhet i sotsialisticheskoe vospriozvodstvo [State Budget and Socialist Reproduction], Moscow, Finansy, 1966, pp. 128ff.

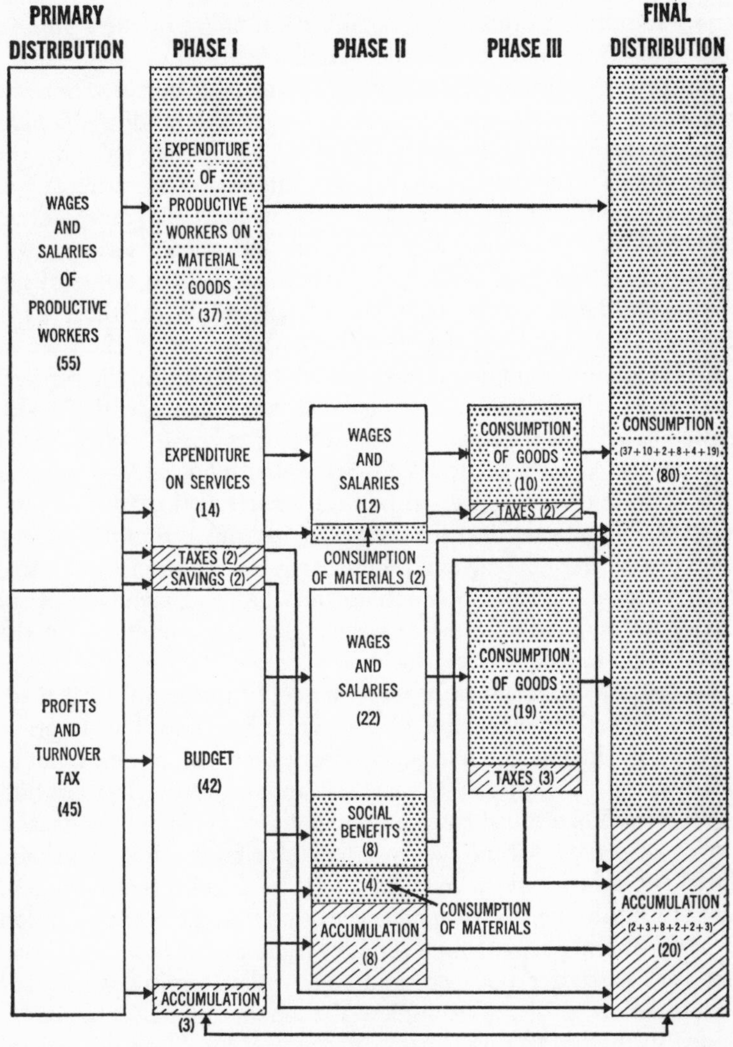

FIGURE 10. *Schema of Distribution and Redistribution of National Income (Hypothetical Percentages)*

SOURCE: L. Zienkowski, *Jak oblicza sie dochod narodówy* [How the National Income Is Calculated], Warsaw, 1957.

points of production to final distribution, by segregating the enterprises according to the main use and distribution of their product into categories I and II as in the Marxian schema.

All personal income and outlays are accounted for in a separate tabulation called *balance of income and expenditures of the population.* A schema of this balance is given in Table 7. On one side, the table groups incomes generated in the state and cooperative sectors and incomes from transactions among individuals and, on the other side, outlays on both goods and services and private savings. This tabulation, tied to the yearly plans, serves as a useful frame of reference for the short-term operational plans which the State Bank draws up for currency emission and circulation, as we shall see in Chapter 9. Limitation of national income tabulations to the physical product and drawing of a partial balance covering consumers' goods as well as services has appeared inconsistent to some leading Soviet economists. As early as the 1920's, Strumilin, followed by a number of other economists, suggested that all services be included in total product. The official doctrine, however, remains committed to the concept that new income and product may not be generated outside the sphere of material production and that the inclusion of all service income, treated now as transfers, would unduly inflate the actual net product. (Thus, Soviet economists deflate Western income totals by as much as 20 to 30 per cent in order to bring them in line with their own kind of income valuation.) The frontiers between productive and non-productive services are, however, not as clearly drawn in each case as may first appear. Material production is interpreted in a broad sense and includes not only any productive service dispensed within the enterprise itself but also, as already stated, outside services, such as those of freight transportation, marketing, catering, etc. Although accepting the idea of the exclusion of personal and governmental services, some Soviet economists suggest that passenger transport and some other services which fall within the scope of the "commercial economy" should also be included in the production sphere. In practice, the scope of the productive sphere and of the national accounts may thus be widely changed without apparent change in the underlying assumptions; it all depends on where one places the arbitrary line between productive and non-productive services.[4]

4. *In Yugoslavia, for instance, social accounting follows the general Soviet pattern but includes passenger transport in "material" production.*

TABLE 7. *Schema of a Balance of Income and Expenditure of the Population*

Incomes	*Expenditures*
From State and Cooperative Organizations:	In state shops
Wage bill	In cooperative shops
Collective farm guaranteed payments and money income distributed as dividends based on workdays	For farm goods on commission
	In collective farm markets
	Services and other:
	Rent
	Private urban house building
Income from sales of agricultural produce to state and on commission	Private rural house building
	Entertainment
Pensions	Payments for personal services
Stipends	
Loan service and redemption	Transport and communication services
Pay and pensions of armed forces, dividends of members of cooperatives, other incomes	Other
	Savings:
From the Population:	
Sales in collective farm markets	Purchase of state bonds
Sale of other goods and services	New savings deposits
	Changes in cash balances
Total	Total

NATURE AND RANGE OF THE OFFICIAL DATA

The differences between the Soviet and the Western income accounting procedures and measurements concern not only the Soviet distinction between product and service but also a number of other elements. The Soviet social product should not be confused with the Western gross national product: the former, always net of services, includes numerous duplications, since it totals all interfirm transactions, whereas the latter includes services and excludes interfirm purchases. Soviet national income (i.e., social product minus interfirm transaction and depreciation allowances) is akin to Western net national product (i.e., national income at market prices), provided that one excludes services. While in the West, national income at factor cost is derived by eliminating total indirect taxes from the preceding, Soviet accounting does not distinguish between market prices and factor costs. As we have pointed out, in Soviet price theory, profit and turnover tax, as well as some local taxes and levies by state enterprises, are viewed as representing jointly the "surplus" of the society (i.e., property income or the *m* of the Marxian schema), and the distinction between them is presented as a matter of expediency, not of substance; they are simply alternative ways of collecting funds for the state. In practice, the turnover tax is the main instrument for bringing value of goods at retail prices up to the level of personal disposable income minus planned personal savings; it is primarily a sales tax – i.e., a charge against sales revenue – though in certain cases, such as agricultural procurement, it might also stand for a factor charge.

A major difficulty with Soviet accounts is that the so-called profits are not entirely related to the volume of capital used per unit of output but rather to the planned needs of capital formation. They are hence not a measure of value created, but a haphazard patchwork dependent not on capital in use but on capital needs. Some Soviet economists suggest that profits should be established at the level at which the marginal producer would not need a subsidy, i.e., at an administratively determined level as in the preceding example. Thus, although a relatively clear analytic distinction may be made between turnover tax and profits, in practice there is no way of fully disentangling the magnitudes of tax and factor charge which are involved.

Valuation methods introduce significant distortions in both the product and expenditure sides of the accounts. On the product side, the share of agriculture tends to be undervalued, principally because of the underpricing of compulsory deliveries and of consumption on the farm; the incidence of the turnover tax increases the share of industry and further distorts the relation between heavy and light industries. On the expenditure side of the accounts, there is a downward bias in the case of accumulation, which is free of turnover tax; this bias, however, is offset in part by undervaluation of individual consumption (notably of consumption on the farm) and by low depreciation allowances. Generally, the distinction between consumption and accumulation does not commend itself either for clarity or for its consistency: it is impossible to ascertain how much defense expenditure is included under either of these headings. The most readily available measure of consumption is taken to be the volume of the sale of goods by state and cooperative retail establishments. But this figure excludes personal services and consumption on the farm, and includes intermediate products sold to the peasant, such as cement, steel, tools, etc.

Ambiguities and exaggerations are compounded in the Soviet computation of real national income. For the decisive years, 1929–50, national income was computed at 1926–27 prices, i.e., in a preindustrial price structure at increasing variance with the scarcity relationships that arose as industrialization developed. Numerous changes in underlying definitions, inconsistencies in assessing the sectoral contributions to net output, and deficiencies in valuations have imparted a serious upward bias to the series. Thus crop output was assessed first on the basis of crops stored, then of crops harvested, and finally of standing crops, although the latter, if not reduced by losses in the fields, may be larger than the barn crops by as much as 30 per cent. Further, some sectoral contributions which are usually troublesome to assess, such as the net output of construction, were simply included in the real income totals on the basis of computations at current prices. In a period of both rapid inflation and sharp increases in new industrial products, 1926–27 prices assigned to these products were simply the current prices of their first year in production. Assigning such weights meant inflating total output and overestimating the contribution of new outputs in relation to old ones.

The related Soviet computations of gross industrial output suffer, moreover, from the fact that any gross measure is sensitive to changes both in structural organization and in volume of production. Inclusion in industry of the previously omitted private and small-scale industries on the one hand and increases in independently reporting units of the state industry on the other — due both to reorganizations and to accounting window dressing — further accentuated the upward bias of these indices.

But the most important single fact about the Soviet performance is that its full official record is not available for inspection by impartial observers. Detailed Soviet data on income in either current or constant prices have not been published since the late 1930's. The official data consist of indices of real income and of gross value of industrial output. Consequently, we do not have complete and acceptable data for either long-term or short-term sectoral changes. Although various Soviet economists have complained about the upward distortion of these indices, the official data have not been revised. The Soviet Union still claims phenomenal increases in income and output: for example, from 1928 to 1950, according to official sources, income increased by 840 per cent, gross value of industrial output by 1,110 per cent, and gross value of large industry output by 1,350 per cent. Since 1950, the 1926–27 weights have been discarded and have been replaced by moving weights for quinquennial periods. Again, however, the industry indices are computed for gross rather than net output, and furthermore, the new data have been welded to the old discredited series without any attempt at correction.

Why have the Soviets continued to use for a quarter of a century the highly misleading 1926–27 weights even though such calculations were bound to distort their own programming schedules seriously? What reasons other than sheer window dressing prompted the retention of this completely unreliable yardstick? What could be done in order to ascertain more accurately the actual performance of the Soviet economy both during these crucial past years and since then? These are some of the questions which we now consider briefly.

ON SOVIET STATISTICS IN GENERAL

The truth of the matter is that statistics in the Soviet Union are not neutral tools. Among the purposes for which they are used, pride of place is taken by the regime's projection of its own image and achievements both inside and outside the USSR. The deep concern of the Soviet system with propaganda and its monopoly over the country's statistical information may and does lead its policy makers to withhold certain data, present them in a highly ambiguous way, or simply falsify them if it appears to be politically expedient.[5]

5. *Thus in December, 1958, Khrushchev declared officially: "With regard to the production of grain, the country has for a long time remained at almost*

In the Soviet Union, statistics is recognized as a science but one with a narrowly determined scope. As officially stated, Soviet statistics is a *social* science based on Marxism-Leninism, and as such, it is and must be "class-conscious and party-oriented." Statistics are to be used for illustrating the contentions arrived at via Marxian analysis and not for experimentally testing certain hypotheses which might contradict this analysis. Hence, statistics is not a universal science but a changing sociohistorical tool. The study of mass phenomena in nature is artificially cut off from these Marxist-Leninist statistics and relegated to some unidentified limbo of "non-statistics statistics," as Professor Stuart A. Rice has facetiously put it. In statistics (social science), mathematical laws and particularly the resort to probabilistic models are anathema to the Soviets. In "non-statistics," the use of mathematics and of probability theory is perfectly legitimate. Thus, Soviet statisticians — i.e., those dealing with the type of information with which we are concerned here — are officially invited to be "active builders of Communist society" rather than "nonparticipating recorders of phenomena."

On the other hand, the USSR is run, as we know, as a huge multibranch, multiplant complex whose centralized control of basic economic activities requires detailed and prompt information on performance and work in progress in each part of the economy, on its resources, production functions, money flows, etc. At each echelon, performance and work must be recorded and evaluated not only for accounting but also for the establishment of rewards or sanctions. Hence, high stakes are involved in these statistics all along the line from their source to their reporting at each echelon, their consolidation, internal utilization, and ultimately their outside release. Within any command economy — of the Soviet or the capitalist

---

the same level that was reached by prerevolutionary Russia. The quantity of the country's grain according to the state resources was extremely insufficient. Difficulties were created in providing the population with bread. Such a situation was undoubtedly known to Malenkov but contrary to the facts, he declared at the 19th Communist party (CPSU) *Congress that the gross harvest of grain in the country in 1952 amounted to 8 billion poods and that the grain problem, which formerly was considered a most acute and serious problem, had been solved for good. This was not in accord with reality and was on his part a deception of the party and of the people. In fact, the collective farms and state farms even in 1952, the year of the best yields for that period, did not gather 8 billion poods of grain but only 5 to 6 billion poods."* (*Closing speech of N. S. Khrushchev at the plenary meeting of the C.P.S.U. Central Committee, Dec. 19, 1958.*)

type, administered by authoritarian methods in either peace or war — a host of similar problems are bound to arise. Economic constraints require the sacrifice of consumption to other goals, the setting of all sorts of "top priorities" by policy makers, the establishment of price and wage controls, etc., and thus create favorable conditions for progressive deterioration of honest statistical information and reporting.

Obviously, there is full public awareness of this fact in the Soviet Union, where economic straits and emergencies are a way of life. There are numerous manifestations of concern with the reliability of the data at the disposal of planners and policy makers. Exhortations to statistical honesty, appeals to lofty Soviet ideals along with stern warnings against cheaters and distorters of statistical information abound in the Soviet literature. The accuracy of the Soviet data at the disposal of Soviet policy makers themselves is affected by the ways in which the Soviet economy actually operates and not the supposed "class-consciousness" of its statisticians. The ideological slant bears mostly on the selection and presentation of the data released to the public. The assorted ills which Professor Berliner calls "simulation of plan fulfillment" — i.e., deviations from scheduled output, deterioration of quality, underreporting in some cases and overstating of performance in others — affect the Soviet system of *internal* statistical reporting from its very source, the enterprise, through all the levels of the economic and administrative pyramid.

Two types of elements distort Soviet statistics: one affects the release to the public of statistical data; the other affects the production of statistical information from the enterprises up, the very "stuff" of which Soviet statistics are made. The authorities vigorously fight the tendencies toward internal distortion and misrepresentation by applying severe sanctions at each level; despite these sanctions, however, the quality of Soviet statistics remains poor and highly unequal as far as accuracy is concerned in the various sectors of the economy. Industrial output statistics, for instance, where a variety of checks and controls are possible and where systematic classification is necessary, are probably the most reliable, even though they, too, suffer from the assorted diseases that may be labeled "simulation of plan fulfillment." Agricultural output statistics — where reporting is of a far lower quality, where checking is more elusive, and where actual results have been continuously poor — are probably the worst. Also of doubtful validity are the scarce and usually conflicting data on employment and wages. In general, as compared to physical output data, the data in value terms are very poor — except for the budgetary data, which qualified outside observers consider quite usable. Aggregative data on gross value of output or on national income must be viewed with skepticism, as we have noted. Equally dubious are the statistics on productivity and related indicators based on the gross output indices. Various checks among all the data officially released indicate that the Soviets do not resort to the use of two sets of books — one for themselves and one for the public: *as a rule*, the data released are the data in use in the Soviet Union itself, even though in some extreme cases the policy makers are led to withhold some important information and even falsify certain published figures for political purposes. Though scanty in the past, Soviet data are now abundant on almost all aspects of the country's economic activity. Quantity does not, however, mean clarity. Many of these data may easily be misinterpreted because of the ambiguous ways in which they are presented, the specificity of the underlying Soviet definitions, and the deficiency of Soviet statistical methods. Despite these numerous caveats, many of these data remain our only possible source for the study of Soviet economic reality. Imperfect as they are, they do give us an understanding of this reality, thanks to the painstaking efforts of those who have learned to revaluate them and to place some of the more valid bits and pieces into a set of coherent and clear pictures of the Soviet economy as a whole and of its internal operations.

METHODOLOGY OF WESTERN REVALUATIONS

The debate concerning the ways in which the Soviet performance could be evaluated now centers largely on the solutions proposed by Professor A. Bergson and his followers of the so-called adjusted factor-cost school. In *Soviet National Income and Product in 1937*, a pioneering study written in 1950, Bergson computed Soviet income in current Soviet market prices and then adjusted these values to a theoretically defined "adjusted factor cost standard" (AFCS). The computations in current rubles simply show the money and income flows at official prices; the "adjusted ruble" computations are meant to penetrate the monetary integument and disclose the actual phenomena occurring in the economy, i.e., the allocation of resources as between consumption and investment in terms of the "real" cost of *inputs*. Bergson's AFCS is principally a standard for efficient allocation in the long run. In it, commodity prices must resolve entirely into charges for capital, land, and labor: thus, we should have "interest" for capital corresponding to "the average internal return of this factor in the economy," depreciation allowances consistent with conventional accounting principles, rent corresponding on the average to differential return on superior land, wages set at a uniform rate for each occupation and differing between occupations according to differences in productivity, and finally uniform commodity prices in any given market. Because of the paucity and peculiarities of Soviet statistical data, however, Bergson's main valuation adjustments consist of the exclusion of indirect taxes from the national product and of the addition of subsidies, along with some relatively secondary corrections in respect to recorded net profit and depreciation. His income-adjusted factor cost thus reduces to the summation of labor income and net income profits of the enterprises — the latter, once adjusted, taken to be an acceptable substitute for interest charges, which are lacking. Bergson's own studies and those written with various collaborators have yielded a detailed and a highly informative view of the growth and structural change of Soviet income during the thoroughgoing planning era. His accounts are cast in a slightly modified U.S. Department of Commerce form. Two basic accounts — income and outlay of households, and a consolidated net income and outlay for government, social, and economic organizations — lead to tabulation of the division of the product by use categories. (See Table 8.)

The validity of the adjusted factor cost procedure has been questioned, notably by Peter Wiles, who has raised the following main objections: First, elimination of the turnover tax and addition of subsidies may correct distortions between producers' and consumers' goods prices, but leaves us with "irrational" net prices. (The *rationality* of the latter, i.e., their reflection of scarcity relationships, hinges on the rationality of wages, which, according to Wiles, do not reflect the relative *scarcities* or *productivities* of labor.) Second, even if wages were rational, the question of what to do about rent, interest, and profit remains insoluble since land, abstinence, and risk bearing do not carry rewards in the Soviet Union. Voicing the skepticism of other students of the Soviet economy concerning ability to evaluate the factor costs other than labor, Professor Gregory Grossman has suggested that Bergson might have given a better base to his computations if he had dispensed with profits altogether, rejected explicitly the relevance of prices for final goods in the Soviet frame of reference, and used a "Labor-Disutility" standard of income valuation (instead of his AFCS). Wiles has, however, recalled in connection with this solution that relative unit

TABLE 8. *Soviet Gross National Product by Use,* Percentages, Selected Years, 1928–1965*

	1928	1937	1950	1958	1965†
Consumption	69.8	63.0	56.3	63.5	60.7
1. Private	64.7	52.5	45.5	56.4	52.2
2. Communal Services	5.1	10.5	10.8	7.1	8.5
Gross Investment	25.0	25.9	27.9	26.6	27.7
Defense (as recorded in budget)	2.5	7.9	10.9	9.9	11.6
Administration	2.7	3.2	4.9		

* *Underlying data: current ruble factor cost.*
† *Based on plan targets.*
SOURCES: Abram Bergson, *The Real National Income of Soviet Russia Since 1928*, Cambridge, Harvard University Press, 1961, p. 237, and Abraham S. Becker, *Soviet National Income and Product in 1965: The Goals of the Seven-Year Plan*, Santa Monica, The Rand Corporation, RM-3520-PR, 1963, p. 38.

wage costs could be no more than a poor substitute for relative unit factor costs, since they are not in a fixed proportion to one another. As can be ascertained from Western statistical data, rent, interest, and dividends enter in varying proportions into any set of factor costs, so that a system of weights which excludes the former could hardly qualify as being rational on this ground alone.

Answering Wiles's main objections, Professor Bergson asserted in his study, *The Real National Income of Soviet Russia since 1928*, that the productive activities of a country could be evaluated either from the point of view of the efficiency with which its resources are used or from the point of view of the satisfaction of its consumers' or planners' preferences. Where the concern is with a country's production possibilities, a proper cost valuation is sufficient. Prices used for this purpose should correspond to marginal costs; it is not essential, adds Bergson, that these prices correspond to marginal utilities and planners' preferences. In other words, what matters in relation to wages is whether wage differentials *within any industry* correspond on the average to relative value productivities, or whether labor and other activities within any one industry are combined so that cost is at a minimum. Interindustry wage differentials should also reflect workers' transfers prices, but correspondence of wage differentials and marginal value productivities *as between industries* is not considered by Bergson as essential for measuring the production potential as it is for ascertaining welfare. Bergson therefore rejects as irrelevant Wiles's assertion that lack of correspondence between interindustry wage differentials and marginal value productivities imperils the income calculation at adjusted factor cost.

Bergson contends that the Soviet economy will operate on its production possibility curve so long as there are no glaring interferences in factor markets. Wiles, however, appears to assert that interferences in the *product* market will in any case prevent the economy from operating on its production possibility curve. If this is Wiles's view, it is wrong from the standpoint of logic; interferences on the product market will merely shift production to a different point on the production possibility curve, but will not move the economy to a point inside the curve (even though relative factor prices would be disturbed).[6] Thus, Bergson is correct in stating that to reduce product prices to factor cost terms is a proper measure of the change of *productive capacity* over time. If there were serious interferences with factor markets, the economy would be moved to a point inside the production possibility curve. In the latter case, Bergson's computations would measure *production* over time, instead of changes in *productive capacity*. Of course, it remains true that Soviet profits do not reflect the scarcity of entrepreneurship or the scarcity of capital and that proper adjustments in this respect are very difficult to make. To the extent that these inaccuracies of factor-pricing exist, Bergson's GNP measures are not an accurate measure of capacity change, but an acceptable measure of output changes.

6. *Graphically, the two positions can be presented as follows. Bergson states that without interference in factor markets, the economy will tend to operate along the envelope* PP *at a point like* A *(chosen by the planners).* Wiles *states that with interference in product markets, the economy will be forced to operate at a point like* B. *The point* C, *determined by the tangency of the consumers' indifference curve* II *and the production possibility curve* PP, *would only be reached if interferences were removed from* both *the product and the factor markets.*

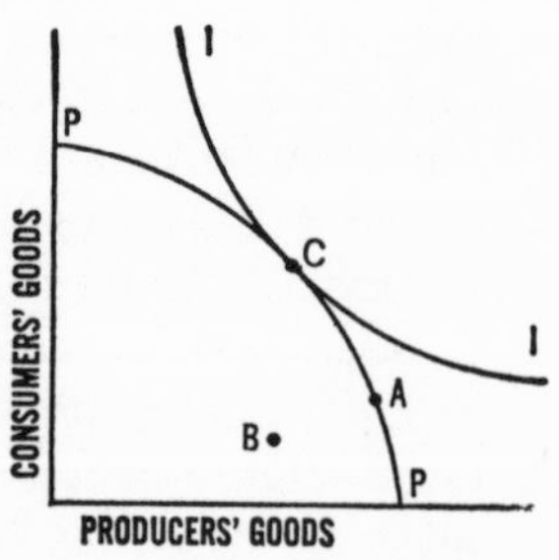

TABLE 9. *Alternative Estimates of Soviet National Product, Indices and Growth Rates, Selected Years, 1928–1965*

	Period	Year-End Index	Annual Growth Rate
Soviet official (Soviet definitions)	1928–1958	1930	10.4
	1950–1958	229	10.9
	1958–1965	157	6.6
Western estimates:			
Bergson: NNP, 1937 ruble factor cost	1928–1958	336	4.8
	1950–1958	170	6.8
Cohn: GNP, net sectoral output indices composite	1950–1958	173	7.1
	1958–1964	136	5.3
Clark: NNP, 1950 U.S. prices	1928–1956	277	3.7
	1950–1956	130	4.5
Jasny: NNP, adjusted ruble prices 1926–27	1928–1955	383	5.1

SOURCES: A. Bergson, *The Real National Income of Russia Since 1928*, *op. cit.*, pp. 85 and 149; C. Clark, *The Conditions of Economic Progress*, London: Macmillan, 1951, p. 186, 192; and C. Clark, *The Real Productivity of Soviet Russia*, Subcommittee to Investigate the Administration of the Internal Security Act, Committee on the Judiciary, U.S. 87th Cong., Washington, 1961, p. 56; N. Jasny, *Soviet Industrialization*, 1928–1952, Chicago: University of Chicago Press, 1961, p. 444–445.

In addition to the detailed tabulations of Bergson in current, adjusted, and "real" terms, various other income estimates in dollars or in rubles are available. Most of the tabulations in rubles do not, however, explore as fully as Bergson and his associates do, the limitations of the Soviet price system. Some summary tabulations of the Soviet income and product for various years have been computed in rubles, notably by Dr. Naum Jasny, and in dollars, by Professor Colin Clark. Dr. Jasny's calculations are at so called "real" adjusted 1926/27 ruble prices; unfortunately, the underlying statistical computations were not released. Those of Professor Colin Clark in 1950 dollar prices are constructed through the perilous process of deriving from agricultural statistics, undoubtedly the poorest Soviet statistics extant, and from some other miscellaneous sources of unequal validity: food consumption, other consumption, investment, and government service. All these computations are, however, insufficiently explained and often vulnerable in respect to coverage, underlying statistical methods, and system of weights used. Table 9 gives a comparison between all of these various estimates and the Soviet exaggerated claim.

The measurement of Soviet *industrial growth* and its changes over time, a most crucial indicator of Soviet performance, raises a host of attendant problems. We have already encountered the problems in assessing Soviet market prices and factor costs; another set of problems concerns the kind and extent of the data needed to construct meaningful industrial outputs series. As already stated, the large amount of Soviet data that has been released since the 1950's is still insufficient for constructing fully satisfactory indices. Numerous solutions of this problem of measuring the Soviet Union's industrial expansion have been advanced in the West; great ingenuity has been exercised, particularly in the choice of weights and product coverage. Naum Jasny has constructed an index for the planning era up to 1950 by using his own "corrected" 1926–27 ruble prices. D. R. Hodgman has computed an index covering large-scale industry until 1932 and all industry afterwards until 1951, using 1934 wage-bill weights. B. Shimkin and F. A. Leedy have resorted to modified Hodgman weights to carry the computations up to 1956. G. W. Nutter has used a combination of Soviet 1955 official prices and employment distribution by industrial groups. F. Seton has constructed his index by using a regression equation to relate the growth of some key Soviet inputs to the output data of some other countries. N. M. Kaplan and R. D. Moorsteen have computed an index for selected years up to 1958 by using 1950 Soviet price weights within certain groups of commodities and 1950 wage-bill weights among these commodity groups. (For some of these estimates, see Table 10.)

Extensive statistical and technical studies support some of these computations — notably the Hodgman, Nutter, and Kaplan-Moorsteen indices. To take the last of the list, its underlying computations are detailed in two studies: one on Soviet machinery prices and production and one on Soviet output of all industrial products. Machinery output, a key part of industrial production, received special attention in an earlier study by Professor A. Gershenkron, who constructed a machinery output index in dollar weights. Related measurements of Soviet performance are those concerning the output of final industrial products (i.e., products for consumption and investment), ratios of producers' to consumers' goods outputs, indices of per capita consumption, and some others.

Generally, the Western revaluations show the existence of significant rates of growth in Soviet income and product and in Soviet industrial output. The Western estimates are not uniform, however. Substantial divergences exist among them because of differences in method of computation, weights used, adjustments made, coverage, etc. (See Tables 9, 10). Many, if not most, of these divergences can be put into proper perspective, thanks to the detailed underlying studies available on procedures and data used. Wide as these divergences may sometimes appear, they are far less substantial than those arising between Western estimates as a whole and the exaggerated official Soviet income and industrial growth indexes. As we have seen, the Soviet official record does not present either fully or satisfactorily sector relations and interactions, income structure, sectoral growth. The deficiencies of the Soviet record stem

TABLE 10. *Alternative Estimates of Soviet Industrial Output, Indices and Growth Rates, Selected Years, 1928–1965*

	Period	Year-End Index	Annual Growth Rate
All Industrial Products			
Soviet Official	1928–1958	2504	11.3
	1950–1958	248	12.0
	1958–1965	184	8.1
Western Estimates:			
Kaplan-Moorsteen	1928–1958	740	6.9
	1950–1958	202	9.2
Nutter	1928–1955	689	6.5
	1950–1955	158	9.6

	Period	Year-End Index	Annual Growth Rate
Powell-Bergson			
1928 weights	1928–1958	1747	10.1
1937 weights	1928–1958	851	7.4
1928 weights	1950–1958	214	10.1
1937 weights	1950–1958	215	10.2
Machinery			
Soviet Official	1928–1958	15900	19.5
	1950–1958	315	15.6
	1958–1965	237	13.1
Western Estimates:			
Kaplan-Moorsteen	1928–1958	2643	11.6
	1950–1958	185	8.0
Nutter	1928–1955	962	8.8
	1950–1955	125	4.6
All Producers' Goods			
Soviet Official (Group A)	1928–1958	4637	13.5
	1950–1958	261	12.7
	1958–1965	197	10.3
Soviet*	1928–1957	2311	11.2
	1950–1957	208	11.0
Western Estimates*			
Kaplan-Moorsteen	1928–1958	952	7.8
	1950–1958	212	9.5
Consumers' Goods			
Soviet Official (Group B)	1928–1958	1062	8.5
	1950–1958	224	10.6
	1958–1965	159	6.9
Western Estimates			
Kaplan-Moorsteen	1928–1958	281	4.5
	1950–1958	205	9.4
Nutter	1928–1955	288	4.0

* *Excluding machinery.*

SOURCES: *Narodnoe khoziaistvo S.S.S.R.* 1960, 1965 [The National Economy of the USSR] Moscow, Central Statistical Office, 1961 and 1966, *passim*, and Kaplan and Moorsteen, "An Index of Soviet Industrial Output," *The American Economic Review* (June, 1960), 301, 303; and A. Bergson and S. Kuznets (eds.), *Economic Trends in the Soviet Union*, Cambridge, Mass., Harvard University Press, 1963, p. 155.

from a variety of causes. In part, they are linked to Soviet economic institutions which do not give certain factors explicit rewards. The deficiencies also arise from cumbersome and often confusing approaches, for instance, the treatment of service payments as transfer income. They are due finally to the peculiarities of Soviet statistics and statistical reporting. Fortunately, among the data released, various basic elements, such as certain physical output data and financial statistics, can be recombined, recast into appropriate molds, and used for gaining a clearer view of the actual performance of the Soviet economy.

9.

Money and Banking

MARXIAN MONETARY THEORY AND SOVIET PRACTICE

In principle, Soviet monetary theory does not depart from the original Marxian concepts concerning gold, circulation of commodities, and law of value. In practice, however, Soviet economists have been forced to entertain rather equivocal relations with the official theory and its underlying assumptions.

The basic postulates of the Marxian monetary theory are

1] Money is a "measure of the value of commodities," i.e., a measure of that specific substance which Marx defines as the "social labor" embodied in each good sold and purchased.

2] Only a commodity which has its own "value" may serve as a measure of other values; hence, only a commodity, such as gold, can fulfill this purpose — bank notes or any other currency meet the task only by virtue of their connection with gold; i.e., only to the extent to which they represent or substitute for gold.

3] Prices of goods do not necessarily correspond to the respective values, but the *sum* of all commodity prices equals the sum of all (underlying) values.

Thus, in the Marxian definition, money is a measure of values, or a unit of account serving as a general equivalent in commodity exchanges, because it has both a use value and an exchange value.[1]

1. *Marx indicates that the variations in the "value" of gold itself do not impair its role as a "standard of price," since, no matter how gold's own value may vary, "twelve ounces of gold still have twelve times the value of one ounce; and in prices the only thing considered is the relation between different quantities of gold." Karl Marx,* Capital *(English ed.; Moscow: Foreign Languages Publishing House, 1954), I, chap. 3, p. 98.*

If commodity exchange is defined as change in the ownership of a good through its sale and purchase via money, how can exchanges take place within the state sectors since no actual change of ownership is possible there? What, then, is the true nature and scope of money, the meaning of prices, and the role of the "law of value" in situations where two forms of ownership — state and collective — exist side by side? These and related questions have placed Soviet economists in a quandary that seemed insoluble and have given rise to violent controversies, some of which we consider in detail later on.[2] For the present, let us note only a few of the more salient implications concerning money.

Since Marxian theory defines money as a medium of exchange of "commodities," Soviet monetary theorists have resorted to paradoxical arguments in order to explain the persistence of money under socialism. First they claimed that money subsisted under Soviet conditions *only* because of the existence, on the fringes of the state sector, of "commodity production and circulation" within the collective farm and cooperative sector. Later they added that money was simply an *objective* necessity, given the existence of "various forms of ownership and of different types of enterprises under socialism."[3] On closer examination, this issue proved to be semantic rather than economic. Clearly, outside the sphere of state interfirm transactions, Soviet money fulfills, with only minor restrictions, its usual functions of a standard of value and a means of exchange. Within the state sphere, the ruble also plays the role of a measure of value, but it serves as only a limited medium of exchange, since it may be used among autonomous state-owned enterprises only for transferring specified goods at predetermined prices according to specific plans. Furthermore, its use as a store of value is limited by sharp restrictions on ruble balances for carrying on transactions. Soviet money is therefore limited in supply and serves as a standard of value both inside and outside the state sphere. The eventual disappearance of the collective-farm and cooperative sector would not

2. *See Chap. 13.*

3. *"And hence," writes V. V. Ikonnikov, "the necessity for money under socialism arises in the socialist system of production, from the existence in certain limits of commodity production and commodity circulation."* Denezhnoe obrashchenie i kredit SSSR [*Money Circulation and Credit in the USSR*] *Moscow, Gosfinizdat, 1954, p. 7. For the newer interpretation, see K. N. Shafiev (ed.),* Politicheskaia ekonomiia sotsializma [*Political Economy of Socialism*] *(Moscow, Sotsekonlitizdat), 1960, pp. 179–180.*

do away with the need for a medium of exchange so long as consumers are allowed to accumulate a generalized claim against goods — for what else is money if not this?

For Soviet monetary theorists, Soviet currency consists of "tokens" for gold: it is only as such that Soviet money is said to be able to perform its functions, including its new assignment under socialism, namely, as an instrument of planning and control over all economic processes. But in fact, the performance of Soviet money has nothing to do with its purported connection with gold. For all practical purposes, this connection is only a fetish, since Soviet currency cannot be converted into gold, is unaffected by changes in Soviet gold reserves, is impervious to international price fluctuations, and is entirely severed from other currencies. At any given time, the purchasing power of each ruble depends not on the stated fetishistic relation to gold, but on government price fixing and on the systematic attempts at equilibrium in the key planned balances, such as the budget, balances of the enterprises, and balance of income and expenditures of the population. Planning of income flows and output distribution is achieved without regard to the gold values on which they are purported to depend.

Soviet monetary theorists regard banking and credit — like money — as transitional institutions arising from the existence of commodity production under socialism.[4] In Soviet theory, both banks and money would cease to exist as such after the installation of a "natural economy" in the "highest phases of communism," i.e., under the Marxian posited conditions of abundant resources and of unlimited supplies. Banking is supposed to be superseded then by a central "bookkeeping" system for the economy as a whole. Clearly, Soviet economists do realize that no complex production is conceivable without accounting; what they suggest is that planning, production, and distribution can be carried out entirely in a pure credit economy. The planners, of course, would still have to compute correctly the specific share of consumption in social output;

4. *"The necessity of banks and credits in the socialist economy," continues Ikonnikov, "is determined first of all by the existence of two forms of socialist production — state and collective-farm cooperative, and the maintenance in connection with them, in given limits, of commodity production and commodity exchange, and the operation in this sphere of the law of value."* (Op. cit., *p.* 45).

and they would still impose strict accounting in the sphere of distribution since, without excess of output over consumption, no further growth could be secured.

MONEY SUPPLY AND CIRCULAR FLOWS

Soviet currency consists of bank notes issued by the State Bank, of currency issued by the State Bank on behalf of the treasury, and of minor coin.[5] As of January 1, 1961, the ruble has been defined as equivalent to 0.987412 grams of fine gold; at this time, old rubles were exchanged for new ones at the rate of 10 to 1.[6] The currency is inconvertible; its volume, as well as the amount of gold reserves and their fluctuation, is not disclosed. By law, bank notes are to have a backing of at least 25 per cent in gold or foreign exchange, and treasury notes may not exceed a fixed percentage of the total bank notes in circulation. The real significance of these provisions cannot readily be ascertained by an outsider. As officially specified, currency is actually injected into the economy in "compliance with the needs of the domestic trade transactions," i.e., at the discretion of the Council of Ministers, which bases its decisions on various planned balances.

Gold holdings are regarded not only as reserves against bank notes but also as emergency "reserve" for eventual transactions with the capitalist countries. The official assertion that the Soviet ruble is the strongest currency in the world is based on the claim that the gold content of the ruble has increased and that the ruble remains stable whatever the fluctuations of the world market might be. Actually, the severance of the ruble from the world financial markets deprives it of international status. Although trade agree-

5. *The banknotes, called* kupiury, *are issued in denominations of 10, 25, 50, and 100 rubles. The currency is issued in 1, 3, and 5 ruble denominations; the coins, of bronze or nickel, represent various numbers of* kopecks *(100 kopecks to 1 ruble).*

6. *Until 1950, the ruble had been successively defined in gold, French francs, and finally United States dollars. In 1950, it was redefined in gold at the rate of 0.222168 grams of fine gold per ruble. Setting the exchange rate of old rubles for new ones at 10 to 1 (in January, 1961) and defining the new ruble as equivalent to one gram of gold instead of 2.2 grams, as in the previous gold-content definition, would have required the Soviet government to devalue the old ruble by more than a half. By simultaneously reducing all monetary values to one-tenth of their previous level, however, the Soviet government was able to introduce a ruble which was "heavier" in terms of gold than the previous one.*

ments with all the other socialist countries are, as we shall see, expressed in "rubles," the rubles of account for international trade are not the rubles of account for domestic trade. The former are taken to be equivalent to $1.10; any other conventional unit of account, say, "bancors," if clearly defined and accepted by the signatories of a trade agreement, could play the same role.

In the Soviet Union, the incomes of individuals — wages, salaries, and interest on savings — are paid in currency. Collective farmers receive a small part of their remuneration in kind. State payments for the officially requested farm deliveries constitute a significant part of the total quantity of currency outstanding. Individuals do not receive rentals or profits, since private ownership of means of production is abolished. Money income is spent at the discretion of income receivers, mostly on consumers' goods and on some construction materials; it cannot be used to finance private undertakings or for trading and speculation. The circular flow — money income, on the one side, and outlays on consumers' goods and services (mostly provided by the state), on the other — is thus carried out in currency.

The transactions between enterprises occur without currency; bank deposits are used instead. Enterprises which, as already stated, are autonomous on the operational plane, receive grants and advances which may take two forms: 1] currency or 2] clearing deposits, according to the inputs which they need to purchase. The ratio of 1] to 2] depends on the ratio of labor to raw materials and semiprocessed goods, the velocity of consumer spending, and the ratio of consumption to all other outputs, all variables being interconnected. The State Bank extends these grants and advances on the basis of transactions in accordance with the governmental decisions concerning investment and planned growth. Only the finished consumers' goods industries and distribution enterprises obtain currency from consumers' outlays and make deposits at the State Bank. The producers' goods industries and manufacturers of intermediate products obtain deposits from their sales; of these, only the amount needed for wages and salary payments may be converted into currency.

The flows of currency and deposits are coordinated through the bank. There are two main circular flows: a currency flow from government to households and a return flow from the latter in the form of expenditures on consumers' goods and services; secondly there is a deposit flow among enterprises for all interenterprise transactions. In a sense, this second circular flow is "distorted," since the enterprises may not deal with capital goods in the usual manner. Instead, these goods must be paid for from budgetary funds earmarked for investment, deposited in the appropriate bank, and put at the disposal of certain enterprises designated as "investors." The investor may then draw on the balances only for specified goods, at designated producers' goods enterprises at prescribed times, in accordance with scheduled plan expansions. (See Figure 11.) The circular flows are somewhat simplified in this chart: consumers also buy some producers' goods from the state and some consumers' goods from the collective-farm markets; the money from these latter purchases returns to the state shops. Collective farms and cooperatives may in turn get deposits or currency from sales to the state firms and may use these for the purchase of producers' goods. In all the transactions considered, be they between state enterprises and collectives, or between state enterprises and individuals, between collectives and individuals, or merely between individuals, money in the forms of currency or deposits has value, i.e., buys goods, because it is limited in supply and is accepted in payment for goods and services. The underlying theories have little significance for those participating in the transactions: what matters to them is that only money, whatever its form, performs the function of buying goods at the established prices. As we shall see below, the State Bank limits the supply of money by means of certain interrelated balances.

THE BANKING SYSTEM

The principles underlying the organization and activity of banking are 1] centralization of banking as a monopoly in the hands of the state; 2] subordination of all banking activity to the economic plans; 3] specialization according to functions; 4] utilization of banks as central bookkeeping units and as instruments of control and verification of planned transactions. The banking system consists of a central bank, called the State Bank (*Gosbank*), an Investment Bank (*Stroibank*), and savings institutions.

The State Bank is the bank of issue, the "commercial bank" of the economy, and the government's agent for fiscal operations. The chairman of the bank is appointed by the Supreme Soviet and has

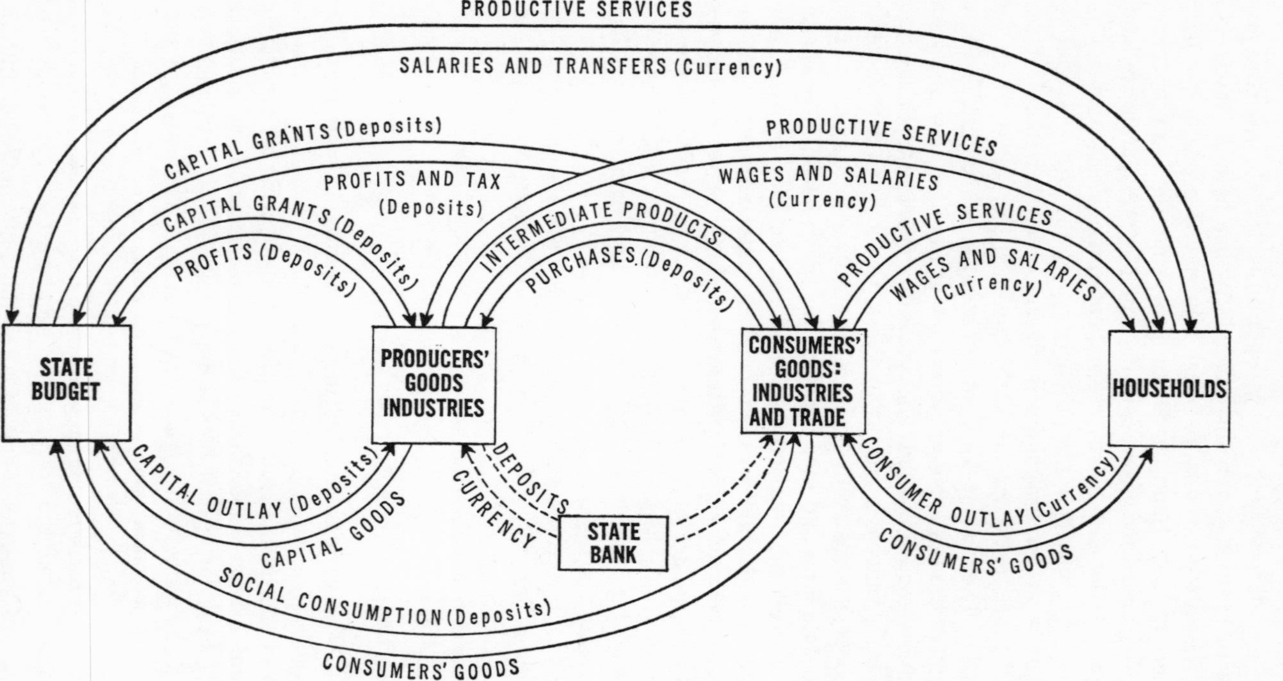

FIGURE 11. *Circular Flows in the Soviet Economy*

a seat in the Council of Ministers. The State Bank's head office is in Moscow; subordinated to it are some 170 republic, regional, and territorial offices which in turn control some 5,000 branch offices and agencies. Following the usual pattern of Soviet organization, the head office of the State Bank has departments organized along functional and operational lines. Among the functional departments are planning (with subdivisions for credit plan, currency plan, and statistics), central bookkeeping, and auditing, as well as capital construction, material-technical supply, labor and wages, and some other areas. Among the operational departments are credits (with subdivisions for economic councils and local industry, defense, transport and communication, and trade), foreign operations, currency issue, and budget operations. Each of the main offices and branches is organized on the same pattern.

As in a bank of similar standing in the West, the State Bank's assets consist of gold, foreign exchange, and loans; its liabilities of bank notes, currency, and deposits; its net worth of its charter capital and its reserves. At this point, the differences between the State Bank and a Western type of bank begin. Gosbank's deposits are of two types: clearing or settlement accounts, reserved exclusively for the state enterprises operating on a commercial basis, and current accounts opened for all other customers, such as institutions and organizations, including state agencies, savings banks, collective farms and cooperatives, and individuals.[7] All accounts are convertible into currency but for specified purposes only — in the case of enterprises, for payroll and for meeting small payments below specified amounts; in the case of individuals, for straight withdrawals or for check payments to the state for services.

Each enterprise has its basic settlement account in the State Bank and, if needed, special subsidiary accounts, e.g., for important repairs. Payments may be made through the "acceptance" method, letter of credit, special account, or check. The acceptance method is most widely used. The seller dispatches the goods to the buyer and presents the invoice to his own State Bank office, which in turn forwards it to the bank office of the buyer so that it can be submitted for his approval. In case of "acceptance," which must be given within a certain number of days, the bank debits the buyer in his account and credits the seller; in case of refusal, the goods remain

7. *Settlement accounts are called* raschetnye scheta; *current accounts,* tekushchie scheta.

under the care and responsibility of the buyer until new instructions are sent by the seller. In the letter of credit and special account systems, the buyer establishes beforehand an account to the order of the seller, who is thus assured of payment as soon as he dispatches the goods. Payments by letter of credit or by check now account for only a small percentage of all transactions.

TABLE 11. *Schema of a Balance Sheet of the State Bank* †

Assets	*Liabilities*
Gold stock *	Gosbank notes *
Foreign exchange *	Currency *
Loans	Deposits
1. Goods in transit	1. Settlement accounts of enterprises
2. Seasonal	a. Subsidiary accounts of enterprises
3. Planned (on basis of output programs)	2. Current accounts
	a. Government
	b. Institutions and other enterprises
	c. Saving banks
	d. Collective farms
	e. Cooperatives
	f. Individuals
	Net Worth
	1. Charter Capital *
	2. Reserves

† *This balance is cast in a "Western" framework. The so-called net balance of the bank does not include the asterisked items, all of which, excluding charter capital, were accounted for in the 1930's by the State Bank's issue department.*

The vast multiplication of mutually compensatory transactions has led to the establishment of various interbranch, interindustry, or regional mutual offset clearing schemes within the State Bank. About half of all interfirm transactions are now cleared in this way in order to reduce the volume of control needed and increase consolidation of operations at the higher levels of the State Bank. In the so-called decentralized accounts system, each participant in a given scheme has a special account segregated from his basic account at his usual bank branch. Only his dealings with the participants in the given mutual offset group are entered in the segregated account; the account is netted and audited at intervals adapted to the specific production conditions of the given enterprise. The nets are then entered in the regular account of the firm at the dates of auditing. This system gives the firm somewhat more freedom to maneuver its total funds; through the periodic control of the end results, the system also frees the bank from the need to control each of the mutual offsetting operations. For speeding clearing operations, the participants in a mutual offset scheme are credited automatically without waiting for the buyer's official acceptance; in any given period, the final result of the procedure might produce an expansion rather than contraction of the total volume of credits outstanding.

The State Bank is the basic source of legitimate short-term loans. No enterprise may extend credit to another, although in practice, numerous cases of mutual indebtedness occur between enterprises and continue to amount to significant sums. In extending credit, the State Bank, like any Western commercial bank, creates new purchasing power. Its loans are made for goods en route ("goods in transit"), increases in inventories of a seasonal character, and planned loans over and above the working capital requirements granted to the enterprises by the state. The minimums are periodically reexamined and revised on the basis of certain norms related to the enterprises' activity. Because of seasonal changes in the supply of agricultural produce and raw materials to food processing, light industry, and trade and procurement agencies and because of the resulting sharp fluctuations in their inventories and working capital needs over and above "minimum" levels, the State Bank's short-term credits have been given to these industries and purchasing agencies, rather than to heavy industries. Consistently over the years, up to as much as 75 per cent of the short-term credit outstanding has gone to light industry and trade agencies.

Since the 1960's, continuous efforts have been made for vastly expanding the utilization of credits. Credit is to be used not only for financing inventories and for bridging seasonal gaps but also for stimulating technological progress and capital formation. Investment loans at terms of up to three years and even more are made available for projects not included in the national centralized investment plans (viz., for acquisition of above-plan equipment; for introduction of advanced machinery and special technological improvements; for increases in the output of consumer goods mainly from local raw materials; and for related purposes). As pointed out by George Garvy of the Federal Reserve Bank of New York, such credits should be regarded as medium-term loans, but they are treated in Soviet accounting as short-term credits because, in general, they are amortized quite rapidly.

The State Bank charges and pays interest, except on budgetary accounts; the difference between charges and payments represents its income. Rates charged are differentiated according to type of credit and cost of handling. In the 1960's, the bank charged 1 per cent for loans on "goods in transit," 2 per cent for all other short-term credit, and 3-5 per cent for loans overdue. For its part, the bank paid 0.5 per cent on the deposits of enterprises and 1.5 per cent on the deposits of collective farms.

Finally, as the government's fiscal agent, the State Bank discharges numerous duties, including collection of taxes, disbursing expenditures, and controlling the execution of specified budgetary tasks for the All-Union or republic ministries of finance. Because of the Soviet custom of sharply differentiating each account according to its purpose and because of the variety and complexity of operations connected with the Soviet budget, more than one-quarter of the State Bank's total accounts are budgetary accounts.

The bank of foreign trade is a subsidiary of the State Bank. Limited, up to the beginning of the 1960's, to a minor range of foreign exchange operations, the role of this bank has since substantially increased in keeping with the sharp expansion in Soviet foreign trade. Along with this bank, a number of Soviet-owned banks and their branches established abroad (e.g., the *Banque Commerciale pour l'Europe du Nord, S.A.*, located in Paris; the *Moscow Narodnyi Bank, Ltd.*, located in London; and the *Voskhod Handelsbank* A.G., located in Zurich) and the inter-socialist International Bank for Economic Cooperation, IBEC (*Mezhdunarodnyi bank ekonomicheskogo sotrudnichestva,* MBES), also participate in the financing of Soviet foreign trade, foreign exchange activities, and international payments.

The second key element of the Soviet banking system is the Investment Bank. This bank is part of the Ministry of Finance, which controls and supervises its activity according to the directives of the Council of Ministers. In April, 1959, the bank superseded a number of specialized banks handling long-term credit for industry, agriculture, trade, communal economy, and housing; it now carries on its operations both through the network of these former banks (totaling some 1,200 suboffices and branches) and through the branches and agencies of the State Bank acting as its correspondents. The Investment Bank is organized on the familiar Soviet pattern with the usual functional departments and a number of departments specialized by economic sectors, industrial branches, and forms of ownership. Its assets are those of the superseded banks, augmented periodically by budget appropriations, specific parts of depreciation allowances (excluding the shares earmarked for important repairs), and shares in the profits of enterprises. The budget grants represent the most important part of these funds and account for some three-quarters of yearly disbursements. The Investment Bank extends both grants and long-term credits. Grants go to state enterprises; credits at low interest rates, to collective farms, cooperatives, local industries, and to individuals for building houses. The bank makes direct payments to the contractors for materials, transportation, and related charges on the basis of orders from the recipients of grants or loans.

The last link in the banking system is represented by some 70,000 savings agencies.[8] They handle accounts for individuals and various organizations and institutions (hospitals, municipalities, mutual aid societies, and others). Savings are kept in the form of time deposits or checking ("current") accounts, which are used for payments for utilities and state services. Dramatic increases in savings deposits since the 1960's – reflecting improvements in income – are leading toward more active uses of savings than in the past and toward the expansion of the functions of the savings system. As in some East European countries, special savings accounts for purchases of apartments, for instances, are to be created, and the savings banks may be authorized to organize the construction and to finance the investments of cooperative apartment buildings. The savings-bank branches, which are, in fact, the only banking facilities available to the population at large, would thus become lending institutions as well as depositories. Interest rates on savings deposits, differentiated in favor of the longer maturities, draw from 3 to 5 per cent interest. The interest may be turned into a contribution to a lottery which pays the winner up to double his savings account.

THE STATE BANK'S PLANNING FUNCTIONS

The State Bank's basic responsibilities are adjusting the

8. Sberegatel'nye kassy, *abbreviated as* Sberkassy.

supply of money to the "real" transaction needs of the economy as determined by the economic plan and preventing expenditures outside planned purposes. Both economic growth — embodied in the planned targets of any given period — and economic stability — embodied in the planned equilibria between such magnitudes as payroll and consumers' goods output, state retail trade volume and "accumulation" level — can be endangered by any diversion of resources outside the planned channels. In order to avoid such dangers, the State Bank aims systematically at keeping both enterprises and households as illiquid as possible and strives to ensure that all scheduled transactions are carried out with minimum monetary means. Thus, the bank's tasks require that it exercise both planning and controlling functions.

The State Bank's planning embraces currency needs and credit expansion. Currency needs are determined by wage-bill requirements and pattern of wage-earners' expenditures. If wage-bill requirements are estimated correctly, any currency surplus or deficit at the end of a planning period will obviously arise only from shifts in the pattern of expenditures. It follows that the transaction velocity of currency can be estimated within narrow margins during any short-term period (say from fifteen to thirty days). In other words, the parameters of the currency plan are fewer in number because of the discretion exercised by the state over the amount and timing of the wage bill.

The currency requirements are projected in a set of monthly and quarterly currency plans [9] which aim at bringing into balance receipts of currency — mainly from state retail trade and transport, taxes, social security, and loans — and disbursements of currency — mainly in the form of wages, salaries, transfers, and advances for state agricultural purchases. Thus, the currency plans deal with gross flows of currency to, and from, the socialist sector, excluding transactions among households. Generally, receipts from trade represent up to 80 per cent of the currency inflow, and payroll payments account for at least as much of the outflow. The State Bank's All-Union currency plan is drawn up on the basis of the observed trends in currency turnover in the country as a whole and on the plans of each of the bank's offices, branches, and agencies; these in turn are based on general trends in their respective republics, regions, or districts and on the quarterly currency plans submitted to them

9. *The Russian term* kassovyi plan *is usually translated as "cash plan."*

by each state enterprise pertaining to its sphere of operation. The currency plans are thus closely tied both to fulfillment of consumers' goods output plans and retail trade and to movement of the wage bill in all enterprises.

In order to keep the quantity of currency at a minimum and to permit the enforcement of tight controls, each enterprise is ordered to hold as little currency as possible, and each socialized shop is required to deposit its daily receipts. The balance between inflow and outflow of currency is made up by the issuing or withdrawing of currency with the express approval of the Council of Ministers. In order to cope with urgent currency needs and eventual transport problems, each main bank office is provided with a certain amount of special reserves of paper money and coins which it may inject into the circulation at the appropriate moment upon approval of the head office. The impact of such factors as the time element in income formation, redistribution of income through transactions among persons, and propensities to save and consume can be ascertained both through the variation in the fulfillment of the currency plans and through correlation of other data grouped in the closely related balance of income and expenditures of the population. As we have observed, this latter balance — drawn up by the State Planning Commission, not by the State Bank — is a part of the general economic plan. Its underlying data are derived from the basic proportions between scheduled outputs of producers' and consumers' goods and planned income distribution.

Unlike the currency plans, which are operational, the balances of income and expenditure are long-range plans drawn for one year or more and their coverage is wider; they aim at encompassing all incomes generated and expended both within and outside the socialist sector.[10] Transactions among the persons may, but will not necessarily, affect total effective demand for state produce. Furthermore, the income created returns to the state shops either directly, via purchases by wage and salary earners or, after a certain detour, via purchases by peasants.[11] Changes in the distribution of income

10. *See Chap. 8.*

11. *Assume that income created by the state sector represents 100 units and that 80 units are expended by wage and salary earners directly in the state shops and 20 units are used for purchases from the peasants. Total income created will be equal to 120. Total expenditures will also ultimately reach 120 and purchases from the state will reach 100, since the peasants themselves must turn to the state shops for their own purchases.*

will, however, affect the velocity of currency balances, the pattern of effective demand for state goods, and possibly, the consumption-saving ratio. Because of the differences in payment and spending habits between wage and salary earners and the peasants, a shift in the relative share of peasant income in total income — due either to higher prices for obligatory deliveries or larger sales to town population or both — will cause a slowing down of velocity of circulation, i.e., an increase in currency issue.[12] Other things being equal, a rise in the relative share of workers' incomes will bring about an increase in velocity; further, a rise in peasant income will condition shifts in the pattern of demand for state produce and possibly a change in total demand, given differences in saving and investment marginal propensities. Peasants tend to buy more construction materials than wage earners do. Assuming that the plan forecasts a given ratio of consumers' to investment goods to be sold to the public, a situation might arise in which consumers' goods remain on the shelves while peasants may not be able to purchase the desired investment goods and end up with unplanned currency holdings. Thus, the currency account rapidly reveals any imbalances between gross inflows and outflows to, and from, the State Bank; but this account alone does not identify directly and clearly the sources of these imbalances. The latter are disclosed in the balance of income and expenditure of the population.

Closely connected with the currency plans are the credit plans: both reflect in specific ways the fluctuations in money supply. Each credit plan aims at balancing, in each planning period, estimated "credit resources" and scheduled credit needs arising from the planned transactions concerning material goods. The plans are drawn quarterly by the State Bank on the basis of forecast receipts and expenditures of each of its offices, branches, and agencies, and of each of their respective customers. After approval by the Council of Ministers, the plan is broken down by republic, regional, and district bank offices, which in turn establish "limits" of the credits to be granted to their clients for the end of each given plan period.

The State Bank can expand loans to the extent of its reserves and of the "idle" resources at its disposal. The latter are defined as 1] current budgetary surplus; 2] previously accumulated budgetary

12. *Since gross inflow to the State Bank would be, say, 70 instead of 80 units as in the example in footnote 11, new currency must be created in order to meet the payrolls.*

surpluses held by the bank for the treasury; and 3] portions of *all* other deposits not currently in active use. The State Bank estimates deposits not in current use on the basis of the minimum balance on hand at the end of an operational planning period. Variations in the minimum balances of enterprises are estimated by the State Bank from the plans of the enterprises. Consequently, any error in the output plans has monetary effects, since it will result in an overestimate of the idle resources at the disposal of the State Bank. The amount of loans to be made during any operational planning period must be equal to planned "credit resources," of which the idle resources are the chief component. If planned credit resources and planned credit requirements are not equal, the bank must reduce either one or the other or both. If at the end of a planning period actual idle resources exceed planned idle resources, actual transactions have fallen short of planned transactions (if velocity has remained constant), or the State Bank has erred in its estimate of credit requirements for the execution of the plan.

The State Bank treats credit as essentially a revolving fund. In fact, it creates new deposits on the basis of its estimated idle resources. In the United States, new deposits are created on the basis of addition to reserves. In the Soviet Union, no reserves are required; the idle resources set the ceiling of credit to be created by the State Bank. In a tight situation, this rule is flexible since a new deposit generates an idle resource — if it does not generate a demand for currency. This process can be easily grasped if one considers how the State Bank may meet some unplanned needs, e.g., increased purchases of agricultural surpluses. The State Bank could credit the state procurement agencies without idle resources on hand since the very increase in the liability of the procurement agency would be matched by a corresponding increase in the current accounts of the collective farms, i.e., in the State Bank's "crediting" means. If, however, the collectives withdrew part of these new deposits in currency, a corresponding increase in currency issue would follow; hence, no increase in idle resources would occur.

Western economists rightly stress that the Soviet practice of achieving a yearly budget surplus acts as an offset to undue credit expansion. Soviet writers, however, deny that budgetary surpluses offset crediting since, according to them, idle budgetary resources are the main source of credit expansion. A. Bachurin asserts that a budgetary surplus is needed "fundamentally in order to increase the credit resources of the State Bank"; Z. V. Atlas adds that budget "reserves" (surpluses) "cover expenditures unforeseen in the plan, without resort to currency emission." Actually both the Western and the Soviet arguments are meaningful but on completely different planes: on the one hand, other things being equal, every increase in tax collections reduces the means available to consumers; on the other hand, "idle" budgetary resources are viewed as a "source" of credit availability in the Soviet frame of reference.

The bank loans, traditionally provided only in response to current expenditure needs (e.g., for building up inventories in accordance with planned processes), have been expanded as a result of decentralization of certain investment decisions, the shift to various credit-financed investments, and the expanded role of interest. Previously, as already stated, each credit has been extended only for a single, well-defined purpose. But since the late 1960's the idea of broadening the rights and discretionary power of the divisions and agencies of the State Bank in their relations with the enterprises and the idea of abandoning detailed regulation of credit operations have been increasingly stressed in specialized literature. It has been suggested that enterprises should pay a specified interest for the total credit received – interest and credit volume to be determined by the local divisions of the bank's agencies – to increase returns per credit ruble. The bank and the enterprise would have an equal stake in improving these returns, part of which would be channeled subsequently into the incentive fund of the bank personnel. As in the past, credit is to remain attached to "real bills," i.e., to movement of "real" goods. Here, the State Bank operates on the basis of an old assumption, the fallaciousness of which is well known; namely, that money requirements and capital requirements are identical. Actually, if the loans provided for inventory build-up remained fixed to these inventories until their emergence as final products, the impact of the State Bank's lending policy might be neutral: the increment in the quantity of money would be matched by an increment in final product. But, as Professor D. H. Robertson reminds us, the money created does not sit and wait "tied around the neck of the goods but goes off on a round of visits of its own." In other words, if the plans of enterprises were entirely consistent with each other and with the total of resources, giving the enterprises just enough credit to carry out these plans would be consistent with stability. But the plans are not fully consistent, and credits are not used for the specified purpose for which they are extended but for a set of both planned and unplanned transactions. Therefore, the policy of lending on "real bills" in no way ensures that the quantity of money thus created matches the actual transaction requirements of the economy, though the credit plan may perfectly equate the two sides of its balance.

THE STATE BANK'S CONTROLLING FUNCTIONS

The State Bank must ensure that, within the framework established by the plan, its main objectives will be carried through without unplanned increases in costs, wage bill, or currency holdings of either wage earners or peasants. In order to fulfill this task, the State Bank is charged with the control of the ways in which each enterprise fulfills the plan and is instructed to make systematic efforts to minimize the quantity of money needed to support the prescribed transactions in the economy.

The State Bank's offices are supposed to exercise a detailed control over the financial activity of each of the enterprises belonging to their respective spheres of operation. In particular, the State Bank must watch closely the movement of the enterprises' wage and their fulfillment of the cost and output plans in the quantitative as well as qualitative terms prescribed. The segregation of settlement and current accounts, and of currency and credit flows, the specificity of each account and of each operation are all helpful devices for the establishment of a comprehensive financial control, or as the Russians call it "control by the ruble." The bank is supposed to treat enterprises which carry out their planned obligations leniently and delinquent enterprises severely. To the former, the bank may grant longer periods for credit repayments; the bank may refuse any credit to delinquent enterprises unless their superior administrative organs — ministry or branch administration — endorse the loan. The bank may further require the delinquent enterprise to use the acceptance payment form only for in-town transactions, and letters of credit, special accounts, or special checks for all out-of-town payments. The bank may also prevent the lagging enterprise from using unpaid shipments until payment is made. Under certain conditions, the bank may ultimately proclaim the deficient enterprise insolvent — no enterprise could take such an action itself — and thus provoke a full-scale inquiry into the affairs of the negligent client by some *ad hoc* party and state organs.

Although the prescribed controls are supposed to be detailed and the array of sanctions increasingly stern, in practice the enormous burden of surveying details forces the bank to resort to what are officially described as *formalistic* controls and leads to a sparing application of sanctions. Since 1954, when the bank was strongly admonished for its formalism and leniency, the relative importance in the total volume of interenterprise transactions of payments by letter of credit, special account, or checks — by no means exclusively reserved for penalized enterprises — has fallen to around 3 per cent per year, a considerable decline since 1950. The bank claims to have been successful in the control of wage-bill movements; by 1957, according to its figures, the state agricultural enterprises and all the other state enterprises exceeded their planned wage bills by only 3.3 per cent and 2.1 per cent respectively, as against 5.9 per cent and 4.3 per cent in 1953. Actually, these "overexpenditures," as they are neatly identified, are no guarantee at all that the wage bill was not actually exceeded by far larger margins. As already stated, wage bills are padded, output figures are manipulated, and ultimately, the wage fund is assessed precisely in relation to the fulfillment of the output plan.

In order to ensure economic stability, the State Bank imposes "financial discipline" on enterprises by the controls just described. The bank disciplines itself by the cumbersome practices of "mobilizing idle resources" and then matching its credits to them, granting each loan in response to "real goods" movements, etc. Inflation, i.e., increases in "unplanned liquidities" which have an adverse effect on the plan, is an ever-present danger; its chief causes in the Soviet economy are faulty planning and faulty plan implementation, especially in respect to volume of wages and volume of minimum working capital requirements and bank credits. Other things being equal, increases in the volume of wages (due, for instance, to illicit or even licit bonuses, overemployment in the producers' goods industries, etc.) immediately affect the liquidity of households; increases in working capital and bank credit affect the liquidity of enterprises and ultimately also that of households. Increases in the wage fund and shortages in consumers' goods output push the free market prices upward and lead to an increased spread between them and the state retail prices (the more so since the latter do not respond readily to changes in supply and demand). Prices of raw materials and intermediate goods within the state sector, though sluggish, react to the upward price push of consumers' goods via cost-wage increases, i.e., through pressures of planned profit margins. Adroit manipulation of turnover taxes, i.e., reduction of actual consumer purchasing power and eventual increases in deduction from profits when enterprises show excess liquidities, keep the inflationary pressures in check. If and when liquidities become heavily concentrated outside the regular state-controlled channels — that is, if they come into the hands of the peasantry — the state may resort to monetary refunding. This, however, is used only as a last resort, since it jeopardizes the peasants' confidence in the currency.

CONCLUDING COMMENTS

Soviet monetary theory and banking practices remain connected to a set of misconceptions which unduly complicate Soviet banking practices.

The dogmatic assertion that Soviet currency is but "gold tokens" could be easily dismissed as inconsequential. As indicated, the actual purchasing power of the ruble and the constancy of its value depend only on the equilibrium or lack of equilibrium in some key planned money balances in the course of the implementation of the plan.

An increase in the liabilities of the State Bank need not be backed by some special idle resources. The extending of credits only up to that highly flexible "limit" rests upon the fallacy that the sole function of the bank is to distribute and redistribute the same funds without creation of new money. This alleged limit has no anti-inflationary virtue.

The State Bank's theory that its loans must be secured against "material values" so as to ensure a "direct connection between credit and the process of production" rests on the fallacious assumption that the money released remains fixed to the intermediate goods which it first purchases. But the connection of credit to "real" movement of goods does not necessarily guarantee economic stability.

Inflationary potentialities in the form of large holdings of currency in the hands of the population have been avoided in the Soviet economy in the postwar years. A potent means for balancing outlays to the population and consumer spending and consumers' goods output has been the manipulation of turnover taxes, i.e., of the level of retail prices. It may be noted, on the other hand, that in the USSR the demand for stocks of money is limited because there are fewer unforeseen opportunities than in a free-market economy. When such opportunities do arise, bank credit may be made readily available. For individuals also, the lack of opportunities, except for a very restricted range of a speculative character, cuts down the demand for stocks of money.

In the last analysis, economic stability depends directly on the very consistency and accuracy of the planned goals, and on the actual division of income between consumption and accumulation which they imply. In the past the State Bank could not significantly alter these fundamental relations since its own planning and controlling functions had only a subsidiary impact on both stability and economic growth. The decentralization of certain investments, the expanded role of credit, the enlarged role of interest, and the increased response to consumers' preferences will, however, significantly enhance the role of the Bank and of financial planning and their direct impact on stability and growth in the future.

10.

Government Expenditures and Taxation

NATURE AND SCOPE OF THE STATE BUDGET

The Soviet budget is a key instrument for dividing the national product between investment and consumption and for channeling and controlling the utilization of investments in accordance with the objectives of the plan. It makes provision for the largest part of the country's capital formation and includes, along with the usual receipts of any state administration, most of the profits of enterprises. Budgetary expenditures amount to more than one-half of the country's gross national product.

The state budget is a consolidated account of the All-Union, republic, and local budgets; it consists of a central budget, some 28 budgets of autonomous republics and areas, and about 50,000 budgets of regional, urban, and rural soviets. It is constructed as a distinct document but in close connection with the economic plan at each stage of the latter's elaboration. At each level, budgeted expenditures and receipts must be based on the key indicators of the plan — in the case of expenditures, notably on projected size of capital works and related magnitudes; in the case of receipts, on gross value of output, trade turnover, and the wage bill. As soon as the Central Committee of the Communist party and the Council of Ministers of the Union establish the directives for the economic plan, the Minister of Finance for the Union instructs each Union minister and the republic ministers of finance in the preparation of their draft budgets on the basis of both past performance and new directives. The ministers of finance of the union republics instruct their colleagues accordingly; the local authorities of the autonomous republics, provinces, regions, districts, etc., do likewise. As soon as the draft budgets of the local authorities are formulated and approved, they are transmitted to their respective republic ministries of finance, adjusted and integrated with the draft of the republic budget, and then submitted for approval to the republic council of ministers. Once approved, they are transmitted to the Union Ministry of Finance which integrates all the drafts of republic and local budgets with a draft of the Union budget which it has prepared; the latter, along with the integrated state budget, is submitted for approval to the Council of Ministers of the Union. The Council makes the adjustments it deems necessary in the final draft which, after its approval, is presented by the Minister of Finance to the Supreme Soviet for eventual adoption in the form of law. After adoption, the adjusted republic and local budgets are presented to their respective state authorities (councils of ministers of the union republics and supreme soviets of the union republics, etc.) for final adoption. The state budget covers the calendar year. The document containing the detailed breakdown of receipts and expenditures is not released to the public; only summary statements and aggregate figures are published.

The budget of the Union is still far larger than all the other budgets put together. Its relative importance, as compared to that of the budgets of the union republics, regions, districts, and local administrations, has, however, decreased sharply since the mid-1950's, owing to changing emphases on the forms of production organization. Thus the share of the All-Union budget in the state budget, which had risen by 1953 to 79.3 per cent of the total, fell to 45 per cent of the total in 1960. Since the mid-1960's, this share has again risen to roughly 57 per cent of the total. These shifts in volume evidently express changes in functions performed at the respective levels. It should not, however, be concluded that decentralization in the handling of budget accounts also implies a weakening of centralized controls; those are undoubtedly less pervasive but not less stringent than previously as far as certain key magnitudes are concerned.

As we already know, the state enterprises of all the branches of the economy are connected to the budget by numerous links, even though each enterprise keeps its own financial accounts outside the budget. They are placed under the financial control of, pay deductions from profits and turnover tax to, and receive capital construction contributions from, the local, republic, or Union budget according to their spheres of operation, size, and importance. Thus the Union budget finances heavy and war industry, the banks, the state farms, the railways, sea, river, and air transport, the highways, the communications system, and the internal and foreign trade state companies. The budgets of the union republics provide for capital outlay of the enterprises of republic importance, while the local authorities are in charge of most food processing and light industries, municipal services, etc. As of 1953, almost 70 per cent of the total industrial output was produced by industries under Union control as against 30 per cent for industries under republic, region, and district control. By 1960 the overwhelming share of industry was transferred to the management of union republics; by 1965 only one half of the industrial output was accounted for by the republic, union-republic, and local industries. The budgets, as we saw, closely reflect these shifting emphases.

STRUCTURE OF GOVERNMENT ACCOUNTS

Government expenditures are divided into three main groups: (1) national economy; (2) social and cultural services; (3) defense and administration. In the plan data for 1968 the first accounted for some 40 per cent of the total; the second, 37 per cent; the third, 23 per cent. (See Table 12.) Both the first and second groups have tended to increase their shares in total outlays over prewar levels.

The financing of new capital investment and the increase in working capital of the enterprises through the budget accounts for a substantial part of the total earmarked for the national economy. Typically, in 1968 the financing of capital construction through the state budget covered roughly 50 per cent of total new investment: the remaining 50 per cent was financed by bank loans, profits left at the disposal of the enterprises as well as depreciation allowances. As has been shown, the largest share of total investments was directed toward selected branches of heavy industry. The expenditures on social and cultural services include outlays on education, health and physical culture, social security (including pensions to war invalids and special allowances to large families), and finally, state social insurance (administered by the trade unions). Outlays on education and health accounted in 1968 for two-thirds of the total earmarked for this category, with the rest assigned to welfare expenditures. No breakdown is made available for outlays on defense, administration, public debt service, etc. Post-1950 defense outlays appear relatively small; however, certain military

TABLE 12. *The Soviet State Budget, 1968 (plan)*

	Billion Rubles		Percentage	
Expenditures				
1. Financing the national economy	50.1		40.5	
Industry		23.9		19.3
Agriculture		9.0		7.3
Other		17.2		13.9
2. Social-cultural services	45.7		36.9	
Education		21.0		17.0
Health		7.6		6.1
Social welfare		17.1		13.8
3. Defense and administration	28.0		22.6	
Defense		16.7		13.5
Administration		1.5		1.2
Other		9.8		7.9
Total	123.8		100.0	
Revenues				
1. From enterprises	112.7		91.3	
Turnover tax		42.2		34.2
Profit deductions		43.8		35.5
Income tax on collectives, social insurance, and other receipts		26.7		21.6
2. From the population	10.8		8.7	
Income tax		10.3		8.3
Other		.5		0.4
	123.5		100.0	

SOURCE: Based on *Pravda*, Oct. 11, 1967.

outlays are camouflaged under various headings. The expenditures for state administration are also deceptively small. These outlays have been varying over the years not because of reductions in the size of the bureaucracy but because a number of employees have been transferred to economic administrations which have been severed from the state budget and placed on their own economic accounting basis. (See Figure 12.)

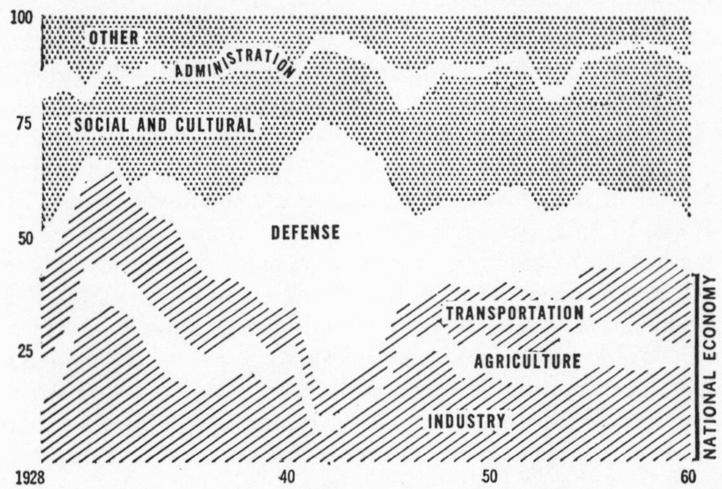

FIGURE 12. *Trends in Soviet Budget Expenditures, 1928/29–60 (in percentage of total expenditures)*

SOURCE: Official Soviet budgetary data and miscellaneous sources.

Where does the money come from to pay the budget expenditures? The revenues of the state budget are listed as follows:

1] From enterprises

A] Turnover tax

B] Deductions from profits

C] Taxes on cooperatives, collective farms, and noncommercial turnover

D] Other revenue (notably receipts from government property, customs duties, and social insurance premiums)

2] Proceeds from the population

As of 1968, turnover tax and deductions from profits accounted for about 70 per cent; income tax from collectives and all other receipts contributed 22 per cent; taxes from the population, roughly 8 per cent. As compared to the prewar period, the main changes are the decrease in the relative share of the turnover tax and the increase in the share of deductions from profits. Jointly, however, then as in

1968 these two sources of revenue made up about 70 per cent of the government's receipts. The other significant change is the decrease in "proceeds from the population" and notably of direct taxes.

As has been pointed out, the turnover tax is the difference between sale prices, as determined by the government, and planned costs plus profit markup. It is placed on consumers' goods with relatively inelastic demand schedules. Since about 85 per cent of the tax is concentrated in the price of 15 to 20 groups of commodities and since it is tied to output and is collected either directly at factories or at the wholesale distributive centers, it guarantees a steady flow of funds to the budget, is easy to collect and cheap to administer. It is, furthermore, a flexible tool for establishing equilibrium prices on the basis of levels of consumers' goods outputs on the one hand and disposable income on the other. In 1960, the turnover tax took some 42 per cent of the value of retail sales in state and cooperative shops and accounted for some 41 per cent of the state budget receipts. In the 1940's and early 1950's, the tax took between 60 and 65 per cent of the value of total retail sales.

The deductions from profits represent portions of profits, planned or higher than planned, other than those left to the enterprise for developing its output or for its other "enterprise funds." [1] As of 1968, the budget absorbed about 78 per cent of the profits of state enterprises and organizations, which contributed over 35 per cent of the state budget receipts. On the other hand, the grants for capital construction made through the budget represented around 50 per cent of the total allocated for this purpose in the economy. The state budget thus concentrates and redistributes very large shares of profits and investment funds. Both the decrease in the relative share of the turnover tax and the increase in the relative share of profits in budget receipts reflect various changes in the structure of plan prices.

Gross income taxes on collective farms, including the money income of peasant members, and taxes on cooperatives now account for only some 3 per cent of total state receipts. A large share of the proceeds of the turnover tax — counted as yielded by the state procurement agencies — is, of course, made up by the difference between prices paid to the collectives and prices charged by the state for agricultural commodities. This differential has been narrowed since 1958 through increases in the prices paid by the state to the collectives; emphasis has, at least in part, been placed on expanding the

1. *See Chap. 4.*

sales to collectives of manufactured goods, which in turn yield fiscal revenues from the turnover tax they carry. Concomitantly, measures have been taken for lessening the impact of the "agricultural tax." This rural counterpart of the urban personal income tax – assessed on the income of the rural household on the basis of the size of its private plot – now plays a limited fiscal role. Thus, the establishment of "unified" agricultural prices,[2] the shift in emphasis toward expanded sales to the collectives, and the eventual abolition of the agricultural tax, as collective farmers switch to cash payments and as their work on their own plots is discouraged, create the conditions for stricter economic accounting in the collectives and for a restructuring of taxation in the countryside.

Personal income taxes still pay only a limited role; since the 1950's they have usually fluctuated between 7.5 to 8.5 per cent of the total budgetary receipts. The tax is paid by workers and employees, writers and artists, professionals of all kinds, artisans, and income earners from agriculture in towns. Salaried incomes below a certain level are exempt; higher tax rates are levied on incomes from private practice. Local taxes – e.g., on construction, land, cattle, peasant markets, and transports – have only marginal significance in the Soviet society. Compulsory mass subscription loans, a typical Soviet method for raising budgetary income for many years, were discontinued in 1958. The decision to discontinue these loans was accompanied by a drastic measure postponing for twenty years the redemption of previously issued bonds. As officially stated at the time, budget outlays on interest and on loan repayment were rising rapidly while the net gain to the budget was decreasing. Since 1958, loan subscription by the population has been limited to a voluntary 3 per cent interest loan.

Given the reduced significance of direct income taxes and the discarding of compulsory loans from the population, budgetary funds are narrowed to the turnover tax, deductions from profits of enterprises, taxes on incomes of cooperatives and collective farms, bank loans, and such minor sources as fees on commercial forestry and fishing, inheritance taxes, licenses, customs, etc. The budget, however, includes also receipts from social insurance levied as a tax on payrolls, which, in 1968, amounted to some 10 per cent of total state receipts.

2. *See Chap. 5.*

Except for the war years, total actual receipts have consistently exceeded actual expenditures.

EXECUTION AND CONTROLS

In order to carry out the state's fiscal program, the annual budget is supplemented by quarterly budgetary layouts. These are established on the basis of various economic indicators: data concerning production and operation of enterprises, the relation of wages to trade turnover, and the movement of capital construction. As each quarter's budget is implemented, conditions are created for adjusting the following quarter's operations. Each quarterly layout is balanced just as the annual budget is, and only certain items are transferred from one period to the next. The turnover tax is collected daily from the larger organizations; income tax of the cooperatives and deductions from profits are collected in different time periods. Ministries and state institutions make expenditures, within the limit of budget appropriations, from credits opened by the banks.

Both collections and disbursements are made through the State Bank which acts as the fiscal agent of the state. The banks keep segregated accounts for union, republic, or local budgets. Funds for capital construction put at the disposal of the Investment Bank are handled by the State Bank acting as the Investment Bank's correspondent. Depreciation funds and profit retained by enterprises for capital outlay are handled through the Investment Bank. The banks give the financial authorities monthly statements concerning disbursement from budgetary appropriation and from retained profits of the enterprises for capital construction. The financial organs control and regulate all the funds involved on the basis of the statements received. At the end of each quarter, the USSR Ministry of Finance prepares an over-all statement on the administration of the state budget. The financial position of public enterprises is thus continuously submitted to the control of the banks and to the additional check of the fiscal organs at each stage of the unfolding of its operational plan.

For the USSR as a whole, except the Arctic territories, the budget accounts are closed on December 31; after that, all unused appropriations are canceled. The disbursing officers must return all unused funds to the State Bank before the end of December. In the Arctic territories, February 1 is the closing date for balancing the accounts of the previous year. The closed accounts approved by the Council of Ministers are submitted for approval to the Supreme Soviet, together with the budget for the following year.

FLOW OF FUNDS, THE BUDGET, AND THE BANKS

The national income accounts relate output, consumption, and saving without reference to the sectoral changes in financial assets and liabilities which render possible the carrying out of the scheduled production, distribution, and investment goals. We now propose to consider the ways in which funds are obtained and disbursed in the Soviet economy. In order to concentrate on the focal relation among enterprises, banks, and the state budget, we make the drastic assumption that there are no cooperative and collective farm savings or investments.

Let EP stand for total profits of enterprises, EP_r, for profits retained, and EP_d, for deductions from profits (that is, profits transferred to the budget). Let D_a stand for depreciation allowances, G_g, for budgetary grants, BL_e for value of outstanding bank loans to enterprises, and ΔM_e for changes in the enterprises' money balances. Let GI stand for gross investment by enterprises, that is, total investment in the economy other than households. Sources and uses of funds by enterprises can then be expressed by the equation:

$$EP_r + D_a + G_g + \Delta BL_e = GI + \Delta M_e \tag{1}$$

Now let ΔB_g stand for bank advances to government through purchase of government bonds, R_{np} for state receipts other than deduction from profits, E_c for government expenditures on current account, including transfers, and ΔM_g for changes in government idle balances (which are at the disposal of the bank). The sources and uses of funds by the government can then be presented by the following equation:

$$R_{np} + EP_d + \Delta B_g = E_c + G_g + \Delta M_g \tag{2}$$

The second equation can be consolidated by replacing the balance on current account ($R_{np} + EP_d - E_c$) with the symbol S_{ca}.

The sources and uses of funds by households can be expressed by:

$$S_h = \Delta M_h + I_h \tag{3}$$

where S_h is household saving, ΔM_h is changes in household cash balances, and I_h is private capital formation (housing). We assume that household borrowing from other sectors is negligible.

Consolidating Equations (1), (2), and (3) yields the expression:

$$S_h + S_{ca} + (EP_r + D_a) + (\Delta B_g + \Delta BL_e) - (\Delta M_e + \Delta M_g) = GI + I_h \quad (4)$$

Expression (4) states that saving by households, by government, and by enterprises, plus the net change of bank indebtedness and minus the net change of cash balances, must equal gross investment by enterprises and households. If there were no net foreign investment, the change of indebtedness to the banking system would necessarily equal the change in cash balances. In more general terms, the difference between the two must equal the negative of net foreign investment. We can, therefore, reduce the expression to the familiar form:

$$S_h + S_{ca} + (EP_r + D_a) = GI + I_h + F \quad (5)$$

where F is net foreign investment.

Up to the late 1960's Soviet practice concerning the instruments used in pooling and disbursing investable funds was unimaginative and rigidly confined to the channels and methods established in the early 1930's. This rigidity stemmed from the assumption that only full centralization could guarantee the adequate provision for the key priorities. There was no awareness that a wider combination of instruments for pooling and disbursing resources existed even within the narrow framework determined in the 1930's and that each combination was bound to elicit different managerial reactions and therefore to produce different impacts on the country's economic performance. As we already noted, since the late 1960's, the Soviet leaders and the East European policy makers who have imitated them, have been scaling down the role of the state budget as an investment clearinghouse while at the same time expanding the role of the banking system and the enterprises themselves. The *extent* to which either the banks or the enterprises are to be called to play a decisive role in investment allocation is still uncertain. However, even without major reshuffling of the existing institutional arrangements, a variety of solutions is possible. For example, at some future time, the banks, instead of the budget, may be called upon to allocate the lion's share of investment funds and exercise the main controls on its disbursement. In this case, the credit plan – a shadow of the material plan – would become a key operational element in the economy, as bank loans, instead of budgetary grants, would become the main element of financing. On the other hand, the enterprises may have an increasingly larger share of retained profits at their disposal (in 1968 that share was still about 22 per cent of total profits as opposed to 78 per cent transferred to the budget).

Although bank loans are apparently limited to government deposits stemming from budget surpluses, to sales of bonds, and to other idle funds at the bank's disposal, such as "indivisible" funds of collective farms and personal savings, no automatic and effective controls are operative on the side of the supply of funds to the economy. The indicated savings are channeled directly into investment via increased bank reserves, which, as we already know, may immediately become sources of multiple expansion. In practice, checks that keep investment expenditure from running ahead of planned savings are discretionary controls on the supply side, combined with a host of complicated and sometimes conflicting checks on the demand side (e.g., controls of the wage bill, checks on means and methods used by enterprises for discharging their obligations under the plan, and direct controls over the allocation of capital goods). Under these conditions, and given the official illusion about an alleged automatic control on the side of supply of funds, any forward push in demand for funds may easily build up inflationary pressures. What in theory is an automatic two-pronged control on both demand and supply of funds is in fact a complicated control on the demand side only.

The USSR experienced a serious price and wage inflation during the prewar period. The inflation had its center in the labor market, where excess demand for workers caused wage rates to rise sharply.[3] Rising wage rates and rising non-consumption outlays produced demand inflation in the consumers' goods market, where the state failed to increase prices sufficiently to soak up excess demand. Since the late 1940's, real inflationary pressures have subsided owing to a combination of causes among which may be listed: the steady postwar expansion in both producers' and consumers' goods, the changing conditions in the labor market with a decline in the number of unskilled workers in agriculture and an increased supply of skilled workers, more realistic planning than in the past, and some-

3. *See Chap.* 7.

what better handling of fiscal and monetary controls than in the 1930's.

PROFIT VERSUS TURNOVER TAX AND EQUITY VERSUS INCENTIVES

Taxes have a direct impact on allocation of resources, distribution of income, play of incentives, and price fixation. Although Soviet planning allocates resources primarily through direct controls, the plan cannot be carried out in its multiple aspects except by financial operations. Within the Soviet institutional framework, what are the roles of the deductions from profits and of turnover taxes in respect to division of the national income and allocation of investment by sector and branches? Are both deductions from profit and turnover tax indirect taxes on commodities purchased by consumers whose incidence is on the consumer? Could profit deduction and turnover tax be replaced by a single instrument of taxation?

Professor Frank D. Holzman tends to think that there is no difference whatsoever between deductions from profits and turnover tax since both must be "borne by the consumer." In the United States, his argument runs, a profit tax may be shifted backward, and so reduce factor prices paid by the enterprise, or forward, and so raise prices paid by the consumer. In the USSR, where enterprises are state-owned, a profit tax levied on them must be borne entirely by the consumer. Actually, however, the answer to this problem hinges on whether prices are set in the Soviet Union to yield a certain profit before or after "deductions" transferred to the budget. In the former case, the size of the deduction is unrelated to the level of prices. In the latter case, however, the "deduction" would be somewhat analogous to a sales tax borne mainly by the consumer. But in the Soviet Union prices are clearly so set, relative to cost, as to yield a given profit before deductions; thus, they cannot be said to be "borne by the consumer" — except, of course, in the sense that all enterprise receipts ultimately flow from the buyer. Deductions from profits transferred to the state budget may, in fact, be large or small, according to a policy seeking to centralize a large share of profits and redistribute them among various branches or to leave most investible resources directly in the hands of the enterprises themselves. The fluctuations in the size of these deductions do not ordinarily affect the consumer; the amount of the transfer in each particular branch does not determine the amount of total gross profits, which is set at the level of planned capital formation. On the other hand, whatever the size of the deduction from profits may be — and this is primarily a matter of administrative expediency — the enterprise cannot "compensate" for it by way of increased prices, since prices are fixed without reference to the deduction.

It is evident that total state receipts may be so planned that total volume of profits — not only the part transferred to the budget — and total turnover tax receipts move in a complementary way. Furthermore, it is also clear that, under their institutional arrangement, the Soviets could dispense with the profit category, equate prices to labor cost within the state sphere, and then increase taxes so that aggregate turnover tax receipts would equal aggregate accumulation. Conversely, they could dispense with the turnover tax and plan profit margins so that aggregate profit income would equal the accumulation targets; these profits could either be left largely in the hands of the enterprises or centralized and redistributed by the state.

Now if the state were to dispense entirely with the profit category, the tax could be used within both the spheres of producers' and consumers' goods so as to equate supply and demand in each of them, the state budget concentrating all resulting investible funds. Conversely, were the state to dispense completely with the turnover tax, prices within, and without, the state sector would be so planned that total profits earned in all sectors would equal all planned accumulation over and above minor amounts arising out of personal saving. As we stated, these profits could be either invested directly by the enterprises or centralized and redistributed through the budget. Let us consider these alternatives closely.

In the first case, profits earned in each industrial branch would presumably be so planned as to cover the planned investment in that particular branch. Obviously, however, it would be rather illogical to tie price-cost relations to investments, which are determined by other criteria. In some instances, it would be impossible to find a price-cost relationship which would generate profits sufficient to cover the investment needs of particular branches. Furthermore, if branch investments were tied to branch profits, success or failure in respect to cost reduction would lead to overfulfillment or underfulfillment of the planned investment program.[4]

4. *Only if cost reductions were fulfilled exactly according to plan would the investment target be met as scheduled.*

Finally, with prices, including profit rates, fixed to match the branch's investment needs, prices of producers' goods would have to be set at relatively high levels, while on the other hand, each shift in investment policies would imply wide changes in prevailing price structures.

In the second case, price-cost relationships would be so planned as to equate total profits to total planned accumulation and then this total would be redistributed as the policy makers saw fit. There seem to be no compelling reasons against using such a solution. Hence the Soviet employment of a combination of turnover tax and profits must be attributed primarily to expediency and tradition rather than to other factors. It is these two elements which have kept in force the distinction between a tax collected in the consumers' goods market and a set of profits manipulated mostly for managerial and incentive ends. Admittedly, it would be difficult to draw a neat line between a complex sales tax and a haphazard set of *profits* — but, within limits, the two have remained operationally distinguishable in the Soviet framework.

The Soviet Union shows strong preference for indirect taxation: for all practical purposes, direct taxes have been abandoned. What is the logic of this measure in relation to equity, cycles, incentives, and allocation of resources?

Western economists tend to believe that equity is an essential element in a tax. *Equity* might be defined as equalizing the tax burden on all citizens by taxing each according to his ability to pay. Since it is assumed that, after a certain point, money income has a diminishing marginal utility and since all taxes are presumably paid from net income, equity is in practice achieved by a progressive net income tax. At the same time, concern with business cycles has spurred Western interest in the use of taxes as anticyclical measures. Indirect taxes do qualify as an automatic fiscal stabilizer, but do not recommend themselves as the main source of revenue, given a government's concern with tax equity. On the other hand, personal taxes and corporate taxes meet both of these criteria, in varying measure. Finally, indirect taxes are used for allocative purposes in only a limited way. (To some extent, such taxes are applied as the modern counterpart of the older sumptuary laws.)

In an economy of the Soviet type, progressive taxation is regarded as interfering with established incentives, whereas the impact of turnover taxes is taken to be neutral with respect to these incentives. The tax system is devoid of equity — if equity is taken to imply equal burden as related to each one's ability to pay. If, however, equity is taken to mean to each according to his work (rather than to each according to his needs), then the Soviet system has equity although its primary objective remains the preservation of established incentives.[5] It may seem paradoxical that capitalism redistributes income through progressive taxation whereas the Soviets place their emphasis on incentives rather than on equity; but as we know, the Soviets assume that the principle "to each according to his work" is the very foundation of their kind of socialism. In the Soviet framework, the turnover tax does qualify under the anticyclical criterion to some extent because it plays an anti-inflationary role akin to that played in the West by high taxation during an inflationary period. It is the resource–allocation element which is of paramount importance in the USSR, whereas in the West this factor plays only a minor role under normal conditions.

5. *Actually, an indirect tax system with differential rates on different commodities would preserve this type of equity only if the expenditure patterns of persons receiving different incomes were identical.*

Part IV

Socialist Economic Models

INTRODUCTION TO PART IV

How can a socialist economy, an economy characterized by public ownership of capital goods, secure *efficiency* in the carrying out of an economic plan and achieve "*congruency*" between the aims of its planners and the operative decisions of its managers? In other words, how can such an economy rationally allocate its resources and achieve correspondence between the goals set at the top and the implementation at the bottom of the production pyramid? These are the perennial problems of any socialist economy.

These same problems lie at the heart of a long academic debate carried on over a number of decades among scholars in Germany, Austria, and later, in England and the United States. Although this debate has attempted to explore the basic elements of optimal allocation of resources under socialism, it is still little known outside the economic profession. Non-Marxist economists were actually the first to examine these problems, often in order to show how collectivism could be rationally implemented, provided that its advocates discarded some of their misconceptions concerning the price system, the market mechanism, and the nature and scope of planning itself. The debate set into a logical frame the interconnections between goals (of consumers or of planners), conditions to be met for optimum allocation of resources in relation to these goals, and planning procedures for carrying out the posited optimum allocation.

These problems of rational allocation and of plan congruency, debated also in the Soviet Union, particularly on the eve of the thoroughgoing planning era, have now acquired renewed importance both in the Soviet Union itself and in the "socialist camp" as a whole. As we have seen, the Soviet economy is not the type of economy that its political leaders envisioned in the early stage of the Russian Revolution, namely, a moneyless system run by statistical bureaus coordinating like clockwork all phases of production, consumption, and labor deployment, without any use for the "antiquated" value categories or for the market mechanism. It is an economy which functions on the basis of centralized plans embodying a different scale of values from that which would prevail under individual industry programming in response to consumers' preferences; its planning system, however, does combine centralized commands and central allocation of capital goods with wide use of value categories and of market mechanisms. The ends of the planners, the question of rational allocation, and the problem of consistency of goals have been discussed in the USSR during two crucial debates. The first, known as the debate of *industrialization*, focused on the choice of a specific developmental path, the appropriate rate of capital investment, and the interrelation of various social and economic ends. The second, now known as the debate on the *economic model*, focused on the scope of planning, the forms of management, of the economy as a whole, the nature and limits of *decentralization*, and the proper *determination of producers' goods prices*. Underlying the debates, of course, was the fact that the state owns the capital goods industries and consequently is both seller and buyer of their products.

In this section, we compare Western and Soviet positions even though the discussants on either side use different principles of allocation — that is, different theories of value — and Soviet economists aim at improving the mechanics of a system in which certain centralized commands are preserved, whereas Western economists emphasize the operation of highly decentralized socialist economies. But it is precisely because Western economists have employed different principles of allocation and because they have shown how planning and competition can be combined that their discussions throw light on the limitation of the Soviet tools for coping with the task of proper pricing and on the complex problems which Soviet policy makers necessarily push to the fore when they attempt to deal with the question of decentralization in planning. Even if Soviet economists continue to disregard the solutions suggested in the West, they no longer claim to ignore the limitations of "war economy" methods; i.e., the shortcomings of a system of planning which relies on certain central commands, on physical allocation of capital goods, and on arbitrary pricing.

The section opens with the examination of the ends posited for the socialist economy in the Western debate, of the conditions for achieving optimum allocation in relation to these ends, and of possible planning procedures for approximating these conditions in practice (Chapter 11). Next, the Soviet selection of planners' hierarchy of values and of the Soviet planning methods are examined, i.e., the formulation of the so-called Soviet strategy of development and of the specific procedures devised in order to make the USSR rapidly "reach and surpass" the advanced capitalist countries (Chapter 12). Finally, Soviet discussions on pricing and law of value are analyzed, as well as the practical solutions proposed or applied both in the USSR and in Eastern Europe concerning the problems of planning and of decentralized economic management (Chapter 13).

11.

Western Theories

PREMISES AND PROBLEMS OF THE ACADEMIC DEBATE

The Western academic discussion has proceeded on these basic assumptions: resources continue to be scarce under socialism, and the socialist economy continues to strive to achieve rational allocation in relation to its given ends. The socialist society has been assumed to be a monetary economy with the following distinguishing institutional characteristics: 1] the means of production are nationalized; 2] a central planning authority (let us call it CPA) controls and coordinates economic activity; 3] there is a free market for consumers' goods; 4] there is freedom of choice of occupation and also inequality of rewards. These characteristics imply the following consequences:

1] The postulated nationalization of means of production agrees with the basic Marxist definition of socialism. The Western debate stresses, of course, that the *form* of ownership (i.e., public or private ownership of capital goods) is not actually relevant to economic calculation; the latter depends, as we shall see, on other elements. Some Western economists, however, and the Marxists themselves attach crucial importance to the *form* of ownership; the first, in order to contest that rationality is attainable under socialism; the second, in order to refute the existence of general economic principles applicable to both capitalism and socialism.

2] The Western discussion focuses on economies in which central planning replaces the functions of the market, but *in various ways and degrees.* In each of the economic models considered, a

CPA coordinates and controls economic life; the scope of its activity determines the type of socialist economy. Two extreme cases of socialist economies can be envisaged: a fully centralized system in which there are no markets for commodities or services and in which the CPA allocates, on the basis of a comprehensive plan, labor and capital goods to the producing units and consumers' goods to the population; and a fully decentralized system in which there are markets for all types of commodities and only investment activities are indirectly controlled by the CPA. The first system could be called *pure administrative socialism*, the second, *pure market socialism*. In between, a variety of combinations is possible, depending on the ways in which the CPA directs production and takes over the market functions with respect to pricing capital goods and productive resources. Since, however, according to assumption 1] the means of production are nationalized, most of the discussants assume that a genuine market for producers' goods is, in the institutional sense, excluded by definition. The question arises, then, precisely how these prices are to be determined and how investment decisions are to be taken.

3] Rational allocation involves the formulation of a scale of values — or of a hierarchy of needs — on the basis of which the alternative uses of resources are considered. In the Western debate, the scale of values which the CPA serves is determined by consumers' effective demand; since consumer preferences alone guide production and expansion, consumers are usually said to enjoy "sovereignty." The ends may, however, be determined by the CPA itself and the consumers' goods produced be distributed by rationing or sold to the consumers, who are left free to choose among the goods. In this case, consumers are said to enjoy "freedom of choice."

4] In the socialist economies considered, the deployment of labor is achieved through price differentials and, therefore, through inequality of rewards. This inequality may, however, be kept within narrow margins if the income of individuals is viewed as consisting of two components: one representing a differential "wage" according to labor performed; the other, an equal per capita social dividend expanding as the productivity of the system rises to higher and higher levels.

In a sense, the Western analytical attempt is, as Professor Robert Mossé puts it, symmetrical to that of Marx. Western economists seek to achieve in respect to the socialist economy, with the tools of marginalist analysis, what Marx set out to achieve in respect to capitalism, on the basis of the labor theory of value.

ON THE POSSIBILITY OF RATIONAL ALLOCATION UNDER SOCIALISM

As it unfolded, the Western debate examined a host of problems ranging from the nature and functions of the price system to the superiority, on strictly economic grounds, of the collectivist system or of the competitive capitalist system. We do not propose to review all these discussions (which have been ably summarized a number of times); instead, we intend to abstract from them the particular elements which are relevant to specific past or current problems of economies of the Soviet type.

The Western analyses of socialist economies culminated before World War I in Enrico Barone's *The Ministry of Production in the Collectivist State*. Barone set out to show how the ministry, aiming at maximizing collective welfare, ought to direct production, given the following conditions: 1] absence of money; 2] absence of market prices; 3] maintenance, for the purpose of accounting, of *ratios* of *equivalence* among products or services, and between products and services as a whole. In a closely reasoned mathematical essay, Barone shows, first, that by appropriate calculations the series of equivalents which "satisfy the equations expressing the physical necessities of production" can be found; second, that, given the aim of obtaining the posited maximum from the services of individuals and of the community, the ministry must reintroduce, no matter under what name, "all the economic categories of the old regime . . . prices, salaries, interest, rent, profit, savings, etc."; and finally, that, because of its aim, the ministry must observe the conditions which characterize free competition, namely, "minimum cost of production and the equalization of price to cost of production."

Following the publication in 1920 of a study by Professor Ludwig von Mises, *Economic Calculation in a Socialist Community*, the discussion shifted its focus to the problem of whether economic rationality was possible in a system with no markets for capital goods. "Where there is no free market," wrote von Mises, "there is no pricing mechanism; without a pricing mechanism, there is no economic calculation." He stressed the idea that even if the prices of finished goods were determined by the market, they could not be properly related to costs in a system where, by hypothesis, the market for producers' goods was eliminated. As von Mises emphasized in various studies, he did not question the ability of a socialist state to order the production "of cannons or clothes, dwelling houses or churches, luxuries or subsistence," but rather its ability to ascertain how its productive resources could be used most effectively to produce these goods. He concluded, "Economic calculation can only take place by means of money prices established in the market for producers' goods in a society based on the private property of the means of production." If Barone (and various other contemporary writers) had essentially attempted to refute the "fantastic doctrine" that production in a collectivist state could actually be "ordered in a manner substantially different from that of anarchist [i.e., free-market] production," von Mises for his part attempted to challenge the very existence of what Eduard Heimann rightly called *objective standards* of rational orientation under socialism. Von Mises thus both rejected the intrinsic validity of any method of imputing producers' goods prices from the prices of finished goods and posited that only under a system of private property was adequate value calculation attainable. In an article published in the 1930's on "Further Considerations on the Possibility of Adequate Calculation in a Socialist Community," elaborating a position he had already taken in 1929, Professor Georg Halm, a disciple of von Mises, gave final form to the basic argument of this school against the method of imputation. He stressed notably that economic calculation was not a process of comparing market-determined prices with the costs derived *ex post* from them, but an *ex ante* comparison "between *known* commodity prices and *known* costs of production." In other words, Halm rejected the circularity of the method of imputation.

Subsequently, particularly in the formulations of Professor Lionel Robbins and Friedrich von Hayek, the thesis of the impossibility of economic calculation under socialism was recast into a theory of the impracticability of attaining rationality owing to the lack of any sound method for assessing the costs of production. In a well-known study of "The Nature and History of the Problem" of economic calculation under socialism published in the collection of essays

Collectivist Economic Planning, Hayek stressed that the CPA, lacking a sound method, could not decide on the prices it ought to establish and would err in its decisions concerning the quantities of consumers' goods that it was desirable to produce. Adding that it would be difficult in practice to solve the hundreds of thousands of simultaneous equations needed before economic decisions could be taken, and rejecting Barone's solution, Hayek concluded: "What is practically relevant here is not the formal structure of this system, but the nature and amount of concrete information required if a numerical solution is to be attempted, and the magnitude of the task which this numerical solution must involve in any modern community."

Two specific solutions were worked out in detail in the debate concerning the assignment of proper values to means of production in a socialist economy. The first solution, usually associated with the name of Dr. H. D. Dickinson, but which had been proposed many times during the German phase of the debate, simply suggested that socialism was not incompatible with actual markets for producers' goods. Nothing would prevent the operating managers of state-owned plants from competing among themselves for the capital goods and productive resources available; as a result, the prices of these goods would be determined by the interaction of supply and demand just as in a competitive capitalist economy.

The second solution, associated with the name of Professor Oskar Lange, accepts von Mises' position on the absence of markets for capital goods in a socialist state. In a remarkable essay, *On the Economic Theory of Socialism* (1938) Lange used some of the suggestions previously made by Professor Fred M. Taylor in order to show how the CPA could find proper *accounting* prices, instead of market-determined prices, by a process of *trial and error.* Taylor had indicated that the CPA might start by assigning a provisional price to all capital goods and productive resources and then let the managers of the socialist enterprises determine their output and expansion decisions as if these valuations were correct. The appearance of physical surpluses or shortages of any capital good would show the CPA whether the respective price was set too high or too low; the CPA would then adjust that price so as to bring demand in line with supply. Taylor suggested that the initial provisional prices could be imputed or assigned on the basis of past price patterns. Lange went a step further and demonstrated, first, that these prices might be picked at random and, second, that the CPA had absolutely no need of complete lists of all commodities and of all the possible combinations of prices and quantities available — despite Hayek's contention. Correct accounting prices, i.e., proper relative prices of any one kind of producers' goods as related to another, and correct costing of capital (interest) could be ascertained through a process of successive adjustment, to be carried out at given intervals by the CPA. With periodically adjusted accounting prices for producers' goods and with market-determined prices for consumers' goods, managers and consumers would have no more equations to solve under socialism than under capitalism. Each manager would be instructed to regard the accounting prices as being independent of his own output or expansion decisions. The acceptance by the managers of these prices as a datum — or, as Lange puts it, the use by the CPA of the parametric function of prices — would in turn enable the CPA to perform the market function of equating demand to supply via periodic *price* adjustments. Even in a fully centralized economy, in which the CPA and not the managers would decide on output and expansion and in which consumers' goods would be distributed to the population by rationing, proper accounting prices — for both producers' and consumers' goods — could, as we shall see subsequently, be ascertained by the same process of trial and error.

For the moment, let us note that the arguments concerning the impossibility or impracticability of properly ascertaining costs in the absence of private ownershp are thus refutable. Commenting on the Lange solution, in a rejoinder entitled "Socialist Calculation: The Competitive 'Solution'," Hayek expressed doubt whether "in the real world where constant change is the rule" equilibrium actually could be approached by periodic price adjustments. Insufficient speed in price adjusting and an assumed inability on the part of the CPA to enter into the necessary details concerning all types of prices, other than the prices of broad commodity groups, would, according to Hayek, prevent the achievement of an actual — if not of the hypothetical — equilibrium. The objections are thus addressed not to the rationale of the system but to its presumed lack of flexibility. Even if they abandon their main target, the Hayek objections in this last form still have some significant implications for the operation of controls within the socialist system.

Having thus seen that the crucial problem of ascertaining proper producers' goods prices does not present insurmountable obstacles — or, in Heimann's terms, that objective standards of rational orientation do exist under socialism — let us now turn to the aims which the CPA is to serve and to the optimum conditions for attaining them.

ENDS AND PRINCIPLES OF ALLOCATION

In socialist economies, economic calculation (i.e., rational allocation of resources so as to achieve optimal satisfaction of conflicting wants from the most intense down to the least intense) raises the following question with particular force: How and by whom is this hierarchy of wants to be established? Secondly, what principles of allocation should be followed in order to secure optimum allocation of resources in relation to these wants? The object of economic calculation is the achievement of the ideal output related to the posited goals; obviously, any change in the hierarchy of needs implies shifts in the allocation of resources and hence in the structure of the ideal output to be produced.[1]

In a socialist society in which consumers were sovereign, their effective demand in the market would establish the scale of preferences — or the hierarchy of wants — in respect to which the producing units would attempt to allocate resources rationally. In a socialist society in which the consumers were either permitted or deprived of freedom of choice, the CPA would establish the scale of preferences by taking or not taking into close account the actual or presumed preferences of consumers.

Let us consider first the case of a socialist society in which *consumer sovereignty* prevails. The scale of wants, from the most intensive down to least intensive, may be affected notably by the income distribution existing in that society and by the recognition that in some key matters — work versus leisure, communal versus individual consumption, investment versus present consumption — collective interests (no matter why they are recognized

1. *Maurice Dobb thus emphasizes the importance of this discussion: "Is the layman's scepticism justified, and is the whole matter . . . a pseudo-problem that has no counterpart in the actual world? . . . The sceptic is clearly wrong. Some problems of economic calculation exist for a socialist society. . . ." (See* On Economic Theory and Socialism, *London: Routledge and Kegan Paul, 1955, p. 239.)*

as such or how they are determined in practice) must take precedence over individually determined preferences. Any shift in income distribution and any arbitrarily posited collective need involves the make-up of the hierarchy of values and of the ideal output mix that will satisfy it optimally.

Some economists stress that under consumer sovereignty, the maximization of *consumer welfare* — defined as the *sum of the utilities of the households of the community* — and the optimal allocation it posits may be attained only if incomes are evenly distributed. In the Marshall-Pigou concept of welfare, maximization requires a decision on income distribution, since the marginal utility of income is the same when incomes are the same for different persons of "equal sensitivity." Some economists separate the decision on income from the conditions of optimum allocation and define the *optimum* as the position in which any reallocation of resources would not increase the welfare of one household without diminishing that of another. Some reject the interpersonal comparison of utility and with it the question of income distribution from the optimal conditions; others reject the former but, on other grounds, stress the need to encompass the income distribution in the decision on optimal allocation. Opinions are also divided in regard to the decision concerning investment: some, like Professor Frank Knight, argue that investment must be made, as in an individualistic society, through the determination of a margin of equivalence between current use and investment; others, like Oskar Lange, suggest that, in a socialist society, the rate of accumulation cannot be guided by consumers' preferences but must be arbitrarily determined by the CPA. Although this arbitrary measure would admittedly diminish consumers' welfare, it would, on the other hand, enable the socialist society to eliminate the dangers of business fluctuations.

Let us now turn to a society in which the *planners* establish the hierarchy of wants. What is the ultimate objective of socialist planning: More output? Growth without depression waste? More military power? More equality? Obviously, a large number of conscious choices are possible. Some of them may be broadly conflicting, but they can be reconciled in certain respects and then pursued simultaneously. Maximum per capita income, for instance, may require the closing down of certain industries, whereas the goal of full employment may demand their preservation. Technological change may require the introduction of automation in one sector, whereas the appearance of technological unemployment may condition the maintenance of highly labor-intensive methods in another sector. However these or other objectives would be determined and combined, the planners obviously could not approximate consumers' preferences to the degree in which an economy with consumer sovereignty does. Unless by accident, the planners could not maximize welfare in the Pigovian sense. An over-all view of the economy and the right to dispose of all its resources undoubtedly induces planners to give considerable weight to what they consider collective needs as against individual households' preferences. Whereas the individual, with his disregard for the future, may go against what may be best from the standpoint of the society as a whole, bureaucratic planning in a society in which consumer sovereignty does not prevail may lay a disproportionate emphasis on investment. But however the scale of preferences is determined, whatever the posited ends may be, the principles followed in allocating resources must be the same if results are to be optimized. From a theoretical point of view, it makes no difference whether the scale of values is determined by bureaucrats or by individuals: a different scale entails allocation of different relative proportions of resources to various industries, but the correct ascertaining of these relative proportions must follow the same principles. And these mathematical principles require that the allocation be carried out in such a way that the marginal physical product per unit of money expended on any factor shall be equal in all lines of use. In other words, factors should be combined in a way which minimizes the cost incurred, and optimally, price should equal marginal cost. Thus, the Western economic debate stresses the universality of the principles of allocation for maximizing returns under any technological conditions, no matter what the institutional framework.

Some of the main criticisms leveled against these principles concern either the meaningfulness of the price mechanism itself or the presumed limitations of the marginalist approach. In *On Economic Theory and Socialism,*[2] Maurice Dobb contends that the planners leave to the "adjudication of any market or pricing system" neither the decision about total investment nor the decision about its distribution between sectors I and II (producers' and consumers' goods, respectively) because this decision on distribution simul-

2. *See in this volume "A Review of the Discussion concerning Economic Calculation in a Socialist Economy."*

taneously governs "the relative rates of growth of consumption and investment in the near future and also the rate of growth of output as a whole." Further, Dobb adds, the decision on the pattern of industrial location must also be determined a priori. But even if one were to accept these arguments — which we shall reconsider later — the problems of allocation between industrial branches and plants and of choice of the scale of output would still have to be solved, and this could not be done rationally without appropriate pricing of producers' goods. Dobb suggests that technical planning could achieve just as much as correct pricing since in fact fewer choices are open to planners than is alleged by the marginalist school. But in practice, as we have seen, numerous choices confront the project maker even within a very detailed centralized planning scheme.[3] To emphasize the existence in the real world of fixed factor proportions and of discontinuities in substitutabilities does not refute the theory of production and its principles: discontinuities help managers instead of hindering them in deciding about combinations of factors and do not in the least disturb the determination of the derived demand for each production factor.

MODELS OF SOCIALIST ECONOMIES

Which appropriate planning scheme could ensure that optimum allocation of resources would be achieved in practice? Western economists have made various suggestions on planning procedure. Our discussion of the operation of economies of the Soviet type will focus only on the so-called "competitive" solution, as formulated by Lange, and on a fully "centralized" socialist system, notably as examined by Lange and Dickinson.

Lange's competitive socialist economy has the following characteristics: 1] consumers' preferences guide production and allocation of resources; 2] a central planning authority fixes *prices*, the *interest rate*, and the *rate of capital accumulation;* 3] financially autonomous firms determine at the established prices how to organize production and how much capital to take; 4] freedom of occupation and inequality of rewards prevail. We have already indicated how the planning authority would, by trial and error, fix and adjust prices and the rate of interest. In order to achieve the

3. *See Chap.* 3.

optimum output, the planning authority would, furthermore, impose two economic rules of behavior on the managers of enterprises. These rules would guide their choices in respect to combination of factors and scale of output. The first would require that plant managers choose that combination of factors which minimizes average costs of production; the rule would thus require that the marginal physical product per unit of money spent on every factor be equalized in all uses. The second would require that output be fixed so that marginal cost equals the price of the product; addressed to managers of plants, this rule would determine the scale of output of the plant and, jointly with the preceding rule, the demand for factors; addressed to the managers of an industry, the rule would indicate how much an industry ought to expand or contract (so that *its* marginal cost would equal the price of *its* product). This rule would apply even if it led plants or whole industries to operate at a loss (which could be covered by a lump tax), since otherwise preferences lower on the scale would be satisfied, while higher-ranking preferences would be neglected. Finally, income would be determined so as to keep inequality within narrow margins without, however, interfering with the optimum distribution of labor. As we have pointed out, wages would vary according to marginal productivities, but individual income would also include a social dividend which would be equal for everyone.

Thus in Lange's competitive model the CPA 1] fixes prices and the interest rate so as to balance, for both products and capital, quantity demanded with supply available, 2] establishes the rules for combining factors and for choosing the scale of output, 3] arbitrarily sets the saving rate. In short, the planning authority substitutes for the market as the instrument of price fixing and adjusting and as the determinant of the total volume of investment. Given the parametric use of prices by the CPA, the managers in this system play essentially the role of "quantity adjusters," as Hayek puts it. In this type of planning administration there is no *ex ante* coordinating scheme.

For this last reason particularly, Maurice Dobb objects to the "competitive" solution.[4] It fails to take specifically into account the problems of economic *change* which constitute precisely the rationale of any central economic plan; "certain kinds of develop-

4. *See "A Review of the Discussion concerning Economic Calculation in a Socialist Economy,"* op. cit.

ment," Dobb adds, "may come upon the agenda only if development is centrally planned as an organic whole," whereas there is no guarantee that an "automatic price system" may be relied upon "to produce the socially desirable result." In a dynamic frame of reference, the data of a static scheme are converted into variables: cost structure and consumers' wants change as the program unfolds. Hence, he concludes, the choice of the type of mechanism — *ex ante* program or elemental coordination through the operation of the price mechanism — is crucial in determining the direction of development itself.

It is certainly true that any centralized program would differ from individual industry programming in response to consumers' preferences; the choice between one type of planning and another involves essentially the value which one attaches to the idea of consumers' welfare. On the other hand, it is equally true that no comprehensive program could be consistently and efficiently carried out without *accurate pricing*. It is one thing to contrast an *ex ante* scheme to the output and expansion "plan" arising from individual industry programming; it is quite another matter to conclude that the former may dispense with the price system because the latter relies exclusively on it. In fact, economic rationality would be both possible and necessary, even in a fully centralized economy where decision at the center determines what to produce and in what quantities, what to distribute to consumers through rationing, and how jobs should be assigned. As suggested by Lange, in such a centralized economy, once the planners' preferences were determined, accounting prices for both producers' and consumers' goods could be established by trial and error. As previously, the CPA would impose the parametric function of prices upon the managers of plants and industries, who would be required to observe the indicated rules concerning the least-cost combination and the choice of the appropriate scale of output. Resources would be allocated only to the enterprises which could "account for" them at the accounting price established by the CPA, thus making operative managerial decisions consistent with the *aims* of the planners. Consistency would be accompanied by efficiency, thanks to the rule of least-cost combination of factors. The essential point stressed by this demonstration is that rationing of consumers' goods does not interfere with rationality, whereas rationing of producers' goods does. If producers' goods are rationed, prices become arbitrary;

if adjustment between quantity supplied and demanded is achieved through price fixing and adjustment, accounting prices remain meaningful and economic rationality is attainable. There is no way of ensuring efficiency without the use of producers' prices accurately reflecting underlying scarcities.

But what guarantees exist to make managers conform to the posited rules either in the competitive model or under the centralized scheme just described? A key element in the operation of the system is *time* — time when purchases are made, when inputs are delivered, when prices are adjusted by the planning authorities, etc. In his criticism of the Lange models, Hayek has correctly pointed out in "Socialist Calculation: The Competitive 'Solution'" that managers may try to meet expected price changes by *anticipatory action* bearing on such decisions as their use of the machines available, their demand for inputs, etc. If a manager could not get additional supplies of a material at the prescribed price, he might use poor substitutes in order to expand production so as to equalize his marginal cost with the prescribed price. In short, the problem of ensuring that the autonomy established at the bottom will conform to the policies pursued at the top appears insoluble to Hayek, who regards the existence of mid-points between centralized decisions of any kind and a fully competitive market system as highly improbable. Dobb, for his part, has rejected Lange's proposals of decentralization on inputs and outputs as too far-reaching. In "A Review of the Discussion concerning Economic Calculation in a Socialist Economy," Dobb has notably suggested that the procedure of trial and error be carried out *within the CPA*, not only in respect to price but also in respect to inputs and outputs, all coordinated within a fully comprehensive *ex ante* scheme.

Certainly, decentralization of decisions on inputs and outputs and reliance on the price mechanism raise numerous practical problems in respect to controls of managerial operational decisions and portend conflicts, particularly in respect to investment, between the CPA and the plant managers. In such a system, it may prove just as difficult to prevent the managers from discounting the action of the CPA in practice as it is to prevent a monopolist from disregarding the action of the market in a private enterprise system. On the other hand, it is equally evident that it is no easier to establish a sound, workable system of controls in an economy in which inputs are centrally allocated and performance is checked against fixed output targets. Physical allocation of producers' goods renders efficiency impossible and, at the same time, complicates to the utmost the task of control. As we have already noted, Soviet planners rely on direct allocation of producers' goods but, at the same time, implement a maze of financial controls. At the top of the pyramid, however, there is increasing awareness of the limits of centralization: cost control rules are periodically "strengthened"; monetary incentives are continuously reshuffled; and executive responsibilities at the intermediate echelons are enlarged. But the financial controls remain both complicated and ineffective precisely because of the continuing reliance on physical allocation of producers' goods, the enforcing of the rules of integral provision for top priorities and of sequential fulfillment for all other tasks, and finally, the distortion of prices for a variety of purposes.

CONCLUDING COMMENTS

The problem which the Western discussion has explored — namely, the necessary relations between planning and decentralization so that both *efficiency*, and *congruency* between the goals at the top and the operational decisions at the bottom, are achieved — has become increasingly significant in the socialist camp since the early 1950's. It is no longer a remote academic debate with no immediate relation to reality; this key problem is on the agenda of Soviet policy makers and planners. Experience of economies of the Soviet type has basically vindicated Barone's prediction that socialist economies would have to "restore all the old value categories," even though the planners have thus far felt free to twist them in various ways. Experience has vindicated, at least in part, the contention of those who postulated that planning could not be efficiently carried out on the basis of technological programming, but that it required the use of a meaningful price system reflective of underlying factor scarcities. Strangely enough, it has also vindicated, as we shall see, the positions of those who, like Hayek, have stressed that full decentralization and reliance on the price mechanism itself would lead to uneconomical managerial practices and abuses under socialism, just as under a private ownership system.

The Western discussion has underlined the vast range of combinations possible between the extremes of pure administrative socialism and market socialism. Against this broad background, the contours of the various phases of Soviet economic development and the experiences of economies of the Soviet type stand out with increased clarity. These economies have used basically three kinds of planning administrations: First, full centralization on production and investment, with direct allocation of producers' and consumers' goods and compulsory assignment to jobs — these were the characteristics of Russia's War-Communism period and of China's first postrevolutionary phase. Second, comprehensive planning of production and investment, physical allocation of producers' goods, consumers' freedom of choice, and freedom of occupation – these were the main features of Stalin's thoroughgoing planning era. Third, broad decisions on production and on the pattern of investment, physical quotas and price controls for a limited number of producers' goods, reliance in various degrees on market mechanisms for operational decisions on output, expansion, and distribution and freedom of occupation — these have been some of the main characteristics of the so-called New Economic Policy (NEP), and are in prospect of becoming *within a markedly changed institutional setting* the basic features of the New System of Planning and Economic Incentives (NEM).

The Western debate has stressed that rational allocation could be achieved under socialism through the experimental costing of factors of production so that the demand for them in all uses would be equated to the available supply; it has underlined that economic calculation posited the need for producers' prices reflecting underlying scarcities. At the same time, however, it has illuminated the various difficulties arising out of the attaining of correspondence between planners' goals and operational decisions of managers either in an economy in which the control of performance depends on the price system or in an economy in which physical allocation of producers' goods is combined with financial controls. In this latter case, the financial controls can play only a weak and unreliable role.

The discussion has further illuminated the possible directions of Soviet effort toward decentralization in planning, in its scope in respect to the setting of production and investment goals, and in its methods in respect to operative decisions and performance controls. The discussion has explored meaningfully these and other aspects of the problem by relying consistently on marginalist principles and by injecting market solutions into planning. It has thus both implicitly underlined the limited use of the labor theory of value as a normative principle for allocating resources under socialism and exploded the old misconception according to which planning and competition were in all respects opposites.

Later, we shall consider in detail the ways in which Soviet economists attempt to make their price system economically meaningful on the basis of the labor theory of value. But before turning to this problem, let us first examine the criteria which the Soviet planners have used as the basis for drawing up their plans and for determining the key aspects of these plans.

12.

Soviet Theories

ISSUES IN THE PERSPECTIVE OF ALL-EMBRACING PLANNING

Since the beginning of the all-embracing planning era in 1928, Soviet economic policy has rested on the premise that the underlying principle of industrialization is a fast rate of growth of industry in general and of heavy industry in particular and that the fastest rates of industrial growth could be attained only through "maximum" capital investment in industry. This premise has again and again been stressed in a variety of party documents published since then. What criteria guided this specific choice of the Soviet policy makers? Were alternative policies envisaged at any time, and if so, why were they discarded? To what extent is this choice connected with a given type of planning administration? In order to answer these questions, which concern the Soviet "model of industrialization" – i.e., the Soviet policy makers' scale of preferences and their choice of a planning procedure – we must turn to the issues which arose on the eve of the thoroughgoing planning era and to the various solutions then advanced and since upheld in Soviet economic literature.

In the early 1920's, full agreement reigned among Communist leaders as to the basic goal of rapid industrialization and the need for comprehensive planning in order to achieve a harmonious and "crisisless" growth. But despite unanimity on generalities there were sharp differences of opinion on both ends and means. The divergences concerning ends centered on 1] the specific path to be selected for achieving rapid technological progress; 2] the weight to be given to various proximate ends (such as the alleged alliance with the poor peasant, the fight against the rich peasant, the development of economic relations with foreign countries); 3] the pace of growth — i.e., the investment rate — which could and should be considered appropriate. The divergences over planning centered on 1] the extent of decentralization and of the use of market mechanisms; 2] the significance of past economic trends for the selection of plan targets; 3] the possibility of achieving both consistency and efficiency in planning. The decisions on ends form the Soviet *strategy* of development; the decisions on means make up the Soviet *planning* procedure; together, they constitute the so-called Soviet model of industrialization.

Two main strategies were proposed in the 1920's. The first emphasized the development of agriculture or, alternatively, its simultaneous growth with various domestic industries. The proponents of this strategy stressed the importance of consumer demand — particularly of the peasant market — for sustained industrial growth, advocated reliance on comparative advantage in foreign trade, and favored a low rate of investment in the state-owned industries in order to avoid hampering the necessary growth of the other sectors. The second strategy stressed priority for the development of heavy industry. Its proponents declared that the potential demand of state industry was unlimited, sought to gear the economy toward self-sufficiency, rejected comparative advantage, and finally, demanded a very high rate of capital accumulation in the state's hands. After deep party strife, the Soviet leadership selected this second strategy and forcibly rallied to it their own party and government machine and their country.

The proponents of the strategy emphasizing agriculture or the simultaneous development of agriculture and industry stressed the need for a sound monetary system, meaningful prices, and accurate economic accounting. Some strategists favoring heavy industry also considered a sound currency indispensable but were inclined to assume that prices could nevertheless be appreciably "manipulated" by the planners. Others in favor of heavy industry — including the most articulate economist among this group, Evgenii Preobrazhenskii — attached only a slight importance to accurate pricing, and advocated the use of "war economy" methods for achieving the highest savings possible. Strategies and respective planning procedures suggested by their proponents were so tightly interwoven that they appeared to be uniquely correlated: actually, any one strategy could be related to a different planning technique.

MARX'S SCHEMA AND THE SOVIET INVESTMENT PRIORITY

The "secret" of Soviet growth is, as Professor Wassily Leontief puts it in an article on "The Decline and Rise of Soviet Economic Science," the channeling of "as large a part of income as possible — and then more — into productive capital investment." Capacity increases in the basic industry group of energy, iron and steel, and machine tools open the way to expanding both producers' and consumers' goods industries. But development of the latter may be slowed down while the expanding heavy industry keeps on feeding, so to speak, upon itself. In *Capital,* Marx asserts that this process is typical of capitalism. Lenin pushes this idea further; in his work on *The Development of Capitalism in Russia,* he stresses that the development of consumers' goods industries might be completely arrested while heavy industry forged continuously ahead. Using the Marxian model of simple and enlarged reproduction,[1] Lenin states that 1] the growth limits of the economy are set by the excess of the output of producers' goods over replacement needs — in terms of our notation, by $i'_g > c_1 + c_2$; 2] under capitalism the larger share of demand is made up of demand for producers' goods and that, consequently, expansion of sector I is always larger than that of sector II, that is, $\Delta i'_g > \Delta c'_g$; and 3] the organic composition of capital necessarily grows, with the result that the increment of expenditures on capital goods necessarily exceeds the increment of expenditures on labor, and the increment in the first sector exceeds that in the second sector, that is, $\Delta c_1 > \Delta c_2$. Lenin concludes that the basic contradiction of capitalism lies precisely in the urge to "limitless expansion of production and limited consumption."

Even though, according to Marxists, Marx is supposed to have examined the process of production in a historically determined system, namely capitalism, Lenin's propositions derived from Marx's schema were subsequently declared to embody the immutable attributes of the Soviet method of industrialization. Professor Gerschenkron has pointed out that the last assumption of Lenin's theory — that *technological progress* necessarily means an increase in the organic composition of capital — is questionable. Technological progress may be achieved through replacement of worn-out equip-

1. *See Chap.* 8.

ment, i.e., at a zero rate of growth of sector I, and hence, a fortiori, at any rate of growth of sector I. On the other hand, steady pursuit of a pattern which posits a growing investment rate would obviously make investment finally absorb the bulk of national income. (In Lenin's study, investment expands at an increasing rate, but Lenin does not carry out his demonstration beyond a few numerical examples.) Gerschenkron's remarks do not, however, refute the reasoning that, all other things being equal, the *growth rate of total product* will tend to increase or decrease according to the proportions in which new investments are distributed between producers' and consumers' goods industries respectively.[2] The systematic emphasis on sector I, the massive channeling of resources toward productive investment, and the ruthless depression of consumption levels during a long period, in fact, bear testimony, as, Leontief puts it, "not so much to the economic sophistication of the Soviet rulers as to their political perspicacity and determination."

STRATEGIES FOR THE ATTACK ON BACKWARDNESS

The Soviet choice of a given investment pattern was hotly debated within the party and in the country at large during the 1920's. The so-called Right Opposition in the Communist party stressed, under various forms, the need for developing both industry and agriculture simultaneously; the Left Opposition emphasized the idea of the priority development of heavy industry. The latter policy was adopted, after a set of maneuvers which led to the crushing of both left and right by the party's leadership under Stalin, and was proclaimed to be the "Soviet method of industrialization." Let us consider briefly the main arguments advanced during this debate,

2. *Starting from Marx's schema of simple and enlarged reproduction, the Soviet economist G. Fel'dman constructed in 1928 a model in which the investment goods sector* (A) *and the consumption goods sector* (B) *are completely severed from one another under given conditions. A's output serves to increase productive investments, i.e., to increase the capital stock or to replace the technically obsolete capital; B's output is directed entirely toward consumption. B, however, may exist completely independent of A as far as sustaining its own output at the current level is concerned, i.e., for simple reproduction. Fel'dman then uses his model to demonstrate that different growth paths will be generated when the fraction of A allocated to the investment goods sector itself varies; but at a certain critical level the increase in the ratio between the capital stocks of sectors A and B will not, under the assumption of constant capital coefficients, push the* rate of growth *of total income beyond a certain limit.*

since the discussion clarifies the underlying assumptions of the economic policy which has been unflinchingly pursued by Soviet leadership ever since.

Various theories — advanced mostly by professional economists and experts — stressing the importance of an expanding consumers' market and of a strong connection with the world market in the development of a flourishing agriculture, exercised a deep impact on the Right Opposition. Lev Shanin voiced the arguments of these economists when he declared that, in a country with a large surplus population, agriculture should be preferred to industry since it can absorb more labor per unit of capital invested, can yield more per unit invested because it has low capital-output ratios, and may build up large savings on account of its low consumption rates. These savings could subsequently be tapped for investment in industry. Assuming a profit rate of 6 per cent in industry as compared to 15 per cent in agriculture, Shanin asserted that a hundred units of capital "diverted" from agriculture to industry in one year would amount the following year to 106 additional units in industry, the third year to 112.3, the fourth year to 119.1. On the other hand, if the original 100 units were left in agriculture, they would total 115 units the following year, 132.2 the third year, and 152.0 the fourth year.

Shanin concluded that by reinvesting in agriculture and by postponing the diversion of resources from this sector to industry, the latter could subsequently develop more rapidly. Given the heavy dependence of domestic industry on the peasant market, the growth of agriculture would allow the rapid recovery of existing industries. Since foreign trade would be intensified and stocks of consumers' goods accumulated, industry could finally forge ahead in new directions without causing commodity shortages. Shanin added that the best sequence to follow in industrial development was the traditional one which starts with agricultural industries working for export, continues with light industries supplying the domestic market, and ends with the expansion of heavy industries at the appropriate moment when any additional demand for consumers' goods created by increased employment in producers' goods branches can be fully satisfied.

Although accepting many of Shanin's "theses," Nikolai Bukharin — first the party's whip against the left; later, the spokesman of the Right Opposition — rejected outright Shanin's "indefinite" postponement of investment in certain industrial branches. Bukharin posited that industry and agriculture must develop together, since their growth is mutually reinforcing. Industry, he stressed, depends on agricultural supplies and on peasant demand; agriculture, in turn, needs both machinery and goods for mass consumption. During an initial period in which appropriate conditions for the domestic production of agricultural machinery were being created, equipment could be imported in exchange for grain, the country's "agricultural currency." As heavy industry grew, dependence on the world market would decrease. But as Bukharin stressed, the limits of industrial growth are directly governed by the growth of key agricultural output such as grain, cotton, hides, wool, flax, etc. Reductions in grain output would entail shrinkages in exports and, correspondingly, in the imports of producers' goods; reductions in the output of raw materials would necessitate a reduction in the domestically produced consumers' goods. All these harmful effects would be magnified if agriculture were prevented from investing and if it were entirely "sacrificed" to industry.

The party's left wing (headed politically by Leon Trotsky) led the all-out attack against Shanin, against the early positions of the party's leadership, and against Bukharin's "theses," which finally were identified exclusively with the Right Opposition. The left's economic theories were expounded by Preobrazhenskii in his book *New Economics*, a crucial Soviet economic document. Preobrazhenskii emphasized first and foremost the need for massive investment if the country's industry were to be completely retooled, adapted to modern technology, and expanded. During a period which he defined as the "infant stage of development of the socialist industry" — specifically during the decades in which the productivity of Soviet industries continued to lag behind that of the United States, the most developed capitalist country — these massive investments must be extracted from agriculture by a variety of means, notably direct taxation and price manipulations. The more backward a country, the greater the importance of small-scale ownership, and the more heavily would "socialist accumulation" depend on the massive diversion of savings ("surplus" product) from agriculture to industry. Preobrazhenskii called this the "law of primitive (or primary) socialist accumulation." Thus, he posited that 1] potential savings exceeded actual savings in agriculture, 2] that for all practical purposes, the investment needed for retooling the state industry, moving it onto the "highest technological plane," and expanding it, was unlimited, and 3] that peasant demand was of secondary importance and could not provide the stimulus needed for large-scale industrial growth.

Preobrazhenskii discarded Shanin's arguments on the advantages of the higher returns immediately obtainable from investing in agriculture and stressed that concentration of investments in producers' goods industries would lead to economies of scale, provide the conditions for developing new industries, and ultimately permit price reductions in goods for mass consumption — through reductions in the prices of the capital goods provided to consumers' goods industries. Declaring that large-scale production was "always" less wasteful than small-scale production since the latter ties up larger amounts of resources in its production cycle and for longer periods, Preobrazhenskii added that introduction of the highest technology was economical even though labor might seem cheaper than capital and even though, in these circumstances, agriculture must remain highly labor-intensive for a long time. The need for a sharp difference in sectoral factor utilization was, he considered, the inevitable "penalty of underdevelopment," to be paid until the Soviet industry finally bridged the gap between its present productivity and the productivity of the most advanced capitalist countries.

The left-wing positions, dubbed in the early 1920's "superindustrialist," were at first resolutely rejected by the party leadership. Preobrazhenskii's economic formulae were solemnly condemned. The idea of developing heavy industry at the expense of agriculture was rejected as representing a major danger to the "alliance" between workers and peasants. The theory of "primitive socialist accumulation" — patterned on Marx's theories of brutal exploitation and dispossession of small landowners at the dawn of capitalism — was branded heretical and a menace to the stability of the Soviet regime. As Bukharin put it later, the goal of the left is to place agriculture "behind" old Russia, whereas the country actually needs to bring agriculture to the level of the United States.

The party soon changed its policy, for a variety of reasons: the most noteworthy were the continuing political and economic isolation of Soviet Russia, the real or presumed economic differentiation among peasants (leading to the strengthening of a rich peasant stratum), and the obstacles involved in persuading peasants to market a larger share of grain so that a higher rate of industrialization and urbanization could be sustained. The party leadership took over the policies of the defeated left and laid even greater emphasis on the need for heavy industry and autarkic development ("Socialism in One Country"). Henceforth party leaders called for a massive investment effort and for rapid industrialization as the *sine qua non* of Soviet survival. Closing the debate on strategy and opening the era of thoroughgoing planning in 1928, Stalin declared in a famous attack against the right that thereafter the party's policy would "proceed from the premise that a fast rate of development of industry in general and of the production of the means of production in particular, is the underlying principle of, and the key to, the industrialization of the country; the underlying principle of, and the key to, the transformation of the entire national economy along the lines of socialist development. But what does a fast rate of development of industry involve?" Stalin asked. He answered, "It involves the maximum capital investment in industry."

The decision on the structure of investment (i.e., the emphasis on heavy industry) implied a number of decisions not only on the rate of capital formation, but also on the organizational setup of the economy as a whole and of agriculture in particular. Preobrazhenskii had bluntly stated that a high rate of investment required the extracting of a large share of marketed produce from agriculture by taxation and price manipulation and the eventual dispossessing of the small peasant. The party officially rejected his theory of "primitive socialist accumulation" as well as its implications, but soon afterwards put all its conclusions into practice. The collectivization of the peasantry was to be instrumental precisely in increasing the marketed share of agricultural produce. The peasant was compelled to deliver a crushing share of his produce at ridiculously low prices, while at the same time losing control over his land. The party's strategy of development thus proceeded from these premises: 1] discontinuities existed on the supply side of savings and large "surpluses" could be tapped by forcibly changing the structural setup in agriculture; 2] Soviet heavy industry could be reconstructed and expanded on a high technological level without planners' being much concerned with the demand of consumers in general or of the peasants in particular; finally, 3] the "reconstruction" of industry would eventually change the technological conditions prevailing in agriculture, but in the meantime, industry could forge ahead only if investments in agriculture received low priority.

The "Soviet method of industrialization" is popularly identified, not with the general idea of developing "capital goods for sector I" (producers' goods industries), but with a set of very specific options concerning certain "leading" industrial branches. The Soviet strategy cannot be separated from these technological decisions. The emphasis on leading industries contributed just as much to Soviet growth as did the basic option for the massive channeling of resources toward "productive investment" in general. On what criteria were these specific choices made? A rich Communist literature has sprung up around many of these decisions. Originally, the logic of the situation of an economically isolated country, shattered by both a world war and a civil war, and strangled by innumerable bottlenecks, dictated the Soviet policy makers' specific preference for the key group: *energy*, *steel*, and *machine tools* — the bases of both autarkic industrial development and a high defense potential. As in any other country, the decision of its engineers, project makers, and managers later helped the regime to frame its innovating decisions in various defense and industrial fields at the technological frontier, where new choices become necessary.

Communist writing on the crucial role of electricity in industrialization is particularly abundant. The first decision of any new Communist regime, from Eastern Europe to the extreme Orient, has been in favor of stepping up electricity production. By now, this is not a reasoned technological choice, but an article of Communist belief. The importance of electricity was brought home to the Soviet leaders during the fuel crises of 1920, which severely hampered economic recovery, not to mention the "reconstruction" of the whole economy on the highest technological plane. The role of electricity was underscored by the Communist leader Gleb Krzhizhanovski, an engineer by training, who pointed out the key role that electricity had played in the development of industrial Germany. Lenin seized upon the idea and created his famous slogan, "Communism is the power of the Soviets plus electricity." [3] The first Soviet plan,

3. *Krzhizhanovski contended at the time that the introduction of electricity in Russian agriculture would solve the European food problem "forever." Others foresaw a variety of marvelous results from the massive use of electricity. The economist V. Bazarov declared that, thanks to its fractionability and transportability, electricity would allow both the mechanization of handicrafts and the reduction of urban construction and thus "relegate to the museums of a future socialist society the barracks-type factory and its fitting addendum, the skyscraper." Others, like the young technician I. Ivanov, in a famous article highly praised by Krzhizhanovski, stressed that electricity would serve as the basis of Communist technology in the same way that steam power had served as the foundation of early capitalist technology. The communist virtues of*

launched in the early 1920's, was indeed a plan for the electrification of Russia (the so-called *Goelro* plan).[4] Though this plan contributed only modestly to Soviet economic recovery, which was brought about by a number of factors, electrification has since been proclaimed the keystone of the Soviet method of industrialization. The so-called energy concept of the economy — i.e., the idea of using massive quantities of electricity to change all the production functions in the economy, simultaneously, as it were, and to secure large increases in output — is still an unquestioned article of faith of Communist policy makers and planners. Although electricity is developed for its own sake — obviously, with the idea of the more the better — in time, it does, of course, further sustained industrial growth.

It was obviously essential to emphasize metallurgy and machine construction in a country intending to develop on autarkic lines and to provide itself with a strong military base. Metallurgy could grow rapidly on the basis of the country's large deposits of coal and iron and of its abundant raw material supplies. But the idea of developing iron and steel has been so thoroughly integrated into the "Soviet method of industrialization" that each Communist country, whether or not it possessed coal and iron, whether it could avail itself of "socialist cooperation" or not, has resolutely engaged in the development of its own metallurgy and machine-construction industries. In each of these countries, these industries have absorbed the largest share of investment during their first quinquennial plans. Communist economic discussion regards metallurgy as a basic instrument of economic and social change, without giving much thought to possible alternative paths of development.

To the crucial electricity-metallurgy group, Soviet policy makers and planners have added a variety of industries as Soviet technology has advanced, e.g., atomic energy, electronics, plastics, etc. In the late 1950's, *chemization* — the grand-scale introduction of chemical processing in petroleum, coal, and other industries — received a great build-up, similar to that of electrification in the early Soviet years. The Soviet model of industrialization, however, remains rooted in its now traditional electrical-metallurgical setting. The *Draft Pro-*

---

electricity were supposed to stem from the fact that electricity "could be dispensed from a single automated central station, through a single mechanism, to a scattered system of working machines." (The Central Committee presumably was to be in control of this automated station.)

4. *The plan was drawn by a state commission for the electrification of Russia* — Gosudarstvennaia komissia po electrifikatsii Rossii (*abbreviated to* Goelro).

gram for 1960–80, repeats the sacramental phrase, "electrification is the backbone of the Communist society," and again stresses the need of ensuring the priority development of electric power output.

APPROACHES TO LONG-TERM PLANNING

In line with the indicated strategies, two basic approaches to planning procedure were suggested. Some of the choices made then have acquired such an air of finality that even now the premises on which these decisions were taken — although they have long since lost their validity — are not questioned in most socialist countries. Let us consider closely the divergent procedures suggested and the impact of some of these ideas on current Soviet planning.

In pointing out that each plan was necessarily a mixture of forecasts based on past economic trends and of directives expressing the changes desired by the planner, the economists V. Groman and V. Bazarov stressed that these directives could not be entirely divorced from past trends. Prevailing relationships among outputs of agriculture and industry, of consumers' and producers' goods, which embody prevailing sector and industry interdependences, impose very specific limits on the planner in his mapping of future changes. The planner must, moreover, deal with a mixture of predictable and unpredictable elements; his plans may, for instance, take the form of directives in industry, but they may be mere forecasts in agriculture, since agricultural output depends on a number of unpredictable elements. Thus, the planner cannot seriously break with past trends, nor can he enjoy the same liberty in making his decisions in every sector of the economy.

This "genetic" approach — a term that underlines the primary significance which its proponents attributed to the distinctive features of every economy's development and to the observable "regularities" existing within it — was sharply rejected by influential Communist planners headed by S. Strumilin. The plan, Strumilin argued, is not a piece of research or a simple forecast; it is a teleologic construct, i.e., a purposeful set of directives for action. It embodies the policy makers' will to change prevailing economic and social relationships so that, in fact, the "over-all aims of that will establish the very premises of the plan." The "teleologist" recognizes two kinds of restrictions in respect to the future, but his definition of these restrictions is radically different from that of the "geneticist." First, past trends may have a decisive impact, but only on short-term targets. This impact will decrease as the time dimension of the target changes. On intermediate or long-term targets, the impact of past trends may become almost nil, so that in a general plan (of 10 to 15 years) the final target may coincide with the ultimate policy objective of achieving a significantly changed economic balance. Secondly, the policy makers' choice of one set of goals implies *ipso facto* the rejection of any other set.

In the teleologists' conceptual framework, a prognosis based on extrapolation of trends is defined as what is objectively inevitable, and planning is defined as what is desirable from the standpoint of the policy maker's aspirations. Where the problem is the creation of a new future, the method of target setting is not that of extrapolation but that of "engineering and designing" new constructs. Accordingly, a general or perspective plan must be conceived as an interrelated program of *engineering* blueprints, coordinated on the basis of a given sequence starting with a number of arbitrarily designed "leading links." The scale of development of each branch is planned with regard to possible investments and various possible bottlenecks, both of which are assessed roughly. The blueprints are integrated into an over-all program by ensuring that each succeeding plan rests upon the preceding ones; the basic programs to which all the others are adjusted are those of the leading industrial branches, followed by industry as a whole, and then by the other sectors of the economy. The guiding sectors thus determine the dynamics of all other branches linked with them; the prospects for agriculture (investment, pattern of output sought, marketed share) are determined by the plans for industry. The goals form a system of assignments for construction; they must be both specific and realistic, i.e., they must conform to the country's present and potential resources. No goal can be considered as an immutable "prediction," moreover; it may be adjusted as the program itself unfolds or as the policy maker shifts his primary objectives.

Criticizing the primacy assigned by the teleologists to these "construction assignments," the well-known economist N. Kondrat'ev pointed out that in fact the engineering blueprints were themselves based on forecasts concerning some crucial magnitudes, such as income, investments, and consumption, and that the goals indicated could attain some degree of realism only if the *projections* were realistic in their turn. Secondly, referring to the linking of each plan to the preceding ones via the familiar method of balanced estimates, Kondrat'ev pointed out that this method guarantees only that the projected rates of development of the individual branches are brought into agreement with one another; it does not guarantee that the projected model of the future economy can be realized. Many such models can be constructed; the problem is finding one which is both realistic and optimal. This, concluded Kondrat'ev, cannot be done simply through the linkage of balanced estimates; it requires a clear determination both of the foundations on which the projections are made and of the economic profitability of the model in which the projections are combined.

Concerned as the policy makers and planners were with achieving revolutionary shifts in factor allocation and with attaining a number of basic priority targets as speedily as possible, they gave only a limited importance to pricing mechanisms, financial balances, and interrelations between the latter and the engineering-technical constructs based on physical plans. They concentrated their full attention on perfecting the physical balances for a number of key products but discouraged as futile the attempts to relate the material balances between them into a single system and to coordinate them with the "synthetic" data on income, financial plans, budget, etc. Bent on perfecting a system that made achieving a number of *limited* objectives its prime goals, the planners also established the rule of integral provision of resources for the activities given top priority and of the fulfillment of the basic targets at all costs, whatever the impact on activities given lower priority.

In the 1920's, P. Popov and M. Barengol'ts attempted to unify the tabulations for both production and distribution, in physical and in value terms, into a single economic account. In a pioneering study, *The Balance of the National Economy of the USSR for 1923/24*, published in 1926, Popov showed how the "credit-debit" (output-input) balance of each branch of production could be integrated into a single system representing the "turnover record" of the economy as a whole. Popov surveyed separately and jointly the role of each branch as supplier and as consumer and uncovered, as he put it, "the volume and the structure of the output which flows into the national economy from its individual branches and is distributed among the separate branches and classes of society." In a remarkable article published in 1928, Barengol'ts explored the "dynamics of inter-industry consumption and production" and compared the behavior over time of certain input coefficients derived from his input-output tabulations.

This pioneering work, however, was both misunderstood and held in low esteem by the policy makers and planners, who declared that Popov's work amounted to only "a game with figures." Strumilin's contention that constructing the plan is "like the far more elementary art of building, . . . a kind of art engineering and not . . . a science in the strict meaning of the term" appeared entirely satisfactory to the Soviet policy makers, especially since Strumilin carefully stressed that "the accuracy upon which strict science insists is by no means necessary for practical purposes." The principles of voluntarism and pragmatism thus became the core of the Soviet "theory" of planning; for over thirty years, it was all that the policy makers considered necessary for implementing what the Soviet literature calls "scientific socialism." After Leontief provided the flexible algebraic framework of input-output analysis and revealed its great potentialities in planning, Soviet planners rediscovered the crude but innovative works of Popov and Barengol'ts and lavished exaggerated praise upon them. As we have pointed out earlier, actual use of input-output, and linear programming methods have expanded in the USSR only since the mid-1960's.

In the 1920's, Soviet policy makers assumed that planning and centralized management were identical. They defined the sphere of centralized management as embracing not only decisions on rate and pattern of investments, but also almost all aspects of production. For the Soviet planner, decentralization in respect to output remained a sort of nagging inconvenience which the system must endure, but which often hinders rather than helps "Bolshevik" planning. Even in the 1960's some Soviet economists (I. Evenko is one example), declared that the highest "centralization" under socialism represented "one of the forms of the manifestation of the objective law of planned proportional development of the economy and one of its requirements." Evenko made clear that he specifically includes in this sphere of centralized direction the concrete tasks of determining the volume of production, the rate and proportions of the development of the economy, the division of materials, labor, and financial resources, the volume of domestic and foreign trade, price fixing, etc. He concluded that political and economic leadership were indivisible.

Analysts of the Soviet system, Czeslav Bobrowski, for instance, have suggested that the identifying of political leadership and economic management was simply a carry-over from the early postrevolutionary years. The maintenance of this identity embodied not only the Soviet policy makers' ingrained predilection for commands rather than for incentives, but also a deep mistrust of the operation of the price mechanism and the achievements of their own planners and managers. As Bobrowski puts it, "When one doesn't know to foresee, he reserves to himself the right of interfering at all times and for all purposes." Only reluctantly did the Soviet leadership finally decide (since the mid-1960's) to modify the past steering mechanism, restrict the field of centralized decisions, and spur the initiative and responsibility of operational management by stressing sales and profit as the decisive criteria of performance at the enterprise level. We shall turn in more detail to these problems in the next chapter.

CONCLUDING COMMENTS

Placed from the outset in full control of the "commanding heights" of the Soviet economy — i.e., its large-scale industry, banks, and distribution system — Soviet policy makers had to concern themselves immediately with both development planning and planning procedure. Their Marxist ideological heritage pointed clearly to the significance of certain variables in economic growth, particularly to the need for large capital investment, but it did not offer ready-made answers to questions like which path of development was open to the Soviet economy in the given historical conditions; which rate of investment was both appropriate and achievable; how investment resources should be allocated; or what kind of planning procedure should be implemented.

The debates of the 1920's helped to map both the Soviet strategy of industrialization and the planning procedure for implementing it. As we know, since the opening of the thoroughgoing planning era, the Russians on the average have invested a quarter of their yearly national income (at current prices), the larger share of which has been channeled toward heavy industry.[5] Can such an investment policy be considered economically rational?

5. *In real terms, the fraction of product invested has actually risen over time even if it has remained more or less constant in current prices.*

To answer that question, one would first have to determine what rate of investment is economically "rational." The decision about the economic *structure* desired by the policy maker, for whatever reasons it may be taken, governs all other decisions, including, notably, the decision on investment and on composition and magnitude of foreign trade. A decision in favor of the priority development of peasant agriculture compels a relatively low level of investment (since consumption on the farm could hardly be reduced below certain levels), large participation in foreign trade, and reliance on comparative advantage. Conversely, in a backward country emphasis on a fully integrated heavy industry program compels very high investment, a shrinking foreign trade — limited initially to exchanging agricultural products for machines — a high degree of protectionism, and hence, depressed consumption levels. Depending on the policy maker's decision on structure, the investment requirement will vary; the differences in rate of "accumulation" will be further influenced by the pace set for implementing the given goals, i.e., by the timetable selected by policy makers and planners.

The case for large investment is well known. Only through a major investment effort can one benefit from large-scale techniques and increasing returns; moreover, costly though certain modern techniques may appear for countries with redundant labor, they make for faster production, tie up less materials, and hence may prove cheaper than more primitive techniques. But as we have seen, in the case of Soviet industrialization, the heavier the emphasis on the rapid development of certain branches with the highest available techniques, the sharper the ensuing differences between their rate of growth and that of all other branches and sectors, and the longer the retention of the most backward methods in the low priority branches. Thus the primary decision on the emphasis to be placed on heavy industry determines the "accumulation" target and the main characteristics of the Soviet growth pattern, namely, the differential growth rates of industrial branches, the mixture of capital-intensive and labor-intensive processes within the same branch, and the divergent development of industry and agriculture.

In respect to theory and to planning procedure, the Soviet debates of the 1920's brought into sharp focus some disparate and rather debatable assumptions which continue to represent the foundations of Soviet planning. The Soviet theory of planning stressed the primacy of the teleologic principle and defined perspective planning as "engineering" construction according to the "assignments" of the policy makers. In this framework, the plan is mainly "a sum of administrative orders." The official theory on planning procedure stated further – at least up to the mid-1960's – that in respect to almost all aspects of production, central orders and operational management decisions could achieve congruency no matter what happened to the price mechanism.

One may recognize that any development plan is by definition teleological in the sense used in the Soviet debate — i.e., it has a purpose deliberately chosen by the policy makers — and that, moreover, both the goal or set of goals and their timetable determine the total investment required. Further, one may agree that specific quantitative targets may be set on the basis of a number of engineering projects conforming to policy makers' goals and that the planner may decide on investment priorities in taking into account the investment budget of each of these projects and the resources available. Yet none of the principles and procedures indicated — the teleologic principle, considering the plan as an engineering construct, the target setting, and the determination of investment priorities — clarifies in any way the problem of the efficiency attainable in the utilization of resources and the problem of the correspondence achievable in this planning framework between decisions taken at the top and their implementation at the bottom.

The search for rules to ensure efficiency and congruency was, in fact, precluded in the USSR for decades by the emphasis on the so-called planning principle as the basic "regulator" of the economy. This principle sanctioned the freedom of the planner to ignore the law of value, i.e., gave him freedom to distort prices at will and to disregard any market signal. For a long time, the search for objective standards in price setting was not one of the Soviet planner's concerns. Thus, not the much-debated teleologic principle but the generally accepted planning principle *ipso facto* eliminated efficiency from plan calculations. The relative freedom of the planners' choice in the long run on matters of structure, target setting, and investment priorities, as stressed by the so-called teleologic principle, was presumed to hold equally for price setting, as expressed by the so-called regulator role of the planning principle. This, in turn, required stressing the identity of planning and operative management — i.e., of detailed commands and controls in respect to operative decisions at the bottom — without setting definite limits to centralization in respect to either investment or output.

Since the planners had only an inherently defective price-setting tool, the labor theory of value (which, moreover, could be ignored at will or disposed of arbitrarily), they were compelled to emphasize the technical-engineering aspects of Soviet planning. For decades, they showed little concern with exploring the path opened by Popov and Barengol'ts, since their primary concern was perfecting an instrument which could ensure the reaching of a *limited* number of objectives as *rapidly* as possible. For this purpose, traditional "war economy" methods — commands, physical allocation of producers' goods, emphasis on the fulfilling and overfulfilling of priority tasks — seemed the most appropriate. These methods implied the rejection of the notion of equilibrium of production, distribution, and consumption — the very notion on which Popov's schema was built — both in drafting plans and in implementing them, and these methods inevitably gave rise to a variety of crises and disruptions, each one of which was solved on its merits without endangering the basic priority tasks. The Soviet strategy of development thus became associated with a planning procedure based primarily on centralized commands, even though the need for decentralization became increasingly obvious and forced the recognition of the principle of business accounting (i.e., autonomy) of each enterprise.

13.

Other Socialist Theories

CONDITIONS FOR DISCARDING WAR ECONOMY METHODS

Is administrative management typical for only a given historical period in the development of the socialist economy? Is it characteristic of an initial phase of impetuous industrialization when only the centralized disposal of resources seems able to prevent the dissipation of the limited means available? How does such a phase actually draw to a close? In a lecture delivered in Belgrade in 1957, "On the Political Economy of Socialism," Oskar Lange stated that the period of administrative allocation of resources, i.e., of "war economy" methods, coincides with the exacting period of forced industrialization and of hasty defensive arming in new socialist societies. This period, however, is bound to draw to a close when war methods begin to interfere with economic growth in many ways, and when new forces mature in the socialist society and pave the way for the introduction of economic rationality. In other words, administrative management is bound to draw to a close when its methods, which nourish a hypertrophied bureaucracy, increasingly hamper technological progress and clearly engender waste of all kinds. The forces which rise and urge the discarding of bureaucratism and its wasteful methods are the newly emerging, well-trained managerial stratum and the growing class of industrial workers. Thus, when various aspects of *backwardness* are overcome, the phase of administrative socialism draws to an end.

The trend toward economic rationality and the changes in planning procedures in the socialist camp bear out only part of Lange's generalization. True, all these countries resorted to war economy methods as soon as each of them launched its industrialization drive. Czechoslovakia, although already industrialized, also applied the same methods in order to carry out an industrial reconversion of vast proportions. Once established, however, administrative socialism and its proliferating bureaucracy die hard. This does not mean that the bureaucracy itself ignores the waste engendered by its own type of management, the distortion of its orders by operative managers, the widespread cheating, theft, and false reporting, the deleterious effect on productivity of a saving rate that is relentlessly pushed up, etc. The desire to curb the most outrageous aspects of Soviet waste has indeed become particularly evident since the death of Stalin. Thus, Lange was right in his contention that once a certain level of development is reached, the questions of efficiency and congruency in planning become increasingly urgent. Various current discussions in the Soviet Union focus on the crucial problems of how prices should be made more appropriate for economic calculation, which investments should be centrally directed and which decentralized, which outputs should be centrally determined and which locally planned, what incentives should be used to achieve congruence between goals and implementation. Even though party leaders may be reluctant to relinquish any of their directing functions, the mere recognition of these problems implies a need for using economic analysis and economic science. After having been dismissed as unnecessary during more than three decades of thoroughgoing planning, Soviet economics is now being brought back to life in order to perform certain functions which, until recently, were regarded as being strictly technical and engineering.

We know, however, that numerous combinations between pure administrative and pure market socialism are possible. The scope of the activity of a central planning authority may contract or expand in many ways affecting allocation of investment, volume and type of central commands to the executing bodies, type of planning and coordination between physical outputs produced, interplay of physical and financial flows, and distribution of goods. But a full break with administrative methods, i.e., the actual separation of the institutions of political government and of economic management, requires the introduction of meaningful prices for producers' goods and the cessation of physical allocation of these goods, the resort to economic incentives on a large scale, and the removal of all arbitrary central commands and interferences with the operative managers. In the USSR there are serious obstacles in the way of such a radical solution.

The leadership of the party is far from acknowledging that its own sphere of commands needs to be sharply restricted, even though it often proclaims that more free choices should be granted to consumers, workers, and enterprises. Characteristically, the *Draft Program* for 1960–80 — years of so-called full-scale Communist construction — specifies that the bodies in charge of planning, accounting, and economic management will indeed lose their political character and will become "organs of public self-government" but only at that remote date when "the Communist society will be a highly organized community of workingmen." Incidentally, the draft program also indicates that, although historical development is bound to lead to the withering away of the state, it will not lead to the disappearance of the Communist party, which apparently is to be eternally necessary for providing "guidance" to the communist society. Further, the Soviet bureaucracy seems to think that its vast centralized power and its manipulation of prices may be the only ways to guarantee a high rate of savings and the attainment of the specific key targets it pursues. As far as costing and pricing are concerned, the bureaucracy is both prone to inertia and lacking in imagination; in any case, the officially accepted labor theory of value is but an awkward tool for rationalizing the price system, as we shall see. Finally, let us note that a complete departure from administrative socialism has thus far occurred only in Yugoslavia. This is not the most industrialized country of Eastern Europe; it is, in fact, one of the least developed. The break took place only after the Yugoslav leadership was cut off in 1948 from the bloc and after it succeeded in obtaining substantial economic aid from the United States. A similar break appeared possible in Hungary and Poland after the popular uprisings in these countries in the second half of 1956. But the Hungarian uprising was crushed by Soviet military intervention, and the Polish uprising fizzled out after a few political changes. The traditional methods of administrative socialism were finally seriously questioned in Eastern Europe and the USSR after the beginning of the 1960's. A series of severe declines in the growth rates of each of these countries — and particularly in the most advanced among them, East Germany and Czechoslovakia — forced a number of important changes in planning strategy, instruments, and management. The traditional emphasis on a higher rate of growth of producers' versus consumers' goods was temporarily abandoned, at least in some of the socialist countries. A significant shift took place in the area as a whole from direct commands to indirect instrumentalities for stimulating the responsiveness of operational management. The sphere of plan indicators was reduced in a variety of ways. Interest-bearing credits, in lieu of grants and capital charges on assets in use, were called into play to reduce the pressure of managerial demand on investable resources; profit from sales, instead of gross value of output, was proclaimed the new "success indicator." Finally, the whole structure of management was revamped to find better equilibria between organizational *concentration* – indispensable for coping with the needs of modern research and technology – and organizational *decentralization* – needed for stimulating managerial initiative from below. Varying degrees of de-emphasis of the CPA, a single, all-powerful center, in favor of more power for planning and control in ministerial branches – and in Eastern Europe in trusts, or industrial conglomerates – and increased initiative at the level of the management of profit-oriented enterprises ushered the phase of New Economic Management (NEM) into the whole European socialist world.

Thus, the administrative methods are seriously challenged only when national crises of great proportions threaten the economy and the entire political and social structure – as in the second half of the 1950's or in the early 1960's. But even under these conditions, the break with the traditional steering system, which is based on *quantity fixation*, and the transition to a new system based on *incentives* of various sorts are reluctant, unstable, and half-hearted. The hypertrophied bureaucracy created in the early phases of a forced industrialization drive seems to visualize itself as eternally indispensable for exacting a continuously high rate of saving, for carrying out some transcendent goal, like an ever-growing heavy industry, an unsurpassed military establishment, or a spectacular feat in outer space.

ECONOMIC CALCULATION AND THE LABOR THEORY OF VALUE

The Soviet price pattern has certain immutable characteristics which set it apart from the price pattern prevailing in either a highly developed or an underdeveloped economy. As we noted previously, investment goods are low in price and yield only small profits, but consumers' goods are high in price and are highly taxed. Throughout the comprehensive planning years, the Soviet price pattern has been molded by the planners' desire to protect producers' goods prices from the effects of inflation, to keep these prices stable for simplifying planning calculations, and to siphon off, via tax plus profits on consumer's goods, the amount decided upon for investment. According to official data, before the planning era, the share of profits and taxes in the prices of producers' goods prices was around 21.5 per cent as against 44.4 per cent in the prices of consumers' goods. The discrepancy between the shares increased during the pre-World War II years and rose even more during the war. After the war, the differential was narrowed by a series of retail price reductions, increases in prices of obligatory agricultural deliveries, and increases in certain producers' goods prices (mostly in the branches in which the wage bill was large and productivity had grown slowly, e.g., coal, ferrous metals, etc.). In 1955, profits, taxes, and markups have accounted for 13 per cent of the price of producers' goods and 40 per cent of the price of consumers' goods. Although Soviet real wages are low, nominal wages are high relative to prices of producers' goods and low relative to prices of consumers' goods. As Naum Jasny has shown, this price-wage pattern contrasts sharply with the price-wage pattern in the United States, where the prices of investment goods are high relative to the prices of consumers' goods and wages are high relative to both. The Soviet pattern also contrasts with that typical of an underdeveloped country, where prices of investment goods are high relative to the prices of consumers' goods and wages are low relative to both. In the process of growth, wages usually tend to rise faster than prices of consumers' goods, and these, in turn, tend to rise faster than those of producers' goods.

By deliberate distortion of the Soviet price-wage pattern, by financing the capital investments of the state enterprises with nonreimbursable budget grants, and by the various peculiarities of economic accounting which we have already discussed, Soviet policy makers have achieved their basic goals. Distortions and peculiarities have not, however, precluded the movement of planning from reliance on physical data to use of value transformation functions expressing the sectoral interdependence of the economy. Thus, for instance, the cheapness of producers' goods relative to labor costs reinforced the project makers' bias in favor of capital-intensive solutions; on the other hand, the reflection of the pattern of labor costs in all wholesale prices (net of turnover tax) allowed the passage from physical data to value transformation functions for intersectoral matrix construction. Nevertheless, numerous Soviet economists have begun to point out the incompatibility of price distortions with optimal use of resources and the imperative need to take into account the influence of factors other than labor on interindustry prices. Since the Soviet discussion is carried out within the framework of the labor theory of value and of the Marxist analysis, let us recall briefly the relevant points of this theory and the specific limitations which it imposes upon the Soviet planners.

Unlike other theories of value, Marx's labor theory is not an explanation of exchange ratios, but a tool devised for examining social relationships arising within a given system of production. As Dobb puts it in his brief pamphlet, *Marx as an Economist,* Marx was primarily concerned "with the relations of production which lay *behind* the market," i.e., with a given system of production and with the distribution of income between property and labor within that system. He developed his theories of exploitation, of accumulation, and of the declining rate of profit by distinguishing sharply between use values and values in exchange and by positing that only abstract, socially necessary labor created the latter, i.e., *value* proper. As the productive power of the economy grows, the amount of use value per unit of exchange value grows; in other words, as technology develops, the amount of socially necessary labor per unit of output decreases. Since Marx regards the amount of socially necessary labor as that intrinsic substance of commodities which he calls *value,* and since the socially necessary labor changes as technology changes, a paradoxical situation arises from the use of capital. Capital goods help to create more *use values* (i.e., more goods), but labor alone is the measure of the new values created, (i.e., the $v + m$ of the Marxist analysis). Since by definition, capital does not create value, its opportunity cost (i.e., the use values foregone in other lines when capital is used in a given direction) plays no role in exchange value. The latter is in fact "embodied labor power"; as we stressed previously, m is "unpaid" labor. If, on the other hand, capital itself is productive, there is a real cost of using it over and above depreciation.

How can the labor theory be used for resource allocation, if it disregards the cost of factors other than labor? [1] The discussion is

1. *A solution of this problem is possible: using the going rate of interest, the values of the labor "embodied" in capital could be adjusted for the time at which they were expended and then summed up.*

further complicated because Marx subsumed under the term *law of value* all the forces which regulate the exchange ratios among commodities, the quantities of each produced, and the allocation of the labor force within a "commodity-producing society"; i.e., a society in which the objects produced are sold and bought by different owners.

Soviet economists use the same point of departure as their Western colleagues: the Soviet state owns the producers' goods industries and at the same time "purchases" its products; but Soviet economists have asserted that Soviet producers' goods were not commodities and that the law of value operated only in an indirect way in the state economic sphere. This approach, which dominated Soviet thinking, particularly before World War II, gave the planner sanction for manipulating prices and the "law" of value as he pleased in planning the allocation of resources.

The reaction against arbitrariness took a specific form within this theoretical framework. Some economists suggested that producers' goods were *quasi*-commodities and that consequently their social cost had to be properly ascertained by the planner. Although the "law" of value undoubtedly no longer operated in the "spontaneous" way in which it used to operate under capitalism, this in itself did not free the planner from the need to ascertain the relative economic significance of the factors in production and, for this end, to use some definite principles, i.e., a theory of value. Even though, as we have stressed, the labor theory is a poor tool for tackling problems of rational allocation of resources, it was called upon to serve as a normative principle of valuation. As Stalin stated in his last book, *Economic Problems of Socialism in the USSR* (1952), the "law" of value has no regulatory function in socialist production, since this "regulatory" role is assumed by the planner who sets the plan targets himself independently of prices; but on the other hand, the law influences production decisions and must be employed for "cost accounting and profitableness, production costs, prices, etc." "The trouble," Stalin says, "is not that production in our country is influenced by the law of value"; it is that "our business executives and planners, with few exceptions, are poorly acquainted with the operations of the law of value, do not study them, and are unable to take account of them in their computations." "This, in fact," he concludes, "explains the confusion that still reigns in the sphere of price-fixing policy."

How is the labor theory to be employed for rationalizing the price structure and the use of resources? Soviet economists and Eastern European economists are divided into a number of groups; even after the price reforms of the 1960's, disagreement continues over the ways in which wholesale prices should be determined under socialism.

What criteria should be used for rationalizing the price structure (assuming, of course, that a large number of prices will continue to be *centrally* determined by the state)? How could the labor theory of value be used for that purpose? Soviet and East European economists disagree both on the question of what function the price system should perform (e.g., the function of reflecting the "socially necessary" inputs or the function of "pumping over" various funds from one part of the economy to another) and of what criteria should be used for devising a price system that allows rational economic calculation and efficient utilization of resources. As pointed out in the official Soviet and East European publications, the socialist economists are divided into the following main schools of thought:

1] Supporters of the so-called *straight value concept* of planned prices, who advocate that the "net income of the society" (i.e., its surplus) should be built into price proportionately to wage costs (i.e., the Marxian v).

2] Supporters of the so-called *averaged value concept*, who advocate that the surplus should be built into price, as traditionally done in the USSR, in relation to prime costs (i.e., to the Marxian $c + v$).

3] Supporters of the so-called *supply price concept*, who argue that the surplus should be built into price proportionately to the fixed assets and to the working capital tied up in production (i.e., in relation to the stock of capital in use).[2] The price reforms

2. *In order to improve the Marxian analytical apparatus, Joan Robinson designates, in the preface to the second edition of her* An Essay on Marxian Economics, *the stock of capital in existence, excluding the wage fund, as* C *and the wage fund as* V. C+V *is hence the stock of capital in existence "engaged in the process of exploitation," while* c+v+m *is, as in the usual Marxian notation, the yearly gross product. What Marx calls the rate of exploitation is* M/V, *while* m/(C+V) *is now the rate of profit. (There is still no way of clearly indicating the third Marxian ratio, that of the organic composition of capital. Neither* c/v, *nor* C/V *indicate the relation which Marx had in mind, the ratio of stock of capital goods to labor time currently employed.) The supporters of the third school advocate then that* m *should be built into price in relation to* C+V.

of the late 1960's were based on this latter concept but with a number of corrections. In fact, several variants of this system are possible, depending on whether the surplus is to be allocated in given proportions to fixed assets and working capital, whether the wage costs should be specifically taken into account, or other possibilities.

Assuming that, with the price system selected, the planner aims at equating the total surplus of the society – to be partly collected centrally and partly left in the hands of the enterprises – with the selected goal of capital accumulation deemed necessary for growth, the price system based on the *straight value* concept could be expressed by the equation: $p^* = A\,p^* + w\,(1 + \alpha)$. In this equation p^* is the new vector of prices in the indicated value type price system; A is the matrix of input coefficients computed on the basis of initial prices; w is the vector of direct wage inputs per monetary unit of output; α is the scalar to be computed, showing percentagewise the allocation of the "surplus" in relation to wages. For the *averaged value* price system the price equation could be: $p^* = (A\,p^* + w)\,(1 + \beta)$. In this equation β is the scalar to be computed showing the allocation of net income in relation to prime costs. Finally, in the *supply-price* type, the price equation would be

$$p^* = A\,p^* + w + (C_{p_i} + V_{p_j})\gamma$$

where C and V are vectors representing the fixed and variable capital per monetary unit of output at initial prices, p_i is a producer type price index of fixed assets of a representative sector (i.e., a sector where cost structure best represents that of the tied-up fixed assets); p_j a producer type index of working capital of a representative sector (i.e., of a sector whose cost structure best represents that of the tied-up working capital); and γ is the scalar to be computed showing the percentagewise allocation of the surplus in relation to fixed and variable capital. In the three systems, the starred letter is the decision variable.

As indicated by V. Sitnin, the chairman of the State Committee on Prices of the State Planning Committee, the two basic principles guiding the Soviet price reform of 1967 were: (1) to make all processing industries profitable so as to allow accounting of full cost – i.e., of fixed plus variable cost per unit – at each level; and (2) to "stabilize" throughout the processing industries the rate of profit to the stock of capital so as to make prices comparable and more readily usable in economic calculations. Actually, as we have already stated, these two principles conflicted in a number of respects. Under the average profit norm selected (viz., 15 per cent to assets), with the prevailing distribution of national income, a considerable number of industries with high current production outlays would have had to operate at a loss, while other industries, with low current production outlays, would have yielded exceedingly high profits. Accordingly, profit rates in the former industries (light and food industries) were raised to 30–35 per cent and even more, while profit rates in the latter industries (electric power industry) were set at 10 per cent. These and a number of other corrections, such as the inclusion of a variety of charges (as, for instance, a charge for prospecting in the oil and gas industry) rendered inoperative the goal of "stabilizing" the same profit rate throughout all the processing industries. Within the uniformly fixed prices for each industry, wide variations in the outlays for the manufacture of similar products remained, of course, very great because of technical lags, incorrect specialization, or poor organization. Consequently, variations in profitability loomed so large that a variety of price charges or of subsidies had to be instituted (e.g., fixed charges on the enterprises with extremely high profitability rates and rent payments in the oil and gas industry according to regions). The basic two goals of price setting had to be circumvented even further when determining profitability of each item, when aiming at encouraging new techniques, when stressing the needs of improved quality and standards, and so on. As in all cases of central price fixing, the end result was a haphazard quilt of patches and adjustments, remotely related to the net principles on which the price fixing was supposed to rest.

Other socialist economists, particularly in countries highly dependent on foreign trade, advocate that the domestic price system be simply based on *world market prices* – a radical solution which disregards the specific scarcities underlying production in each of these countries. Finally, still others suggest that central price fixing could be based on the *shadow prices* obtained in the course of programming for an optimal national plan. Thus, the Soviet economist L. Kantorovich, whose pioneering work in linear programming in the late 1930's is now universally acknowledged, proposed that optimal programming could be achieved by systematic use of shadow prices and of coefficients of standard efficiency at all levels of plan elaboration. In his early work, Kantorovich advocated the use of shadow prices for solving specific practical problems, such as optimal utilization of machinery, optimal utilization of arable land, best plan of freight shipment, etc. In 1960, Kantorovich went a step further, and in making his theory more general, suggested the need for interconnecting all the sets of shadow prices used for optimal planning in the economy as a whole. This proposal implicitly discards the current Soviet price system, stresses the need to replace it for planning purposes with a price structure reflective of underlying scarcities, and at the same time suggests that such prices alone make the criterion of profitability fully applicable in planning. Given, however, the lack of sufficient information and the vast computational difficulties involved in working out and operating a nationwide price system based on shadow prices, such a solution for the economy as a whole seems as yet remote.

DECENTRALIZED SOCIALIST MANAGEMENT MODELS

During the initial phase of development of the Communist regimes in Eastern Europe, the policy makers and planners of the countries of the area slavishly followed the "Soviet model," i.e., the Soviet strategy of industrialization and the Soviet planning procedure as shaped during Stalin's thoroughgoing planning era. Now, not only a number of economists but even some bureaucrats have become aware of the vast range of combinations possible between the extremes of administrative socialism and market socialism. Immediately after the Poznań uprising of 1956, the Polish premier, Gomulka, declared: "The model of socialism can also vary. It can be such as that created by the Soviet Union; it can be shaped in a manner as we see it in Yugoslavia; it can be different still. Only by way of experience and achievements of various countries building socialism can there arise the best model of socialism under given conditions."

The Poles have improved little on Russian planning practice, even though a variety of new models were proposed in that country after the Poznań uprising. The principal proposals were formulated in 1957 by the Polish Economic Council, an advisory body of the Polish Council of Ministers, consisting of economists of all political tendencies. Let us briefly consider the Council's solutions, since they concern the key problems with which we are directly interested, namely, securing efficiency in the allocation of resources under planning and ensuring congruency between the aims set and their practical implementation. The Council proposed that the economy be guided by a central plan drawn up in value terms rather than in physical terms; that all firms maximize profits and minimize costs, unless otherwise directed; and that prices of both producers' goods (except for raw materials) and consumers' goods should be based on their domestic costs. These costs were defined as the average variable cost of the group of enterprises which have the highest cost in any given industry. To this so-called marginal variable cost, a proportional profit should be added in all branches so as to cover the "accumulation" decided upon for investment and social consumption. These so-called initial prices may be modified by adding a negative or positive markup so as to bring supply and demand into line; but the planners should have price stability as a primary aim and act on the underlying supply and demand relations before changing prices.

During this discussion, it was widely recognized that previous planning methods had rendered technological progress impossible unless it were forcibly imposed from above, had introduced a system of distorted incentives which made enterprises afraid of progress because any change in production methods required a switch to a different plan, and had forced enterprises to produce not the output mix most desirable to customers, but the one most appropriate for obtaining bonuses. But the Polish government hardly proved ready to introduce the institutional reforms which could clear the way for the operation of the market mechanism. As in the other countries of the area, the Polish leaders shied away from vesting decision making in the producing enterprises and divesting the center of its roles of output planning, investment allocation, and price fixing, except within very narrow limits. The line of change finally adopted has been quite similar to that taken in the USSR itself. It has consisted of expanding the operational and managerial role of industrial trusts and conglomerates, stressing the planning role of these intermediate echelons, and devising only limited improvements in coordinating the activity of the center, the conglomerates and the enterprises. But even after these reforms were achieved, the questions of price fixing and its implications, of the effectiveness of investment, of the material interests of any enterprise's personnel in its financial results, of the methods of planning and of resources allocation, remain more alive in Poland than anywhere else in the "socialist camp."

The Yugoslav planning and management system which emerged after that country's break with Moscow and after a number of years of search for an appropriate economic policy and adequate planning procedure offers an extremely useful contrast with the planning and management models prevailing in the Soviet camp. Although affirming their devotion to Marxism, the Yugoslav theoreticians have felt little bound by any of the canons of the dogma and have resolutely rejected the idea of a "unique road to socialism," i.e., of either a unique strategy of development or of a unique planning procedure. Let us consider briefly the specific characteristics of the Yugoslav system with respect to 1] nationalization of the means of production; 2] role of the central planning authority; 3] management and activity of the production units; and 4] deployment and rewards of labor.

1] Industry, banking, transport, and most of the distribution system are nationalized. Private ownership continues to exist in small-scale production and trade. Farms no larger than 10 to 15 hectares and small-scale handicrafts are operated on a private basis. In the state-owned sector, the principle of *self-management* of each production unit is emphasized: this is viewed not only as economically expedient for proper management but also as politically imperative for achieving the separation of political government and economic institutions and preparing for the eventual "withering" away of the state. Formally, the control of each state enterprise is vested (since 1952) in its workers' council. The workers' council elects an executive board and in consultation with the local authorities appoints its director. The firms are grouped into trade associations, which must promote specialization among their members, share out the imported scarce raw materials, organize market research, etc.

2] Policy guidance is transmitted by an arm of the executive branch (the Committee for Social Planning) to professional planners (of the Federal Planning Institute) who draft the so-called "social plan" on the basis of continuous contacts with the ministries and the Committees of the Federal Government, the Republic Planning Institutes, the economic chambers, the central and other main banks, and the Federal Statistical Institute. The draft, containing only key economic principles and rough quantifications of the broad goals set forth by the Committee of Social Planning for a five-year period, is enacted into law by the Parliament. By a similar process, Republic plans and communal plans, which need not harmonize in detail with the plan above them, are prepared.

Before the mid-1960's the instruments for securing plan realization were: rates of taxes on profits, assets, and incomes, regulations concerning basic wages, price ceilings, farm price guarantees, etc., as well as the distribution of the investment funds by federal, republic, and local authorities and by enterprises. The federal share of the investable resources – roughly two-thirds of the total – was used for stimulating investment initiative in accordance with the centrally designed development of branches and regions, the foreign trade balance, and the international situation. The investment bank and some related banks granted loans so as to attain investment targets by taking into account the credit-worthiness of the borrowing firm and the profitability of each project. The "instrument" for securing optimum selection of projects was competitive bidding for loans (applied wherever technical alternatives are open, or where the question of location is a problem). The borrower had to guarantee repayment, provide part of the estimated cost, and pay any excess expenditures incurred in completing the project. In the sphere of foreign trade, the central influence was maintained through the allocation of anticipated foreign exchange for imports in agreement with the foreseen output and employment patterns. Foreign exchange was allocated by sectors but was not used for a specific commodity import program; the type of import was determined by the firm obtaining the foreign currency. A small quota of currency was available for bidders outside the main allocation sectors. Since the mid-1960's the Yugoslavs have sharply reduced the role of state planning, increasingly stressing the idea of *de-etatization* rather than centralized guidance of the economy. The massive withdrawal of the state from economic decision making (particularly from investment allocation), the abolition of a number of taxes on the enterprises, and the formation of local banks by the enterprises themselves (with the aim of building up their own position in the economy) have so attenuated the economic role of the state that it is doubtful whether any decisive instruments are left at the center for implementing the "social plan."

3] Within this framework, each enterprise is entirely free to buy and sell and to determine the scale and pattern of its activities in response to *consumers' preferences*. It is free to decide on its prices, profits, and wages, on disposal of profits after taxes, on distribution of its investment. It is free to engage in foreign trade. The determination of all prices through the market is a primary principle of the Yugoslav system, although a number of price controls have been introduced since the mid-1950's.

4] The deployment of labor is achieved through price differentials and inequality of rewards. Any state-owned enterprise must first provide for the cost of materials, rent, tax on fixed and working capital, depreciation, interest, and borrowed funds; the remaining funds are allocated to wages, investment, and other purposes. The distinction between workers' wages and share in profits, which was prevalent for a time, has tended to disappear.

Yugoslav market socialism thus contrasts vividly with Russian administrative socialism. Throughout the 1950's, the Yugoslavs dismantled their previous planning administration and developed a new planning system based on giving wide scope for independent decisions by the producing units and the local authorities (the communes). As Hayek has correctly foreseen, however, market socialism may also encourage the development of various forms of uneconomical managerial behavior. With markups over cost set at the discretion of local plant managers, a distortion of resource allocation must occur whenever the rate of markup over marginal cost differs from one plant to another. In addition, the Yugoslav arrangement often led to inertia in adjusting to market change. National monopolies became entrenched in some branches of industry, for instance. The trade associations, encouraged by the government principally for promoting specialization among their members or for allocating scarce imported materials, have tended to act as cartels, i.e., to manipulate prices and to play the role of mutual protection societies. On the other hand, various price regulations and the use of the turnover tax have tended to prevent longer-term market adjustments, while the controls on imports have contributed to distorting the investment pattern. In order to improve the efficiency of the system, strengthen the role of the market, and encourage modernization on a large scale, the state dismantled finally even its indirect controls, abolished its export subsidies, lowered the level of import tariffs, devalued sharply the currency and exposed the economy to international competition at world prices. Decentralization was thus carried to the point where the idea of centralized planning guidance and controls has lost much of its significance. But the small and still poorly developed Yugoslav economy, even after passing through the wringer of this drastic set of reforms, has not been able to achieve noteworthy successes in the efficiency of investment, the level of employment or the balance of payments. The attractiveness of the Yugoslav model of successive and expanding decentralization has hence seriously diminished for the other socialist countries as the Yugoslav economic difficulties, particularly since the 1960's, have increased.

In order to develop at an accelerated pace and to compete on the world markets, various socialist economies have started since the beginning of the 1960's to stress the needs of *both* centralized decisions on broad investment allocation, and decentralized decisions on production, but at the scale of profit-using giant *trusts* or *conglomerates,* i.e., associations of enterprises capable of implementing advanced technology and able to participate meaningfully in international competition. By the beginning of the 1960's East Germany took the lead in outlining and implementing what was to be known as the "new economic model of planning and management" (NEM) – and what might perhaps be called more properly "managerial socialism," a steering model relying neither on economic administrations *à la Russe* (viz., ministries), nor on full decentralization as suggested by the Yugoslav experience, but on big socialist corporations run by highly skilled managers on an effective business-accounting basis.

SHIFTS IN SOVIET PLANNING

Until the mid-1950's, Soviet economists had a stereotyped set of answers with which to oppose the Western theories of rational allocation of resources under socialism, the question of proper costing and pricing of producers' goods, and the question of decentralized management. They contended that rational allocation of resources could be achieved on the basis of manipulated prices and that to think otherwise is to be misled by "subjectivist theories of value." They declared that the planner could manipulate producers' goods prices and that the "competitive" solution, for instance, was simply "incompatible" with socialism, embodying, as it does, "the contradictions and weaknesses of capitalism." Finally, they vigorously attacked the Yugoslavs' discarding of war economy methods in planning and management and declared that such "revisionist" measures were provoked by the bourgeois theoretical leanings of the Yugoslav leaders. The Chinese Communists in particular accused the Yugoslavs of implementing the policies of Ferdinand Lassalle, Marx's nineteenth-century rival, as well as the theories of Eduard Bernstein, a Social Democrat who, at the beginning of this century, rejected some Marxian tenets. A variety of Communist bloc writers, from Albania to Czechoslovakia, accused the Yugoslavs of copying Mussolini's corporatist state or the "Keynesian state-capitalist theories" — a statement which does both Keynes and Tito an injustice. Even today, Yugoslavia appears through Chairman Mao's looking glass as a country of widely heterogeneous theories and of conflicting experiments, an incomprehensible mixture of systems and methods.

Since the 1960's, however, the need for improving the over-all efficiency of the system, for rationalizing the use of resources to maintain a high rate of growth, for keeping in pace with the vast technological change occurring in the advanced economies of the West, and for increasing the initiative at all operational managerial levels has become obvious throughout Eastern Europe. But it is also apparent that both the unattractiveness of the Yugoslavian results, derived from the successive expansion of decentralization procedures, and the reluctance of certain communist leaders to divest themselves of their privilege of continuously intervening in the economy (particularly in respect to directions of such areas as investment, price controls, profit sharing, and product allocations) are bound to render the processes of transition from war-economy methods to decentralized patterns of planning and management halting and contradictory.

At particularly critical junctures — in 1932, during the Soviet collectivization drive; in 1953, after the death of Stalin, and after the multiplication of signs of unrest in the satellite countries; in 1956, after the crises which shook Hungary and Poland — various warnings have been sounded concerning the consequences of Soviet or "satellite" bureaucractic planning and management. These warnings have all stressed 1] the disparity between the growth of productive forces due to the investment emphases and the slow pace of improvement in living standards, and 2] the terrible and permanent "disproportions" existing in the economy, such as the continuous breakdowns in supplies, incomplete utilization of equipment in certain branches, production of substandard and often unusable consumers' goods, and the inefficient distribution system.

Georgi Malenkov in 1953, and various "satellite" leaders in 1956, all sensed that these problems pointed toward the need to shift the investment pattern so as to improve the living conditions of the people and the need for a complete overhaul of the planning and management system. In "For a New Economic Program," an article written for Poland after the Poznań events, but applicable to the Soviet Union, and to all of Eastern Europe, Oskar Lange suggested the following measures, among others, as indispensable in order to cure some of the "disproportions" endangering the economic machinery of Poland. In industry, he suggested that the leaders should 1] stop the race for purely quantitative indices and relate bonuses to the profitability of enterprises, not to the quantitative fulfillment of the plan; 2] reduce the rate of quantitative growth of industrial production, which in certain branches is purely fictitious; 3] extend the participation of workers in the direction of enterprises, and proceed with vast decentralization. In agriculture, he suggested that the leadership 1] establish real incentives for increased production, notably by providing the villages with consumers' goods and 2] establish firm guarantees against further encroachments upon private property, including livestock, etc. In distribution, the leaders should 1] reorganize distribution by taking account of consumers' needs, 2] analyze efficiency of foreign trade and expand foreign trade so as to satisfy consumers' needs immediately.

Clearly these are the main lines along which the NEM reforms have developed in the Soviet Union and the rest of socialist Eastern Europe. But the NEM is far from being a way out of a crucial dilemma. The maintenance of vast central controls concerning allocation of key materials, production directions, and prices and wages is bound to hamper managerial decision making and initiative and to blur the market signals that are supposed to influence greatly current production and long-term decisions on investment and labor utilization. On the other hand, the danger of rising prices in the absence of serious downward influences on costs and the continuous bidding up of wages in conditions of certain labor scarcities, are bound to reinforce the maintenance of centralized controls despite rising pressures of the socialist managers and plant directors, who are eager to achieve fuller managerial responsibility. However, the changes carried out, along with improvements in planning techniques and in the choice of instruments for guiding the economy, should create conditions for a better and more efficient performance. The Soviet and East European economists and managers show an increasing interest in the tools of Western economic analysis systems control and information theory, and are increasingly interested in applying them to a planned-market economy. Even though the economists were once almost exclusively *macro*economically oriented, they have stressed, since the end of the 1950's, that the neglect of *micro*economics has been dearly paid for by low efficiency, despite spectacular quantitative growth. In order to achieve a practicable synthesis of macroeconomics and microeconomics and of planning and market mechanisms, these economists are ready to experiment with a number of schemes adjusted to the particularities of the different countries involved – to their level of development, size, participation in foreign trade, and so on. But, as Leontief remarks in his previously-mentioned article on the "Decline and Rise of Soviet Economic Science": "It will take some time before the planners will be able to apply in practice the new techniques their economists are now acquiring in theory." Even within the limits described, however, "there can be little doubt," Leontief adds, "that in the years to come the introduction of scientific planning techniques will increase the over-all productivity of the Soviet economy, just as the adoption of new methods of scientific management by our own large corporations has raised the efficiency of their internal operations."

Part **V**

Socialism v. Capitalism

INTRODUCTION TO PART V

The Soviet Union and each of the socialist countries attempt to "catch up with and surpass the highest indices of capitalism." If the Soviet Union is racing against the United States, China races against Great Britain, Poland against France, and so on. But the desire to *catch up* with the most developed capitalist economies does not lead these countries to reproduce feature for feature the economy of its chosen opposite from the Western world. Rather, each country, following the Soviet example, strives to raise its main industrial outputs to the levels attained by its selected competitor. Obviously, in its goal of exceeding the capitalist countries – both singly and collectively – in basic outputs, the socialist camp aims to become the mightiest industrial-military complex on the surface of the earth.

The socialist camp is cemented by ideology and a variety of economic interests; there can be little doubt about its representing a convergence of interests. It is equally certain, however, that it also harbors powerful centrifugal forces. Vast differences in size, factor endowment, and levels of development create different economic potentials. The drive toward industrializing each national unit by means of an identical strategy of development which emphasizes the same industrial branches generates severe competition for the securing of the same inputs and the sale of similar outputs. Furthermore, the least developed countries apply relentless pressure on the more developed for extensive economic aid and for the growth-inducing goods which could bolster their particular industrialization schemes. These pressures engender deep and numerous cleavages in the socialist camp.

In 1948 Yugoslavia was expelled from the bloc, supposedly for "revisionism." In 1961 Albania was, in its turn, ostracized by the USSR and the East European satellites, allegedly for "adventurism" and "dogmatism." But whatever the purported doctrinal differences, it is clear that both Yugoslavia and Albania had hoped to compel the Soviet Union and the other more developed countries to hand them more economic aid and more growth-inducing goods than these countries were willing to give.

The rise of China, the ensuing bipolarization of the bloc, and the clustering of the smaller countries around either the USSR or China portend even deeper conflicts in the socialist camp. The need to coordinate the outputs and the trade plans of at least some of these economies is acute, but efforts in this direction meet with almost insuperable difficulties. The interaction of some of these elements and the possible outcome are examined in the opening chapter of this part (Chapter 14).

The basic characteristic of the Soviet economic performance has been a persistent and significant rate of growth in income and industrial output. How does this result measure up to United States output? Can one actually make a meaningful comparison between the performances of two economies with different goals and different institutions and social organizations? What will be the outcome of a race in which one of the competitors, the United States, is both reluctantly involved and deeply committed? Chapter 15, which concludes this book, seeks to put into focus the over-all and sectoral achievements of the USSR, to review some problems involved in their measurement, and finally to compare the Soviet to the United States performance. In assessing the results of this race, the chapter stresses the idea that, for all practical purposes, Soviet policy makers may be only incidentally interested in outdistancing the United States in per-capita outputs of certain consumers' goods: the true objective of the Soviet regime during the next ten to fifteen years is overtaking the United States in the key industrial and military branches.

14.

Problems of Socialist Cooperation

PLANNING AND AUTARKY

Economically, the socialist camp is not exactly a great family sharing in some utopian way the investable resources of all. Each of the countries of this increasingly heterogeneous ideological "camp" is autonomous on the economic plane; i.e., each one's growth depends first and foremost on its own resources. Differences in factor endowments, however, difficulties in foreign trade with the West, and a general policy of developing mutual economic relations for a variety of political, strategic, and economic reasons render the output and foreign trade plans of some of these countries dependent in varying degrees on the output and foreign trade plans of all the others. Because the Soviet Union has advantages of size, resources, and level of industrial development and because the other countries, though less richly endowed, follow similar industrialization policies, the Soviet Union's output and foreign trade plans assume a cardinal position in relation to the output plans of some of these countries. In effect, the Soviet Union is the main supplier of industrial raw materials to CEMA's members and was for a time, at least, the key supplier of machinery to China. The output and development of certain basic East European industries — notably steel and chemicals — are increasingly dependent on Soviet supplies. On the other hand, the emergence of China as a center of power within the socialist camp increasingly limits the USSR's freedom of political and economic action. In time, China may lend its support not only to a small and insignificant country like Albania, but also to some other more important CEMA country ready and willing to assert its own demands vis-à-vis the USSR.

It has often been stated that national planning is by definition hostile to international trade since it disregards the needs and requirements of other countries. In the 1940's in "The Influence of National Economic Planning on Commercial Policy," Professor Jacob Viner stated, "The less the degree of dependence of a national economy in its ordinary operations on trade with other countries, the less, *ceteris paribus*, will be the difficulties of setting up and operating a comprehensive national economic plan." "There is planning logic, therefore," Viner added, "in the marked association in recent years between the movement toward comprehensive economic planning and the movement toward autarky, most conspicuous in Soviet Russia but by no means confined to it."

Statements like Viner's imply that the planned economy bent on balancing domestic supply and demand for a number of what it considers cardinal commodities necessarily omits any test of comparative advantage; in other words, the planned economy naturally tends to become autarkic since isolation from world market prices and trade fluctuations (on which that country's trade may have little or no influence) simplifies the tasks of domestic planning. Indeed, so long as the Soviet Union felt politically and militarily isolated, it restricted its foreign trade to a "tolerable minimum" — to borrow Viner's expression. But this changed rapidly when a number of other economies of the Soviet type came into being. The USSR expanded its foreign trade as it discovered that it could thus cushion the imbalances of its own output plans and as it established long-term foreign trade agreements ensuring that certain supplies which could help its own domestic plans would be available at fixed delivery periods and at stable prices.

It is now clear that foreign trade and comparative advantage may benefit a planned economy just as much if not more than a non-planned one. For countries like Czechoslovakia or Hungary, which are completely devoid of certain natural resources, restricting foreign trade to a "tolerable minimum" is simply suicidal. The emergence of a number of socialist economies has in fact opened up significant possibilities for interlocking their output and foreign trade plans and hence for vastly expanding mutual interchanges. And, indeed, this trade has expanded appreciably. Some of the basic output plans of certain Eastern European countries are now securely tied to the scheduled outputs of certain Soviet raw materials. If the division of labor, however, has not been broader, the explanation lies — outside power politics — in the difficulty of ascertaining, given the prevailing pricing systems, the kind or amounts of goods to be traded and in the dogmatic approach of most bloc policy makers to the problem of industrialization. Economic calculation and dogma are the key factors behind the reluctance of these countries to adjust both their short-term output plans and their long-term investment choices to the need for expanding their interchanges.

CALCULATION OF "EFFECTIVENESS" IN FOREIGN TRADE

The manipulation of prices within these countries complicates enormously the computation of the profitability of any given foreign trade operation. Let us note that Marxists do not reject the basic Ricardian approach to comparative advantage. Indeed, bloc economists stress that the objective of foreign trade is to save domestic labor; hence the smaller the socially necessary (domestic) labor embodied in exports relative to the socially necessary (domestic) labor used for producing the imported goods, the more profitable trade should be assumed to be. In practice, however, enormous difficulties were encountered in assessing the economic meaning of any inter-East European foreign trade operation, particularly before the price reforms of the late 1960's.

In the past, because of haphazard distortions of the price system in each country, primarily "coefficients of foreign exchange" were used for assessing the economic efficiency of a foreign-trade sale or purchase. Since the mid-1960's, with the introduction in each of these countries of new price systems uniformly based on the "supply-price concept," more meaningful comparisons have become possible between *domestic* and *foreign* prices. However, even though some dogmatic ideas concerning prices have now been overcome, the new price patterns still diverge in a variety of ways among the socialist countries. This occurs for several reasons: the "surplus" margins included in price are neither identical nor similarly distributed; domestic and foreign demand and supply pressures do not exercise the same impact on each country; the exchange rates are still more or less arbitrarily set; and so on.

In these conditions, as in the past, each foreign ministry computes, at various intervals, a so-called coefficient of foreign exchange, based on the country's export operations, and a so-called coefficient of domestic realization, based on its import operations. Involved in the computation of both coefficients are the domestic and foreign prices paid and obtained and the official rate of exchange. Assume that, in the case of Hungary, for instance, the established rate of exchange is $1 for 6 forints and 1 (old) ruble for 1.5 forints. Assume also that a given commodity is purchased by the exporting enterprise at 1,400 forints and sold for $200 (i.e., 1,200 forints at the official rate of exchange). The *coefficient of foreign exchange* is taken to be the ratio of the domestic price to the price obtained, computed at the official rate, i.e., 1,400 ÷ 1,200 = 1.16. The coefficient is then 16 per cent above parity. If the commodity is sold for $250 dollars, the coefficient is 0.93 (1,400 ÷ 1,500), i.e., 7 per cent below parity. The lower the coefficient, the more profitable a transaction is presumed to be. In the case of imports, if a commodity is purchased for 200 rubles and resold for 360 forints, the ruble has been "obtained" at the rate of 1.8 forints. This figure is called the *domestic rate of realization.* Since at the official rate of 1.5 forints 200 rubles equal only 300 forints, the *coefficient of domestic realization* is 1.20 (360 ÷ 300 = 1.20), or 20 per cent above parity. If the domestic sale price is 279, the coefficient of domestic realization is 0.93, or 7 per cent below parity. This time the operation is presumed to be unprofitable.

Obviously, since all the magnitudes involved — domestic price of an exported commodity, domestic price of an imported commodity, and rate of exchange — are distorted in various ways, these calculations at best allow a comparison between two foreign trade transactions of a closely related nature, but they can hardly serve as an indicator of what is actually occurring in foreign trade as a whole. The profit rates for producers' versus consumers' goods, differentiated for other purposes altogether, may make one export operation seem more profitable than another, when actually a loss is incurred. Some CEMA countries compute the differences between the foreign exchange obtained and that expended for importing the raw materials that are used in producing the given exports — a difference which may be relevant for balance of payments considerations but which no more furnishes a general criterion of "effectiveness" than the preceding computation. The difficulties appear compounded when one considers the problem of choosing whether to export a finished product, a semifinished product, or its basic raw material, and the need, for that purpose, of calculating value added at each stage of production. Furthermore, this trade moves in bilateral channels: thus, what must be evaluated and compared are the end results of given sets of export-import operations to be carried out with one country or another. No reliable criterion is available for ascertaining "profitability" when the domestic price differentiation does not reflect the underlying scarcities and when import-export operations must perforce be lumped together because trade is strictly confined to bilateral channels.

Further, the area policy makers are not satisfied with static considerations. They stress correctly that the division of labor between countries is not static; the development of each country on the basis of its own domestic plans changes the structure of its trade as well as the ratios of the socially necessary (domestic) labor for producing the goods exported and imported. But the vital initial question is how to draw up the domestic output and investment plans themselves and ensure that they are "realistic" in their assessment of the present and potential development of the respective country with regard to the goals pursued by its policy makers. In this respect, the policy makers of most of these economies are dogmatically committed to a policy of autarkic industrialization. There is thus an ideological block against taking into account the plans of other countries when drawing up long-term investment plans. In this case, dogma rather than the convenience of setting up an isolated domestic all-round plan appears to lend substance to Viner's statement.

Finally, the area's economists accept the logic of comparative advantage, but only after giving it a particular twist. Followers of Marx have many misgivings about resorting to the international price pattern in intrasocialist trade since, according to Marx, a more developed country is "always" in the position of exploiting a less developed one. In Marxian terms, "an advanced country is enabled to sell its goods above their value even when it sells them cheaper than the competing countries," whereas a less developed country "may offer more materialized labor in goods than it receives and yet it may receive in return commodities cheaper than it may produce them."[1] According to the Marxian argument, the split of the gains from trade is always against the underdeveloped country because of its lagging technology. The differences in technology account for the differences in the socially necessary labor for each product within the framework of any given economy. The inter-

1. K. *Marx,* Capital (*Untermann transl.*). *Chicago: Kerr & Co., 1909, Vol. III, pp.* 278–279.

national market reduces the socially necessary labor of any given commodity (and hence its value and price) to its level within the most advanced country. Thus, an underdeveloped country always relinquishes more "materialized labor" (value) than it gets in exchange.[2] Differences in technology may indeed go a long way in explaining the nature of foreign trade at any given moment. But it is meaningless to assert that, because of these differences, a ton of Soviet coal has more "value" than a ton of Polish coal or of any other goods of equivalent international price because the respective Soviet industry is more labor-intensive than the Polish one.

Since 1948, this theory of implicitly unequal exchange (more materialized labor of the underdeveloped country as against less labor of the more developed country) has been stressed by the Yugoslav Communists in order to indicate that unequal relations may also exist among socialist states. Although the Yugoslavs have been expelled from the bloc as revisionists for suggesting the possibility of socialist exploitation, the question of the utilization of the international price pattern in the socialist camp is still unsolved. In the various councils of CEMA, Soviet, Czech, and East German economists — the representatives of the more industrialized countries — have generally expressed agreement with the further utilization of the international price pattern, whereas Bulgarian and Rumanian economists have indicated serious reservations about this solution. Thus the Czech economist Vladimir Kaigl asserted that, in their present technological development, economies of the Soviet type could not evolve in their mutual trade a separate price structure completely severed from that of the world market. For this reason, he suggested that the gulf between developed and underdeveloped areas be bridged by other means than price manipulations and arbitrary deviations from world prices. On the other hand, the Rumanian economist Josef Anghel declared that the application

2. *To use a Ricardian-type illustration of comparative advantage, let country A devote 80 man-years to producing a certain quantity of wine and 90 man-years to producing a certain quantity of cloth. Let country B need to devote 100 man-years to producing the same quantity of cloth and 120 man-years to producing the wine. By exchanging country A's wine for country B's cloth, both countries would gain: in terms of the domestic cost of producing the cloth, A would save the labor of 10 man-years; B would gain in terms of the domestic cost of producing the wine the labor of 20 man-years. Here the Ricardian theory ends. For Marx, however, country A has gained from this exchange a net value of 20 man-years (100 received against 80 paid), whereas country B has incurred a net loss of 20 man-years (100 given up against 80).*

of world prices to area trade had "harmful effects" and that the role of the "law of value" must be limited in intrabloc relations. He suggested that mutual trade prices be "adjusted." Until now, however, the practical consequences of this suggestion have been minimal.

As we have pointed out, world prices are used as the "base" of intrabloc trade, but the prices are kept stable during the implementation of any given foreign trade contracts, so that volume, value, structure, and delivery periods of imports and exports may be securely tied to the domestic plans. In principle, each bloc seller should charge the same price to all bloc buyers of the same commodity, but there is some evidence that sellers may charge more than the world market price in transactions with purchasers who can offer only "soft" goods in exchange. In other words, monopoly positions arise and are put to use in the imperfect intrabloc market, particularly when substantial difficulties occur in the trade of these countries with non-bloc areas (e.g., the Western embargo on "strategic" goods). Discrimination is thus practiced among the members of the Eastern trading area: it is possible, however, that in some cases a level higher than world market prices exists on *both* sides of any given bilateral trade agreement.

The impossibility of carrying out meaningful economic calculations in foreign trade because of the distortion of bloc prices and the dogmatic approaches both to the Soviet strategy of development and its emphases and to foreign trade as viewed through Marx's theory of unequal exchanges thus have seriously impeded systematic broadening of the division of labor within the bloc.

CEMA: NATURE, ROLE, AND PERFORMANCE

In order to strengthen socialist cooperation, the Council of Economic Mutual Assistance (CEMA) was formed in January, 1949, by the Soviet Union and the Eastern European countries (East Germany, Poland, Czechoslovakia, Hungary, Rumania, Bulgaria, and Albania).[3] Among the Asian socialist countries (China, Outer Mongolia, North Korea, and North Vietnam), only Outer Mongolia has taken up membership in the Council. Since "optimal

3. *Albania was expelled from* CEMA *without any formalities after its official denunciation at the 22nd Congress of the Soviet Communist Party in October, 1961. Yugoslavia has, on the other hand, been admitted as an observer.*

proportions" between sectors and industrial branches at the scale of the bloc, even if they could be ascertained, could not be imposed on economically autonomous countries, the Council has only advisory and consultative functions. It may make recommendations, but it lacks the executive authority to enforce them. The Council has no fixed headquarters and meets about once a year in the capital of a different member country. At its sessions, it examines the recommendations of its expert commissions — now some thirty in number and of a permanent character since 1956 — each of which has its headquarters in the country best suited for its specific work. Thus, for example, the Soviet Union is host to CEMA's heavy metallurgy commission, Czechoslovakia to the machinery construction commission, East Germany to the chemical commission, Poland to the coal commission, Rumania to the oil and natural gas commission, and Bulgaria to the agricultural commission. On each commission sit the member countries' permanent representatives of the ministries and planning authorities concerned.

In the first years of CEMA's activity, the essential method of economic cooperation among the area countries was the establishment of long-term foreign trade agreements designed to guarantee the minimum supplies of basic materials needed for carrying out the independently drafted national output plans. Each country was attempting to reproduce in miniature the Soviet development, and at that time, coordination at the level of trade seemed to be the most appropriate method of "socialist cooperation." After a while, since the countries of the area began to glut their common market with a host of similar products, the problems of coordinating all the output plans and all investment plans began to receive increased attention, and CEMA was encouraged to turn its efforts to these issues. It was soon conceded that autarkic policies were harmful, that each country need not develop all the branches of heavy industry, and that cooperation was necessary precisely because all these countries were genuinely interested in increasing their interchanges of highly processed products.

Thus, it was recognized that each socialist economy need not reproduce in miniature the economy of the USSR, although each one was supposed to continue to implement the same strategy of development, with its emphasis on heavy industry. But insurmountable difficulties arose in determining concretely which particular branches of industry and which products should be developed for export and by whom — i.e., how the comparative costs of different output and trade patterns should be assessed within the area. Moreover, because of the prevailing patterns of organization, incentives, etc. — notably the emphasis on "reaching and surpassing" some gross value of output target — each industry, sector, region, or country tends in practice to insulate itself, guarantee its own supplies, produce its own spare parts, and break its own bottlenecks. In this sense, too, Viner's contention is vindicated: insulation is related to planning, provided that one applies this contention not only to each country, but also to each region, branch, industry, or plant.

As the area's market became glutted with identical products, however, coordination began to be worked out cautiously through technical and engineering decisions rather than by cost and price assessments. Each of CEMA's permanent commissions of experts started to examine and discuss each type of product, taking into account the production facilities offered by the various member countries. On this basis, specific technical and engineering apportionments of production among the member countries were recommended. The experts proposed, the Council recommended, and the various countries implemented, if they so decided, the specific decisions involved via their bilateral agreements. As a result of this extremely laborious procedure, certain plants in a given country were entrusted with production for the whole area. In some outstanding cases, certain industrial branches (e.g., the East German aviation industry) were converted to other purposes. In other cases, agreements were secured for dividing outputs of close specifications among a number of countries. In still other cases, the cooperation achieved consisted of establishing joint companies in which one country furnished the raw materials and the other the industrial facilities to exploit them. This step-by-step technical and engineering apportionment could, however, be upset or at least rendered of doubtful value if two important countries suddenly developed a very broad framework of bilateral cooperation (e.g., the Soviet-Czechoslovak agreement of the late 1950's, in which the two countries agreed to cooperate on production of a group of key commodities). It is difficult to know in what measure such agreements actually completed or canceled out the bloc-wide apportionments already suggested by CEMA commissions. It is certain however, that future bloc-wide apportionments will have to be adjusted to agreements already reached bilaterally by the most important members of the area.

During the next decade the more developed East European countries will attempt to gear some of their basic investment plans to the Soviet plans of investment and output in some key industrial branches. As the main exporter of iron ore in the bloc, the Soviet Union holds sway over the expansion of steel facilities in the whole East European area. The period of investment gestation in certain industries is extremely long, and the relevant decisions, therefore, must be taken immediately. This sort of coordination, however, concerns only certain key investments and affects only part of the foreign trade of the countries concerned; a large part of this trade both within Eastern Europe and with the West will still be governed by short-run considerations.

The transition from coordination at the level of trade to coordination at the levels of production is thus both cautious and one-sided, among other things because of the reluctance of the very large countries — the USSR and China — to relinquish any of their own basic decisions concerning their domestic investment choices. Among the smaller but differently endowed countries, a clear differentiation is occurring in this respect. Although Czechoslovakia and East Germany, for instance, are willing and ready to engage in a very broad division of labor both between themselves and at the scale of the area — since they have already attained a high level of technological development — the more backward countries of the area still hope to industrialize faster by travelling a more isolated road, i.e., by following not only the Soviet strategy of development but also its emphases, thus avoiding too rapid and detailed a division of labor in the socialist camp as a whole.

PRICES AND MULTILATERAL COMPENSATION

After the 1961 ruble reform, the Soviet Minister of Finance claimed that the new Soviet rate of exchange conformed to the actual relations of the purchasing power of currencies. He added that this exchange rate would facilitate comparisons between world prices and the average Soviet wholesale prices, since at this exchange rate, the former would be brought to the level of the latter, thus allowing a clearer valuation of the relative profitability of each export and import operation. The statement received credence in the West, but with qualifications. Professor Morris Bornstein agrees that the devaluation of the old ruble has actually brought the Soviet average price level into closer agreement with world market prices converted into rubles at the new rate. He has, however, correctly pointed out that this measure could not be viewed as sufficient in itself for solving the problems of computing the profitability of Soviet trade since it did not affect in any way the distortions prevailing in the domestic structure of Soviet prices.[4] Until now, no one has proposed the adoption of the Soviet price pattern in intrabloc transactions. Such adoption would make the foreign trade ruble convertible within the limits of the trade agreements into goods at the delivery prices prevailing in the USSR. The divergences between the Soviet price pattern and that of each other country is of such nature, however, that no one could ascertain who in the area would benefit and in what amount from any foreign trade transaction carried on at Soviet prices.

As already indicated, the prevailing system of bilateral agreements and clearing eliminates the need for the transfer of currencies as imbalances appear during, or after, the period set for carrying out a given commercial agreement. The balances may be covered by transfer of commodities, similar to the commodities included in the trade agreements and at the previously established prices, or through the already discussed arrangements through the IBEC. The limited attraction of the nonconvertible "transferable" ruble, and of the goods that might be purchased with it by the net exporters, and the incapacity of the net importers to adjust to unexpected export demands (over and above the obligations incurred via bilateral agreements) restrict the amounts of clearing rubles which each CEMA country can and is willing to accept. This kind of limited arrangement, similar in some points to the one that prevailed in the defunct European Payments Union, could be expanded only if the balances built in clearing rubles could be readily converted into gold. Given the restrictions prevailing even after the formation of IBEC, the avowed need to ensure planned supplies and hence the preference for bilateral arrangements, the scarcity of certain key exportable goods above and beyond the plan, the need to limit the amounts of freely convertible clearing rubles and to provide for the conversion of the latter into gold up to a

4. *Morris Bornstein, "The Reform and Revaluation of the Ruble,"* The American Economic Review, *March, 1961, p. 120.*

certain amount — all these elements, along with other factors, are likely to keep multilateral compensation within narrow margins.

CONCLUDING COMMENTS

The monopoly of foreign trade has proved to be an important political defensive and offensive tool for the USSR. Defensively, the monopoly has ensured maximum protection against capitalist competition and maximum assistance to the national plan because it has made imports from every source dependent on plan needs and has tailored exports to pay for the required imports. As an instrument of political attack, the monopoly has ensured the Soviet Union's freedom to shift rapidly from one market to another, to adjust purchases and sales to political considerations,[5] and to maximize the impact of its operations, especially when the international market is in distress. In fact, the more unsettled the world market, the more effective the monopoly appears as an instrument of commercial warfare. Furthermore, the more delicate the balance of power in the so-called non-committed countries, the more powerful looms the Soviet capacity to adjust its trade to its political objectives. Since 1954, systematically and in strict accordance with those objectives, the Soviet Union has expanded its trade with, and aid to, underdeveloped areas. It has concentrated its efforts on a few key spots: in the Middle East, notably on Egypt; in Asia, particularly on India. The USSR, Czechoslovakia, and China are now a source of military supplies for almost any group or faction ready to take arms against the West. In periods of international tension there is always talk in the West of counteracting the Soviet monopoly of foreign trade by creating a similar foreign trade monopoly on either a national or an international scale. Such a move, however, is extremely difficult to implement within

5. *The rapid adjustment of Soviet foreign trade and aid to political considerations can best be observed in the case of former bloc countries. Immediately after the political denunciation of Albania, the USSR discarded its trade agreement with that country, cancelled its credits for the period 1961–65, withdrew the Soviet technicians from Albania, and expelled the Albanian students and cadets from the Soviet Union. Khrushchev thus applied in 1961 exactly the same gamut of economic measures that Stalin did in 1948 when he expelled Yugoslavia. The same measures were also taken against China.*

the framework of free enterprise economies, and as yet no specific measures have been taken to this end.

The pursuit of industrialization in the socialist countries and the implementation of the Soviet strategy and techniques of economic development by each of these economies have made Soviet plans the hub of the plans of many of these countries. The Soviet share in the world's trade has increased from slightly over 1 per cent in 1938 to nearly 5 per cent in 1965; three-quarters of this increase is accounted for by trade within CEMA. In 1965, the USSR accounted for over 30 per cent of the foreign trade turnover (imports plus exports) of Poland and Hungary, over 35 per cent of the foreign trade of Czechoslovakia, and 50 per cent or more of the trade of the other CEMA countries. Deliberate industrialization has facilitated imports of Soviet raw materials into Eastern Europe and exports of East European manufactured goods to the Soviet market. On the other hand, as in the past, the Soviet Union is on balance a net importer of machinery.[6]

Until now, division of labor in the bloc has occurred on two different planes. On one plane are the decisions concerning the technical and engineering apportionment of various outputs according to existing plant facilities in this or that country; engineering science thus attempts to provide the answers which distorted costs and prices cannot give. On the other, East European decisions about investment in certain branches of industry during the next decades are planned according to the scheduled availability of raw materials, mostly from Soviet sources. A limited adjustment will most probably occur on this second plane between one or another East European country. It should be noted that this second type of coordination arises, at least in part, because these countries cannot secure

6. *The following table shows the changes in the structure of Soviet foreign trade:*

	Percentage of Total Exports					Percentage of Total Imports				
	1913	1928	1938	1958	1965	1913	1928	1938	1958	1965
Machinery and equipment	0.3	0.1	5.0	18.5	20.0	15.9	23.9	34.5	24.5	33.4
Fuels and raw materials	42.8	63.1	57.7	65.9	69.2	63.4	67.8	60.7	51.6	32.2
Grains	33.3	3.3	21.3	8.3	} 10.8	—	—	—	—	—
Consumers' goods	23.6	33.5	16.0	7.3		20.7	8.3	4.8	23.9	34.4

SOURCE: *Narodnoe Khoziastvo SSSR v 1958*, op. cit., pp. 800–01, and *ibid.*, 1965, pp. 673–4.

certain raw materials from non-bloc sources.

In the short run, planning of the Soviet type creates serious bottlenecks in some branches and "unplanned" surpluses in others. Trade is and will be welcomed in so far as it can cure some of these imbalances. Certain imports may indeed break impending bottlenecks, whereas certain exports may serve as an outlet for certain surpluses, even such surpluses as obsolete military equipment. Thus, the intra-CEMA market and the trade with the underdeveloped areas can and undoubtedly will cushion some of the imbalances of the growing outputs of the USSR. On the other hand, it is also true that overriding political considerations will lead the USSR to export capital goods to, say, Southeast Asia or the Middle East, against raw materials and consumers' goods, even though in terms of the emphases of Soviet planning this may slow the pace of Soviet capital formation and lead to "unwanted" increases in the share of domestic consumption.[7]

Soviet economists declare that the CEMA trade is "a new type of trade" in which the partners enjoy "full equality," in contrast to the relations prevailing in the capitalist world markets. It is stated that equality arises because the clearing operations are carried on simultaneously by the appropriate organization of *both* partners, not by only one of the two; and that equality is ensured by the fact that "the law of value does not operate anarchically," but is kept under control with prices being established on the basis of "mutual interest and voluntary understanding." Actually, having both partners keep the record of their operations is a simple double-checking procedure rather than a sign of "equality." As far as prices are concerned, whether they are kept stable or not is irrelevant to the questions of equality and mutual interest. Finally, the procedure of omitting prices in the basic trade agreements and of leaving them to be decided afterwards in the contracts concluded by the export and import agencies often places the weaker country completely at the mercy of the stronger partner. Characteristically, in trade with capitalist countries, the prices set by the Soviet agencies have always been a sore point. Quite often these prices have proved higher than international prices and quality has been lower, so that many countries have had serious difficulties in implementing their trade agree-

7. *Sino-Soviet credits to the underdeveloped areas from the beginning of 1954 to the end of 1960 amounted to $4.584 billion, of which $3.461 billion was economic aid. Of the total, $1.881 billion went to the Middle East.*

ments with the Soviet Union.

All in all, the balance sheet of socialist cooperation is a very mixed one. In the first two decades following CEMA's formation, the joint efforts of its member states built the "friendship" pipeline, created a railway car pool (with over 100,000 cars), linked their energy supply system, established some joint cooperation in certain industries, founded the IBEC, exchanged a vast amount of engineering information, and helped dovetail certain physical flows of materials needed for their respective domestic plans. But, on the other hand, socialist "cooperation" has been rent by dramatic crises leading notably to complete breaks in foreign trade – e.g., with Yugoslavia, Albania, and China. Most of the small East European countries remain heavily dependent on Soviet raw materials or on the Soviet market for their manufactured goods and are for all practical purposes at the mercy of their powerful partner – unless they can succeed in becoming more competitive than in the past in the world markets and unless true opportunities open up for them for trading with the West.

15.

Competition and Convergence

DIFFERENCES IN GOALS AND IN RESOURCE ALLOCATION

The process of industrialization, i.e., economic development, may occur at varying speeds. The pace of development is ascertained by gauging the rates of growth of various aggregates, such as gross or net value of industrial output; GNP, its origin components and end-uses; and per capita income. In a less general fashion, the pace of development may also be measured by determining the rate of growth of some specific physical outputs, the fluctuation in the labor force and its components, and so on.

Attempts to reduce the multidimensional process of growth and the variety of structural changes which it entails to some undimensional aggregative value measurement meet numerous and in some respects insuperable difficulties. Some of these difficulties were discussed in Chapter 8, when we dealt with the so-called index problem in relation to changes over time in Soviet GNP and its components. To the difficulty of aggregating different products changing quantitatively over time into a generalized product total, a special difficulty is added when one attempts interspatial comparisons. The new problem involves linking the various sets of value aggregates and all their changes as measured in different value terms. This linking may be done in a number of ways, for there is a variety of weighting patterns and conversion ratios rather than one definite solution, and the choice of any one link leads to different results, all equally legitimate statistically.

How then should one treat these various solutions? To answer this question, let us recall the specific limitations of the data which we are handling. Income and product data are regarded as the best indicators of a country's economic capability; changes in per capita income are considered the most appropriate measure of its economic growth. But there are different opinions about what income actually is. We have examined the divergences in this area between the Soviet and the Western schools, and there are differences within the West besides. Once this first hurdle has been surmounted, one may note that in a developing economy, money income may increase faster than real output of goods and services, as certain kinds of goods previously produced within the household (food and clothing, for example,) begin to be manufactured by firms working for the market. Since growth involves the contraction of the non-market sector, measures of money income tend to overstate the pace of growth of such countries and consequently exaggerate differences between countries. Furthermore, linking these magnitudes by exchange rate conversions may be misleading, because exchange rates diverge from the purchasing parities of the currencies in which these aggregates are computed.

To circumvent the difficulties involved in using money incomes, the GNPs of two or more countries might be linked by using the price pattern prevailing in any one country: the goods and services produced in, say, countries X and Y could be computed in the price pattern prevailing in either X or Y, or in both of them. But price patterns differ sharply because of divergences in underlying scarcities, disparities in the spread of technology in each sector and branch, etc. The value of, say, one ruble compared to that of one dollar may be greater or smaller in the purchase of one type of good rather than of another. Thus, the utilization of any one price pattern will tend to overstate certain outputs relative to others and will yield completely different ratios between the magnitudes involved as compared with the results obtained when another price pattern is used. Each set of results will be meaningful only in terms of the price pattern used. It is entirely futile to try to extract a single general answer out of a variety of diverging results by computing the geometric means between them, for instance; for there is no such thing as an abstract price pattern "in between" the patterns prevailing in either X or Y. The economist can only choose weighting procedure as judiciously as possible, explain his methodology, and underline the limited validity of his results.

Let us note finally that composition of the respective GNPs (and of each of their components) may be as decisive a factor as relative size in determining the respective growth potentialities of various economies. Although Soviet GNP is substantially smaller than that of the United States, its different utilization enables the USSR to match United States military capabilities and allows that country to expand its industry more rapidly than the United States. The vast differences between the two nations' utilization of their respective GNPs and their components are but a reflection of the vast differences in the goals, institutions, and socioeconomic environment of the two countries. Comparisons of aggregative data between countries so differently oriented may easily be biased or misleading. The best one can do is to determine clearly the relevance of each comparison he makes to any given issue and, by means of a variety of supplementary data, such as physical output figures, to give each of his comparisons as many additional dimensions as possible.

Now that we have made these necessary qualifications, let us turn to some of the pertinent data for Soviet–United States comparisons.[1] Consider first the relative shares of GNP by their end-uses and the factor payments generated in production in both the USSR and the United States, as valued in their respective prices. In non-war years, gross investment in the Soviet economy has been about 27 per cent of GNP (at adjusted current rubles); whereas consumption by households has fluctuated roughly between 60 and 63 per cent.[2] In the United States, investment has been smaller in relative terms: it has oscillated between 16 and 20 per cent of GNP, whereas consumption of households has ranged from 60 to 75 per cent. Soviet investment effort is thus consistently larger than that of the United States.

Secondly, consider the structure of the national income. Given the character of the underlying data, the sectoral contribution to income is somewhat distorted and more difficult to adjust: broadly, however, these data reflect the differences in resource allocation already observed in the pattern of employment. In 1955 only 37 per cent of Soviet 1955 income was generated in industry, as against 41 per cent in the United States; the share of Soviet agriculture far exceeded and that of Soviet services fell substantially short of the respective relative shares in United States income. Agriculture,

1. *This chapter draws heavily on the excellent materials presented by specialists to the hearings of the Joint Economic Committee of the 86th Congress and released in the three-part report,* Comparisons of the United States and Soviet Economies, *Washington, D.C., 1959.*

2. *See Chap.* 8.

that vast and still far from efficient sector of the Soviet economy, accounted for as much as 27 per cent of Soviet income as against only 4.6 per cent for the United States.

According to the computations of Professor Morris Bornstein, Soviet and American GNP, measured in Soviet prices, were in 1955 1,285 and 4,802 billion rubles, respectively, and the ratio between them was thus only 26.8.[3] Measured in United States prices, Soviet income was of the order of $212 billion as against $397 billion for the United States, and their ratio stood at 53.4. These large differences occur because goods with relatively lower (higher) prices in either the United States or the USSR are produced in the respective countries in larger (smaller) quantities, so that in comparing the two GNPs, a greater price weight is given to the goods more abundantly produced in the USSR when dollars are used, and conversely, a greater price weight is given to the goods produced more abundantly in the United States when rubles are used. Since the question of the respective sizes of the contrasted GNPs eludes a single answer, one may perhaps consider further the implications of the dollar valuation, since it is cast in more familiar though no more meaningful terms than the ruble valuation. Again according to Bornstein, whereas the ratios between the two GNPs were 53.4, the ratios of consumption were only 39.0, of investments, 68.3, of defense, 94.3, and of government administration, 152.1. Although Soviet GNP per capita was of the order of 44 per cent of that of the United States, Soviet consumption per capita was less than one-third that of the United States. Thus, in 1955, from an income half as large as the American income for that year, the USSR invested an amount equivalent to 68 per cent of United States total investment and spent on defense a sum equivalent to 94 per cent of United States expenditures. Subsequent computations indicate that by 1960 the total Soviet investment effort was probably on a par with that of the United States. Since the size and structure of Soviet capital investment are determined by the regime, Soviet investment in producer durable equipment expanded methodically throughout the 1950's, finally matching the United States effort; Soviet investment in industry, in agriculture, and in transport and communications has probably exceeded the respective United States total from 1959 on. Whereas in the USSR only one-third of total investments

3. *Bornstein's estimate of Soviet income in 1955 is slightly larger than that presented in Chapter 8.*

was directed into housing services and sociocultural areas, in the United States, where consumer demand carries much more weight, from 50 to 60 per cent of the total went for these purposes.

Parity of annual productive investments suggests near parity of absolute increments in GNP because of the USSR's introduction in certain branches of the most modern technology, more intensive utilization of equipment, and greater specialization of output—all of which offset up to a point small productivity in various other branches. This seems consistent with an estimated average yearly growth rate in the GNP through the 1950's of over 7 per cent in the USSR and of less than 3 per cent in the United States.[4] However, notwithstanding the systematic allocation of as much as one quarter of its GNP to investment to a single-minded emphasis on growth-inducing and technologically well-equipped industries (an allocation that ultimately probably matched total United States investment in dollar value), the Soviets were not able to keep up a high rate of growth throughout the 1960's. The Russians failed to outpace the United States significantly and experienced, as we have already stated, a severe loss in economic dynamism; according to their own statistics, their over-all growth rate declined to 5 per cent. The underlying causes of the slackening in growth rates of total product and of industrial output and productivity in the USSR and in Eastern Europe were multiple. The growth achievable through expansion and commissioning of *new* plants in the privileged sectors, the traditional recipients of the bulk of investments, tended to diminish. Second, the over-all gains in output in the leading heavy manufacturing and mining sectors could no more offset the increasing loss in momentum occurring in most of the consumers' goods branches. Large strata of consumers, dissatisfied with the low quality and assortment of consumers' goods, virtually boycotted them and finally forced, as we already indicated, certain changes in investment allocation, planning, and management. The yearly rates of growth in total product through the late 1960's oscillated finally between 4.5 to 5.5 per cent for the USSR, as opposed to 4.0 to 4.5 per cent for the United States. In historical perspective, the Russians experienced both a broadly declining secular trend in growth rates and fluctuations of a cyclical nature within broad quinquennial or decennial periods. The claims that a planned economy of the Soviet type can always achieve higher growth rates in total and per-capita product than capitalism and that it can achieve them steadily proved without foundation in fact. Such claims completely overlook the differences among economies in factor endowments, size, capital-output ratios, and so on; moreover, they gloss over the impact which investment fluctuations, differences in project implementation and maturation, and failure of the various plans to mesh exercise on the yearly growth rates of any economy.

OVER-ALL PERFORMANCE AND THE CONSUMER

Heavy industry, the sector favored by Soviet policy makers, has shown persistently high rates of growth for machine tools, metal working, fuel and power, since, in conformity with their principle of providing integrally for activities with top priority and of tackling other priorities serially, the Soviets have concentrated their principal efforts, their best brains, and their highest-quality inputs in their preferred industries. In order to maximize the effectiveness of their capital outlays within each industry, the Soviets concentrated their attention further on the main processes in the decisive branches of these key industries. As a result of this high degree of selectivity, even the most modern Soviet industries are a composite of sharply differing technological blocks, ranging from advanced capital-intensive processes to rather backward labor-intensive auxiliary services. But this very unevenness is an expression of economical use of scarce resources, awareness of the great impact of selective technical improvements, and flexibility in the utilization of investments despite the Soviet bureaucratic environment. The close cooperation of industry with various technological institutes, the emphasis on research, immediate introduction of the newest techniques in these expanding key branches, the possibility of "popularizing" techniques throughout a whole industrial branch by direct training and exchange of workers among plants — are all clear advantages which may noticeably and rapidly improve the performance of some of these industries. The Soviets are now bidding strongly for world technological leadership and are pressing at the frontiers of research and development not in spite of, but because of, their incredible concentration of means in the key industries and processes.

4. *For a detailed discussion of this question see* A. Bergson, The Real National Income of Soviet Russia since 1928, *op. cit., chap. 14, p. 259ff.*

According to official Soviet claims, this very unevenly developed industry produced about 47 per cent of United States industrial output in 1957 and, 65 per cent of the United States industrial output in 1965. Western estimates place the Soviet industrial output of 1960 at only between 50 and 55 per cent of American output. Whatever the precise percentage may be, one must note that the total subsumes different production ratios and different utilization of industrial commodities. That the USSR produced, say, 50 per cent of the United States output does not, of course, imply that its growth capacity and military capabilities were half as large as those of the United States. What we have said for the national product as a whole holds good also for each output; namely, that the pattern of utilization may be of paramount importance when assessing the growth potentialities of an economy. Soviet steel output in 1955, for instance, equaled the United States steel output of 1913. But in the USSR, the preponderant share of this output went to heavy industry and defense; moreover, technology in the 1950's was totally different from that of the 1910's, so that efficiency in use was obviously incomparably higher in the USSR in 1955 than in the United States in 1913.

The rate of growth of Soviet industrial output has actually been consistently higher than that of the United States. According to the detailed computations of Kaplan and Moorsteen, to which we referred in Chapter 8, the Soviets doubled the volume of their industrial output between 1950 and 1958. During that period, the volume of industrial production grew at the rate of 9.2 per cent per year, of machine tools at 8 per cent, of other producers' goods at 9.5 per cent, and of consumers goods at 9.4 per cent. The increment in physical outputs of certain basic commodities — electric power, oil, gas, coal, steel, mineral fertilizer, sulfuric acid, and so on — were massive and even exceeded the American increments during the 1950's, but by the mid-1960's the Soviet Union still remained significantly behind the United States. In electric power — the crucial production in which the Soviet Union has truly made a decisive effort — the Soviet-United States output ratio stood in the mid-1960's at 42. The Soviet positions were, however, much more favorable in the output of primary energy (gas, oil, and coal), where the ratios stood at 53, 92, and 122 respectively. Finally, in the mid-1960's, the Soviet Union reached 75 per cent of the American steel output. Given the vigorous growth of industry in the United States and the alleged "competition" in which the Soviet industry is engaged with it, the Soviet government has to continue to work on the assumption that the basic Soviet industrial plant must be expanded further. The Soviet leadership deems it necessary to add new productive capacities in fuel, power, metals, machinery, chemicals, and so on, on a large scale. In addition, it also assumes that it must ward off, on the one hand, the pressures of the less-developed socialist countries for more massive Soviet development aid, and on the other hand, the domestic pressures for substantial increases in consumers' welfare. The slogans of "competition with capitalism" and of the Soviet Union's race to "catch up with and surpass the United States" thus serve as a convenient pretext for furthering Soviet national interests, suppressing any serious centrifugal tendencies within CEMA (*vide* Hungary, Czechoslovakia, Romania) and for perpetuating the inequalities of development within the socialist camp in general.

In contrast to their concentrated effort in the key industrial branches, the Soviets have, as we know, neglected the consumers' goods industries and have assigned a low priority to agriculture. Because of the lopsided character of their investment, not only have their per capita consumer goals remained significantly smaller than in the West, but the goods produced are of a notoriously poor quality. Shoddy goods remain typical for certain consumers' goods industries just as highly advanced "space-ships" and rockets are now typical of the military and capital goods industries.

As we have noted, agriculture stagnated until the mid-1950's but has since then forged ahead. Although the aim of rapidly extracting a large marketed share of grain has led to brutal collectivization of the countryside, stagnating output, massive loss of livestock, and a declining income trend in the villages, there have been substantial changes in this sector since the mid-1950's. The exact prospects for growth in output remain difficult to ascertain, however, because Soviet agricultural statistics are of very doubtful reliability. Soviet agriculture uses much more manpower and land than American agriculture does, is far less mechanized, and has low yields per acre and per capita. Its mechanical power has essentially replaced animal power, rather than contributed to saving labor. Whereas the Soviet regime is pushing relentlessly for further increases in output and in the marketed share of grain, the United States is wrestling with the opposite problem, namely, finding markets for its large agricultural surpluses. Moreover, differences in dietetic patterns mean that, while the Soviets seek to increase certain outputs, butter and potatoes, for example, the United States is trying to decrease them. As a result, the Soviets may rapidly gain on the United States in these products. Notwithstanding larger resources devoted to agriculture in the USSR and output restrictions in the United States, according to official Soviet computations, the Soviet-American ratios for key agricultural outputs in 1959 were as follows: for all types of grains, 68 (wheat 225, but corn, 0.10); for potatoes (the typical food of low-income diets), 781; for milk (only half the United States production in 1953) 109; for butter 129, but for meat 48, and for eggs only 38.[5] Although the USSR is still far below American per capita levels for meat and eggs, it is close to the United States average for milk and has already surpassed it in butter, since American butter production has contracted rapidly upon public response to warnings against cholesterol in solid fat. According to data prepared by Professors D. Gale Johnson and Arcadius Kahan, between 1928 and 1955–57, average product per agricultural worker rose between 36 and 43 per cent in the Soviet Union, and by some 149 per cent in the United States. The Soviet prospect is for more rapid growth in the next decade, even though agriculture will remain beset by a substantial amount of disguised unemployment.

There is a striking contrast between Soviet and American patterns of resource allocation in transportation because of both factor endowment and selected direction of growth. In this crucial field, it is particularly difficult to appraise aspects of the Soviet economy by the standards usually applied to free-enterprise economies. As pointed out by Holland Hunter and by Ernest W. Williams, Jr., "the answers to the desirable roles of the several forms of transport which emerge under our regulatory and promotional system in servicing a free enterprise economy depart sharply from those which emerge from the Soviet planning approach." The Soviet transportation system is characterized by intensive utilization of the railroad plant, with methodically planned high traffic density and even flow of traffic over time, and limited investment in other facilities, particularly in highways, inland waterways, pipelines, etc. The very emphasis on heavy industry requires a strong effort to

5. *These data are from* Narodnoe khoziaistvo SSSR v 1959 [*The National Economy of the USSR in 1959*], Op. cit., *pp. 104–111.*

minimize inputs into transportation as a whole, while ensuring the accomplishment of the key planned tasks. Whereas the United States railroad plant had to be built ahead of the development of traffic and is now substantially overbuilt, in the USSR there is no competition among railroads and there is little competition between railroads and other forms of transportation. The American transportation system carries twice as much total freight traffic as the Soviet system, but in rail freight traffic the Soviet–United States ratio is 2:1. It is in transport by inland waterways, motor trucks, and pipelines that the USSR lags far behind the United States.

Although high-speed industrialization has long ago achieved for the USSR the conditions of "take-off into self-sustained growth," the planners do not gear their industrial machine toward "the age of high mass consumption," to use W. W. Rostow's terminology. The American economy has reached its present high output level by more than a hundred years of steady growth; throughout this period, the share of consumption has actually stayed at relatively high levels. In contrast, in the USSR between 1928 and 1950, the output of consumers' goods rose only very slowly. According to Professor Lynn Turgeon, the output of Soviet light and food processing industries is hardly more than half that of the United States, and the Russians have 30 million more people to feed and clothe. In the rural areas of the USSR, however, more people rely on homegrown food. If Soviet per capita food consumption is now slightly above half that of the United States and the clothing consumption is somewhat less than half, the American consumer's great advantage over his Soviet counterpart continues to be centered in the field of consumer durables and services. The Russians may close the gap in respect to food and clothing in the not too distant future, but their policy makers do not envisage the same pattern of per capita durable consumers' goods utilization as prevails in the United States.

Since the mid-1960's rising trends in disposable money incomes – brought about by increased wages, liberalized social insurance payments, and increased money incomes of the collective farmers – have fostered growing strains in the provision of personal services, transportation, lodging, retailing, and similar areas. Despite increased investments in these directions, expansion of facilities remains grossly inadequate. According to Western calculations, through the decade between the mid-1950's and the mid-1960's, the following patterns of growth occurred in respect to consumption categories. The yearly growth rate in food consumption was either low or declining; that of services was higher than that of food and was generally rising; that for soft goods was greater, though tending to slow down; finally, that of durables was rising steadily and markedly. Among the most decisive efforts in Soviet attempts to expand consumption categories is the program of developing passenger-car output, with the goal of over one million cars per year by 1975, an output still oriented primarily toward the needs of the bureaucratic managerial elite. Typically, the Soviet Union produced in the mid-1960's only 5.5 per cent of the American motor-vehicle output, and only 2.2 per cent of the American passenger-car output. The scheduled 1975 production – based on the construction in the USSR of an Italian Fiat plant using United States machine tools – would bring the Soviet Union closer to the automotive age, but by 1975 the USSR will still be left with an automobile stock roughly equal to that of the United States in 1917 and on a per capita basis with about 5 per cent of the current United States inventory. Thus, despite the new efforts in the direction of consumers' welfare, much remains to be done. Indeed Soviet per capita consumption, which was about 27 per cent of the United States per capita consumption in the mid-1950's, still reached less than one third of the United States standard by the mid-1960's. The efforts in this direction, however, do not require as yet any significant alteration in the traditional Soviet economic priorities.

PROJECTIONS OF COMPARATIVE GROWTH

According to estimates we have already mentioned, the average annual rate of growth of GNP in the USSR in the 1950's was more than 7 per cent, as compared to slightly less than 3 per cent for the United States. If the Soviet–United States income ratio stood at roughly 55 in the mid-1950's, and the indicated comparative rates would have continued, the Russians would have caught up with the United States in the 1970's. Actually, the rates of growth changed in the 1960's and the relative positions have remained roughly the same as in the 1950's. An impressionistic idea about the respective position of the two powers in levels of aggregate industrial output over the next decades is given in Table 13. Again assuming that in the starting year, the Soviet–United

States industrial output ratio was about 50:60, the table shows the number of years Soviet industry will need to catch up with United States industry, given various rates for the two contenders. At the Kaplan-Moorsteen estimate for the 1950's of a roughly 9 per cent rate of growth for the USSR as against 3 per cent for the United States, Soviet industrial output would reach that of the United States in the 1980's. Incidentally, the *Draft Program of the Communist Party* for 1960–80 uses precisely this kind of differential rate for claiming that the Soviet Union will "leave the U.S. output far behind" by 1980. But this is only an impressionistic projection with nothing final about it. As the Soviet Union industrial machine expands, competing needs appear for increased consumption, for larger exports of growth-inducing products to socialist underdeveloped areas, etc. Thus, Soviet policy makers have the problem of keeping consumption in relative terms at about the same plateau of, say, 60 per cent of GNP, and of not over-extending foreign commitments, so that domestic investment and military expenditures can be kept at their previous relative levels. As we shall see, there is a strong possibility of maintaining the current high rate of growth during the relatively short period of ten to fifteen years in which the Soviet policy makers are crucially interested, but what will happen to United States rates of growth in the meantime is not yet certain and this, of course, is equally decisive for the comparison with which we are concerned.

TABLE 13. *Projected Industrial Growth Rates, USSR and the United States*

USSR Rates of Industrial Growth	*United States Rates of Industrial Growth* 2%	3%	4%
7%	17 years	21 years	28 years
8	14	17	21
9	12	14	17
10	11	12	14

The gap between the socialist camp and the rest of the world remains very large. At the end of the 1950's, the Sino-Soviet camp as a whole, comprising 26 per cent of the world's surface and well over one-third of its population, produced less than one-third of the world's industrial output. In 1959, the camp produced some 35 per cent of the world's pig iron, 30 per cent of its steel, 50 per cent of its coal, 15 per cent of its oil, 20 per cent of its electrical power, 26 per cent of its cement, 31 per cent of its lumber, and between 20 and 30 per cent of a variety of consumers' goods. Thus, the gap between the two worlds is large, and the temptation to change the relationship of forces by means other than peaceful economic competition is extremely strong. One should note, however, that the decisive element in the near future may be neither the present Soviet–United States nor the over-all socialist posture, but the result of the battle of *science* and *technology* waged between the USSR and the United States. The outcome of this battle will ultimately determine both the military strength and the growth potentials of the two power groupings. Among the chief goals of modern science and technology is the control of thermonuclear reactions so that nuclear energy may be released slowly instead of producing vast explosions. A breakthrough in this field would provide an unlimited source of energy and open new and incredibly vast avenues for industrial growth.

THE SOVIET MODUS OPERANDI AND ITS ADVANTAGES

For relatively short critical growth periods, developmental planning and "war economy" procedures may prove better instruments for achieving rapid growth than the profit system and the market mechanism. For industry at least, the operation of the Soviet economy on the basis of a given development strategy, combined with improved modern planning methods, may yield results matching those obtained by the play of market forces in the developed economies. The following factors have enabled the Soviet system to achieve certain striking successes: 1] capacity to attain high rates of capital accumulation because of the high concentration of both political and economic power in the hands of the government, the absence of demand problems, and the lack of certain types of labor problems (work stoppages, etc.); 2] ability to concentrate heavily on research, to bring technological advances into certain selected areas rapidly, and to enforce the spread of such advances without concern about interfirm competition; 3] a feedback mechanism rendered increasingly responsive to changes in industrial production; 4] the capacity for working toward a target for decades without deviation. In a profit-directed economy, the needs of consumers — not maximum growth and an ever-expanding heavy industry — are the primary concern of producers. Economic growth may become a government preoccupation, but if government preferences clash with consumers' wants (in peacetime, of course), government has no guarantee of success. For in a free economy, consumers have stronger means of influencing both production and governmental action than they have in a centrally planned economy.

If centralized decision on investment and their strategy of development have paid off for the Soviet planners in terms of growth in key strategic industrial and military branches, their long-term blindness with respect to pricing, their bureaucratic emphasis on commands rather than on appropriate incentives, and their deep commitment to overcentralization and bureaucratic proliferation have in many respects offset some of the advantages accruing from their capacity to carry out the key priorities resolutely. As we have seen, however, the Soviet system has room for combining centralization of basic investment decisions with more decentralization of output and with flexibility of plan implementation.

Can the growth rates secured so far be maintained in the future? The consensus is that as higher and higher levels of output are reached, declining rates of growth will tend to set in because it becomes progressively more difficult to increase the growth rate by increasing the relative size of the capital goods sectors as compared to the consumers' goods industries. If we designate the percentage of total investment devoted to sector I of the Marxian schema as ϕ, with I standing for total investment, we may write $I_I = \phi I$, and $\phi = I_I/I$. A ceiling will be set by the minimum rate of expansion of sector II required for supplying the consumption needs of the additional workers employed in sector I. As formulated by Maurice Dobb,[6] methodically raising ϕ in order to attain higher rates of growth requires a faster expansion in employment than in consumers' goods output and hence a permanent reduction in consumption. In order to avoid this permanent reduction, real wages might be allowed to fall during only a given period until the desired potential was reached; then ϕ could be reduced while wages were raised. This solution, however, would produce a lower rate of growth during the latter period.

6. *Maurice Dobb,* An Essay on Economic Growth and Planning (*London: Routledge and Kegan Paul, 1960*), *pp. 66–75.*

The considerations just cited ignore technical innovations which could ensure a rise in ϕ without a fall in the per capita availability of consumers' goods. This is actually what has happened, except in the early decades of Soviet planning. Furthermore, the extremely disparate structure of Soviet industry may present a special type of advantage in respect to investment opportunities. Since each plant, industry, and branch is a composite of a variety of technological blocks, the Russians may be able to shift the pattern of investment without running into diminishing returns — a possibility which would be precluded if technology were equally developed in all aspects of production in a given plant, industry, or branch.

ON INDUSTRIALIZATION AND "CONVERGENCE"

The human costs of the Soviet take-off into massive industrialization have been staggering. Well known and repellent are such aspects of Soviet history as the forced collectivization of the 1930's in order to extract agricultural surpluses deemed necessary for launching the Soviet Union on the road to speedy industrialization, the physical and moral regimentation of the population, the savage purges and repressions, the labor camps dotting the vast USSR from one end to the other, the ostentatious privileges of party bureaucrats and of their police guards, and the introduction of colonial types of exploitation during the early years of the spread of Soviet-patterned systems to Eastern Europe. As the early phases of the so-called primitive socialist accumulation are left behind, as higher levels of industrial output are reached, and as industry depends less on tribute from agriculture for its further expansion, some of the crudest aspects of the early industrialization drive tend to disappear. The shift from Stalin's centralist administrative planning and management system to NEM is viewed by many as the confirmation of the old theory of convergence — a theory stressing an alleged tendency of the Soviet system to "converge" with the American system, i.e., to *grow alike* to it. Phenomena of evolutionary convergence, well known in biology, are processes in which *unrelated* lineages of animals come to resemble each other as their members become progressively adapted to similar ways of life. In a similar way, it is argued, the identity of the problems raised by industrialization and modern technology and of the solutions they elicit are bound to lead toward the convergence of socialism and capitalism. Professor Jan Tinbergen of the Netherlands School of Economics suggests that the two systems tend to approach asymptotically the same type of institutional structure necessary for maximizing welfare. Welfare economics, as it is known, tries to define the maximum welfare attainable under certain constraints (e.g., the initial quantities of the factors of production and given production laws), without reference to the social structure. The social structure is the unknown of the problem to be determined in such a way that welfare is maximized. Professor Tinbergen finds that the structure of the optimum order is a "mixed order" toward which both systems tend to gravitate. It would have the following characteristics: a large public sector taking care of all externalities; decentralization in instruments utilization; and public responsibility for regulating total demand, the level of total investment, the instability of markets, and income distribution. The Soviet writers state for their part that no matter what changes may occur under socialism, the public property remains essential to it, while private property remains characteristic for capitalism. To reconcile the two positions, Professor Gunnar Adler-Karlsson of the Swedish Institute for International Economic Studies has pointed out that ownership, O – which the Russians stress – is identical to the *bundle of functions a* plus *b* plus *c*, etc., which the owner can exert on the owned objects, that is, $O = a + b + c \ldots\ldots + n$. It is this "bundle of functions" which, according to Tinbergen, grows alike in the two systems. Thus far, says Karlsson, neither the Russians nor Tinbergen have realized that the two sides of the equation represent the same identity no matter who the "owner" is. Moreover, says Karlsson, a formal socialist society may even allow individuals to "handle more ownership functions than a formally capitalist society, in which many functions have been socialized."

The differences and similarities *between* capitalism and socialism as systems, and *within* each of these systems, actually are multidimensional, continually evolving and hardly reducible to a simple and neat scheme. These differences and similarities concern not only the economy as such, but also the political, social, and legal framework in which the economy performs. To start with, the *goals* of the policy makers of the socialist societies remain colored by the "Marxist-Leninist" persuasion, and their economic policies (concerning patterns of growth, public versus private goods, planners' versus consumers' preferences, and so on) remain substantially different from the approaches to economic policy prevailing in the individualist-centered Western societies. Furthermore, since present-day socialism (i.e., the socialism of the Soviet-type as distinct from the earlier Western and Central European socialist philosophies) is the one that has taken hold mostly in *industrializing*, rather than in *already* industrialized, societies with the exception only of Czechoslovakia, massive efforts of rapid industrialization and of structural change have also become typical of the goals of the policy makers of these countries. Finally, "Marxist-Leninist-Stalinist" socialism has taken root within a number of *independent* states, each one molded by its own previous history, by its own aspirations, factor endowments, level of development, behavioral patterns, and so on. The German Social Democrat G. Volmar – rather than Marx or Engels – correctly foresaw in about 1879 the emergence of *isolated* autonomous, underdeveloped socialist states, rather than the simultaneous victory of socialism in the developed countries merging willingly into a utopian fraternal association. This isolation creates "geographic speciation," i.e., differences among the socialist states themselves, differences that may become fixed and irreversible. Thus even in respect to goals, certain socialist states may converge while others may diverge from the capitalist countries.

Concerning *instruments* (and underlying structures) the main differences between socialism and capitalism still center on the generation, distribution, and utilization of *profit* as incentive, source of income, or criterion of economic decision. Massive nationalizations have, inter-alia, served as a means by which private-profit making, private-profit motivation, and private profit as a criterion of economic decision could be erased or weakened. The Soviet-type socialist societies remain indeed societies in which *public or collective profits*, rather than private profits, are typical. However the collectives themselves tend in the more developed socialist countries to be profit-motivated, i.e., to use profits as incentives and as the most sensible criterion of decision making over a wide field. But one should also not forget that in countries like China and Cuba, for instance, even collective profits are not viewed as acceptable incentives and are still treated as unreliable guides for resource allocation.

The socialists have traditionally believed in the planning of the economy as a whole as a means of replacing the market mechanism. But today, over-all planning of inputs, outputs, and distribution from a single center appears even to dogmatic socialists as not fully attainable even with the help of the most sophisticated computers. Planning is indeed in the process of changing from a method of rigorously charting a course of action over a fixed time period (as during the Stalinist era) to a flexible means of structural change and loose economic coordination. In combination with the market mechanism – rather than in opposition to it – planning remains typical of all the socialist countries. One should also note, however, that the market mechanisms concerning price formation, factor rewards, capital or goods markets, and so on continue to be hampered in a variety of ways in each of these countries. Few of their policy makers have entirely surmounted their distrust in the market mechanism.

As far as *management* is concerned, some small or very underdeveloped socialist countries are still run essentially as a company town or as a single corporation; others, vaster in size and higher in level of development, have deliberately created a number of largely autonomous corporations which run their industries. Others have decentralized even more, taking the state entirely out of the administration game. No form, however, is final; organizational structures are indeed reshuffled at various crucial junctures since they can be adequate *only* for *specific* periods, tasks, or skills distribution.

Even if socialism and capitalism were to combine planning and the market in closely related ways, and even if both would rely on large corporations (public versus privately owned respectively) as their preferred form of economic management, they could still *diverge* significantly concerning *goals* (the nature and the mix of public-private preferences), economic *structures* (viz., extent of the free play of the market), or the utilization of certain *instruments*. Finally, the confinement of socialist systems to isolated states, at different levels of development, is bound to lead to heterogeneity and geographic speciation; it is gratuitous to assume that any socialist state would necessarily evolve, in time, like any other socialist state did before it. As "modern" socialism spreads, particularly to the underdeveloped countries of Asia, an area even more backward than the Russia of 1917 or 1928, primitive socialist accumulation recurs in an even more ruthless fashion. In certain respects, China's drive to industrialization is even more cruel and unremitting than that of the USSR, and the liquidation of the so-called rich peasants is even more staggering than in the Soviet Union of the 1930's.

Even though the Soviet system has reached "industrial maturity" – i.e., even though industry has become the overwhelming and expanding sector of the economy with respect to output and employment – the policy makers resist the pressures to turn their industrial machine toward the rapid expansion of consumers' goods. Heavy industry and its basic branches continue to be systematically emphasized in the plans for the next decades, just as in the past. The ratio of heavy industrial production to consumers' goods output is to shift in value terms from roughly 2 to 1 in 1960 to 3 to 1 in 1980, according to Soviet forecasts. The policy makers of the socialist countries still adhere to a goal which transcends the object of industrializing backward areas. This goal is the destruction of a rival social system and of the older industrialized countries – the United States and the Western Powers. While this drive is on, the strategy of development emphasizing heavy industry and stressing a lopsided pattern of investment is not likely to be substantially modified. Barring sweeping changes in technology, the Soviet economy will continue to operate under the primary pressure of "reaching and surpassing" the United States in various fields, whether for total or per capita output or for parity in available capacity. Until now, production costs under the Soviet developmental strategy and planning techniques have been incalculable. Waste has occurred in subtle and concealed fashion as well as in crude and obvious forms. The lavish concentration of resources in preferred areas achieved by literally starving the industries and branches deemed secondary, the development of "pushers" and other arbitrage specialists who feed on the plan's inconsistencies, the extent of falsified output reporting – all these are typical manifestations of an economy that has depended on commands rather than on incentives. Many of these crudities could be smoothed out, however, if pricing reflective of scarcities and a balanced system of incentives were employed within the framework of the planned economy.

Some backward areas wish to take over the Soviet strategy of development and certain of its planning techniques without adopting the Soviet institutions which have helped to enforce them. Instead of trying to lift their whole economies by the slow methods of the past, these countries could indeed, as Wassily Leontief suggests in "The Second Industrial Revolution: The Economic Impact," take the dramatic short-cut of building a few large modern automatic plants whose relatively low capital and labor requirements per unit of output would radically change these countries' prospects of industrialization. As Leontief adds, such plants "towering up in the primitive economy like copses of tall trees in a grassy plain . . . would propagate a new economic order." But if underdeveloped countries want to go beyond this, if they want to imitate the whole Soviet strategy, with its lopsided investments and its reduction of the consumer to a residual claimant to society's product — one wonders whether it can be done without resort to coercive mechanisms.

For ultimately, the choice between a market-oriented system and an economy of the Soviet type cannot be made on economic considerations alone: it is a total choice which involves the human goals of each member of the society and his scale of values.

Bibliography

SOURCES IN ENGLISH

I. The Economic Steering System

(1) * Management of the Economy as a Whole

Albers, H. H. *Organized Executive Action.* New York: Wiley, 1961, Part 2, Organization for Management, chaps. 4–9; Part 3, Planning Strategies, chaps. 12–13.

Dale, E. *Planning and Developing the Company Organization Structure.* Research Report No. 20, American Management Association, New York, 1952.

Dobb, M. H. *Soviet Economic Development since 1917.* London: Routledge & Kegan Paul, 1948, chap. i.

Frank, Z. and Waelbroeck, J. "Soviet Economic Policy since 1953, a Study of Its Structure and Changes," *Soviet Studies,* July, 1965.

Holden, P. E., Fish, L. S. and Smith, H. L. *Top-Management Organization and Control.* New York: McGraw-Hill, 1951. Part A.

Kirschen, E. S. *et al.* (eds.). *Economic Policy in Our Time.* Amsterdam: North-Holland Publishing Co., Chicago: Rand McNally, 1964. Vol. I: *General Theory.* Part I.

National Policy Machinery in the Soviet Union, Report of the Committee on Government Operations. Washington, D.C.: 1960, chaps. i, ii, iv.

(2) Plan Construction and Coordination

Dobb, M. H. *Capitalism, Development and Planning.* London: Routledge and Kegan Paul, 1967, chaps. 3–5.

Hardt, J. P., *et al.* (eds.). *Mathematics and Computers*

* Numbers in parentheses refer to chapters.

in Soviet Economic Planning. New Haven and London: Yale University Press, 1967.

Kornai, J. *Mathematical Planning of Structural Decisions*. Amsterdam: North Holland Publishing Co., 1967, Parts 1, 2.

Lange, O. *Essays on Economic Planning*. Calcutta: Indian Statistical Institute, Asia Publishing House, 1960.

Leontief, W. "Input Output Analysis and the General Equilibrium Theory," in Barna, T. (ed.), *The Structural Interdependence of the Economy*. New York: Wiley, 1957.

Levine, H. S. "The Centralized Planning of Supply in Soviet Industry," in Joint Economic Committee, 86th Cong., 1st Sess., *Comparisons of the United States and Soviet Economies*. Washington, D.C.: 1959, Part I.

"Methods of Plan Construction in Eastern Europe and the Soviet Union," *Economic Survey of Europe 1962, Part 2. Economic Planning in Europe*, United Nations. Geneva, 1965, ch. IV.

Report of the United Nations Seminar on Planning Techniques, Moscow, USSR, July, 1964, New York: United Nations, 1966.

Tinbergen, J. *Central Planning*. New Haven and London: Yale University Press, 1964.

(3) Pricing, Market Mechanisms, Controls

Bergson, A. *The Structure of Soviet Wages: A Study in Socialist Economics*. Cambridge, Mass.: Harvard University Press, 1944, chaps. ii, xiii, xiv.

Bornstein, M. "The Soviet Price System," *The American Economic Review*, March, 1962.

——— "The Soviet Price Reform Discussion," *The American Economic Review*, Feb., 1964.

——— "Soviet Price Theory and Policy," *New Directions in the Soviet Economy*, Joint Economic Committee, U.S. 89th Congress, 2nd Sess. Washington, D.C. U.S. Gvt. Printing Office, 1966, pp. 63–94.

Campbell, R. W. *Soviet Economic Power*. Boston: Houghton Mifflin, 1960, ch. 5.

Dobb, M. H. "The Problem of Choice between Alternative Investment Projects," *Soviet Studies*, January, 1951.

Galenson, W. "The Soviet Wage Reform," *Industrial Relations Research Association, Proceedings of the Thirteenth Annual Meeting,* Madison, Wisc.: 1961, pp. 255–65.

Grossman, G. "Scarce Capital and Soviet Doctrine," *Quarterly Journal of Economics,* August, 1953.

Hunter, H. "The Planning of Investments in the Soviet Union," *Review of Economics and Statistics,* February, 1949.

Jasny, N. *The Soviet Price System.* Stanford, Calif.: Stanford University Press, 1951.

——— *Soviet Prices of Producers' Goods.* Stanford, Calif.: Stanford University Press, 1952.

Kaplan, N. M. "The Choice among Investment Alternatives in Soviet Economic Theory," *Journal of Political Economy,* April, 1952.

Political Economy. Institute of Economics of the Academy of Sciences of the USSR. London: Lawrence and Wishart, 1957, chaps. xxix, xxx, xxxii.

"Recommendations of the All-Union Scientific-Technical Conference (June, 1958) on Problems of Determining the Economic Effectiveness of Capital Investments and New Techniques in the USSR National Economy," *Problems of Economics,* January, 1959.

Robinson, J. "Mr. Wiles' Rationality: A Comment," *Soviet Studies,* January, 1956.

Sharpe, M. (ed.). *Planning, Profit and Incentives in the USSR,* Vol. II: *Reform of Soviet Economic Management.* White Plains, New York: International Arts and Science Press, 1966.

Wiles, P. "Are Adjusted Rubles Rational?" *Soviet Studies,* October, 1955.

Zaleski, E. *Planning Reforms in the Soviet Union, 1962–1966.* Chapel Hill: The University of North Carolina Press, 1967.

II. Sectoral Management and Planning

(4) Industry

a. The Firm

Berliner, J. "The Informal Organization of the Soviet Firm," *Quarterly Journal of Economics,* August, 1952.

——— "Managerial Incentives and Decision Making: A Comparison of the United States and the Soviet Union," in *Comparisons of the United States and Soviet Economies,* Part I.

Frank, A. G. "The Organization of Economic Activity in the Soviet Union," *Weltwirtschaftlisches Archiv*, Spring, 1957.

Gsovski, V. *Soviet Civil Law*. Ann Arbor, Mich.: University of Michigan Press, 1948, chap. 11.

Kornai, J. *Overcentralization in Economic Administration*. Oxford: Oxford University Press, 1959, Part I, The System of Instructions, chaps. 1–3.

Nove, A. "The Problem of Success Indicators in Soviet Industry," *Economica*, February, 1958.

Sharpe, M. (ed). *Planning, Profit and Incentives in the USSR*, Vol. I: *The Liberman Discussion*. White Plains, New York, International Arts and Science Press, 1966.

Schwarz, S. M. "The Industrial Enterprise in Russia," *Harvard Business Review*, April–May, 1945.

b. Cost Accounting, Prices, and Wages

Bergson, A. *Soviet National Income and Product in 1937*. New York: Columbia University Press, 1953, chap. 3.

Bergson, A. *The Structure of Soviet Wages: A Study in Socialist Economics*.

Campbell, R. W. "Accounting for Cost Control in the Soviet Economy," *Review of Economics and Statistics*, February, 1958.

Kornai, J. *Overcentralization in Economic Administration*, Part IV, Relationships between Enterprises, chaps. 1–4.

Turgeon, L. "Cost-Price Relationships in Basic Industries During the Soviet Planning Era," *Soviet Studies*, October, 1957.

(5) Agriculture

Clark, M. G. "Productivity and Incomes on a Soviet Dairy Farm," *I.L. Research*, Cornell, Fall, 1958.

Durgin, F. A. "Quantitative, Structural and Institutional Changes in Soviet Agriculture During the Khrushchev Era, 1953–1964," *Cahiers de l'ISEA* May, 1966.

Finegood, I. M. "A Critical Analysis of Some Concepts concerning Soviet Agriculture," *Soviet Studies*, July, 1952.

Gsovski, V. *Soviet Civil Law*. Part II, Special Topics, chaps. 19, 20.

Hubbard, L. E. *The Economics of Soviet Agriculture.* London: Macmillan, 1939.

Jasny, N. *The Socialized Agriculture of the USSR.* Stanford, Calif.: Stanford University Press, 1949.

Johnson, D. G. and Kahan, A. "Soviet Agriculture," in *Comparisons of the United States and Soviet Economies,* Part I.

Karcz, J. (ed). *Soviet and East European Agriculture.* Berkeley and Los Angeles: University of California Press, 1967.

——— "Quantitative Analysis of the Collective Farm Market," *The American Economic Review,* June, 1964.

Mertsalov, V. "The Position of the Peasantry in the USSR," *Soviet Society Today,* A Symposium of the Institute for the Study of the USSR. Munich: The Institute, 1958.

Nimitz, Nancy. "Soviet Agricultural Prices and Costs," in *Comparisons of the United States and Soviet Economies,* Part I.

Volin, L. "The Kolkhoz in the Soviet Union," *Foreign Agriculture,* November–December, 1947.

Vucinich, A. *Soviet Economic Institutions.* Stanford, Calif.: Stanford University Press, 1952, chaps. 2–4.

(6) Supply and Distribution

a. Domestic Trade

Goldman, M. I. *Soviet Marketing, Distribution in a Controlled Economy.* Glencoe and London: The Free Press and Collier-Macmillan, 1963.

Hubbard, L. E. *Soviet Trade and Distribution.* London: Macmillan, 1938.

b. Foreign Trade

Baykov, A. M. *Soviet Foreign Trade.* Princeton, N.J.: Princeton University Press, 1946.

Condoide, M. V. *Russian American Trade.* Columbus, Ohio: Ohio State University Press, 1946.

Goichbarg, A. G. "The State Economic Organizations of the USSR," *Annals of the American Academy of Political and Social Science,* July, 1935.

Pryor, F. L. *The Communist Foreign Trade System.* Cambridge, Mass.: The M.I.T. Press, 1963.

Spulber, N. "The Soviet Bloc Foreign Trade System," *Law and Contemporary Problems,* Summer, 1959.

(7) Labor

Berliner, J. S. *Factory and Manager in the USSR*. Cambridge, Mass.: Harvard University Press, 1958, chaps. ii, iii.

Brown, E. C. *Soviet Trade Unions and Labor Relations*. Cambridge, Mass.: Harvard University Press, 1966.

Chapman, Y. G. *Real Wages in the Soviet Union since 1928*. Cambridge, Mass.: Harvard University Press, 1963.

Clark, M. G. (ed.). *Steel in the Soviet Union*. American Iron and Steel Institute, 1959, Part VI, Management-Labor Relations.

Deutscher, I. *Soviet Trade Unions*. New York: Royal Institute of International Affairs, 1950.

DeWitt, N. *Education and Professional Employment in the U.S.S.R.* Washington, D.C.: National Science Foundation, 1961.

Dodge, N. T. *Women in the Soviet Economy*. Baltimore: The Johns Hopkins Press, 1966.

Douty, H. M. "Soviet Wage Structure: Discussion," *Industrial Relations Research Association, Proceedings of the Thirteenth Annual Meeting.*

Feshbach, U. "The Soviet Statistical System: Labor Force Recording and Reporting," *International Population Statistics Reports*, Series P-9, No. 12, U.S. Bureau of the Census, Washington, D.C.: 1960.

Galenson, W. *Labor Productivity in Soviet and American Industry*. New York: Columbia University Press, 1955.

Gliksman, J. "Recent Trends in Soviet Labor Policy," *Monthly Labor Review*, July, 1956; *Problems of Communism*, July, August, 1956.

Granick, D. "Initiative and Independence of Soviet Plant Management," *American Slavic and East European Review*, October, 1951.

——— *Management of the Industrial Firm in the USSR*. New York: Columbia University Press, 1954.

Gsovski, V. "Elements of Soviet Labor Law," *Monthly Labor Review*, March, April, 1951.

James, R. C. "Management in the Soviet Union," in Harbison, F. and Myers, C. A. (eds.), *Management in the Industrial World*. New York: McGraw-Hill, 1959.

Kornai, J. *Overcentralization in Economic Administration.* Part II, Incentives for Top Management, chaps. 1–3.

"Manpower and Employment in Eastern Europe and the Soviet Union," *Economic Survey of Europe* [in] *1957*. Geneva: 1958, chap. vii.

Reed, R. H. *Estimates and Projections of the Labor Force and Civilian Employment in the U.S.S.R.* Washington, D.C.: U.S. Bureau of the Census, International Population Reports, Series P-91, No. 15, 1967.

Schwarz, S. M. *Labor in the Soviet Union.* New York: Praeger, 1953.

Weitzman, M. S. and Elias, A. "The Magnitude and Distribution of Civilian Employment in the USSR: 1928–1959," *Population Reports,* Series P-95, No. 58, U.S. Bureau of the Census, Washington, D.C.: 1961.

Yanowich, M. "Trends in Differentials between Salaried Personnel and Wage Workers in Soviet Industry," *Soviet Studies,* January, 1960.

III. Social Accounting and Finance

(8) Income and Product Accounts

a. Marxian Schema and Soviet Income Definitions

"A Note on Some Aspects of National Accounting Methodology in Eastern Europe and the Soviet Union," *Economic Bulletin for Europe,* United Nations, Geneva: November, 1959.

Elias, A. "Soviet Practice in the Classification of Economic Activity," *International Population Reports,* Series P-95, No. 57, U.S. Bureau of the Census, Washington, D.C.: 1961.

Marx, K. *Capital.* Moscow: Foreign Languages Publishing House, 1957, Vol. II, Part III, The Reproduction and Circulation of the Aggregate Social Capital, chaps. 20, 21.

Marx, K. *Critique of the Gotha Programme,* Political Economy in the Soviet Union Series. New York: International Publishers, 1944.

Nemchinov, V. "Relationship of Expanded Reproduction," *Problems of Economics,* February, 1959.

Political Economy, Institute of Economics of the Academy of Sciences of the USSR, chaps. xv, xxxvii.

Robinson, J. *Marx, Marshall, Keynes.* Delhi: The Delhi School of Economics, 1955.

Samuelson, P. A. "Wages and Interest, Marxian Economic Models," *American Economic Review*, December, 1957.

Sweezy, P. M. *The Theory of Capitalist Development*. New York: Oxford University Press, 1942, Part II, The Accumulation Process; Part III, Crises and Depressions, chaps. v, viii.

b. On Statistics

Clark, C. A *Critique of Russian Statistics*. London: Macmillan, 1939.

———, Baran, P. A., Bergson, A., Gerschenkron, A., Harris, S., Yugow, A. *et al.* "Appraisals of Russian Economic Statistics," *Review of Economics and Statistics*, November, 1947.

Egermayer, F. "The Evolution of Soviet Views on Statistics," *Czechoslovak Economic Papers*, Vol. I, 1962.

Grossman, G. *Soviet Statistics of Physical Output of Industrial Commodities, Their Compilation and Quality*, Study by the National Bureau of Economic Research. Princeton, N.J.: Princeton University Press, 1960.

Hodgman, D. R. *Soviet Industrial Production, 1928–1951*. Cambridge, Mass.: Harvard University Press, 1954, chap. i.

Jasny, N. "Intricacies of Russian National Income Indexes," *Journal of Political Economy*, August, 1947.

——— "Soviet Statistics," *Review of Economics and Statistics*, February, 1950.

Rice, S. A. *et al.* "Reliability and Usability of Soviet Statistics," *The American Statistician*, April–May, June–July, 1953.

Schwartz, H. "On the Use of Soviet Statistics," *Journal of American Statistical Association*, September, 1947.

c. Western Methods and Estimates

Bergson, A. *Soviet National Income and Product in 1937*.

——— *The Real National Income of Soviet Russia since 1928*. Cambridge, Mass.: Harvard University Press, 1961.

——— and Kuznets S. (eds.). *Economic Trends in the Soviet Union*. Cambridge, Mass.: Harvard University Press, 1963.

Dobb, M. "Rates of Growth under the Five-Year Plan,"

Soviet Studies, April, 1953.

Gerschenkron, A. "Soviet Heavy Industry: A Dollar Index of Machinery Output, 1927/28–1937," *Review of Economics and Statistics,* May, 1955.

Granick, D. "Are Adjusted Rubles Rational? A Comment," *Soviet Studies,* July, 1956.

Grossman, G. Review of A. Bergson's *Soviet National Income and Product in 1937,* in *Journal of Political Economy,* October, 1953.

Hodgman, D. R. "Measuring Soviet Industrial Expansion: A Reply," *Soviet Studies,* July, 1956.

Hoeffding, O. *Soviet National Income and Product in 1928.* New York: Columbia University Press, 1954.

——— and Nimitz, N. *Soviet National Income and Product 1949–1955,* RAND, RM 2101, Santa Monica, 1959.

Hoover, C. "Soviet Economic Growth," *Foreign Affairs,* June, 1957.

Holzman, F. D. "Adjusted Factor Cost Standard of Measuring National Income: Comments," *Soviet Studies,* July, 1957.

Jasny, N. "Soviet Economic Growth," *Social Research,* Spring, 1954.

——— *Soviet Industrialization 1928–1952.* Chicago: University of Chicago Press, 1961, chap. i and Append. B.

Kaplan, N. and Moorsteen, R. "An Index of Soviet Industrial Output," *American Economic Review,* June, 1960.

Moorsteen, R. and Powell, R. P. *The Soviet Capital Stock 1928–1962.* Homewood, Ill.: Irwin, 1966, Part II.

New Directions in the Soviet Economy. Parts II–A, II–B.

Nutter, G. W. "Industrial Growth in the Soviet Union" and discussion by Heymann, H., Jr. *American Economic Review* (Proceedings), May, 1958.

Robinson, J. "Mr. Wiles' Rationality: A Comment," *Soviet Studies,* January, 1956.

Rothschild, K. W. "A Note on the Rationality Controversy," *Ibid.,* July, 1957.

Seton, F. "The Social Accounts of the Soviet Union in 1934," *Review of Economics and Statistics,* August, 1954.

——— "Soviet Progress in Western Perspective," *Soviet Studies*, October, 1960.

——— "The Tempo of Soviet Industrial Expansion," Manchester Statistical Society, *Transactions*, January, 1957; reprinted also in *Bulletin of the Oxford University Institute of Statistics*, February, 1958.

Shimkin, D. B. *et al.* "Soviet Industrial Growth—Its Cost, Extent, and Prospects," *Automotive Industries*, January, 1958.

"The Rates of Soviet Economic Growth," *The American Statistician*, June, 1958.

Wiles, P. "Are Adjusted Rubles Rational?" *Soviet Studies*, October, 1955.

——— "A Rejoinder to All and Sundry," *Ibid.*, October, 1956.

Wyler, J. "The National Income of Soviet Russia," *Social Research*, 1946.

(9–10) Finance

Ames, E. "Banking in the Soviet Union," *Federal Reserve Bulletin*, XXXVIII, 1952.

Arnold, A. E. *Banks, Credit and Money in Soviet Russia*. New York: Columbia University Press, 1937.

Berliner, J. S. "Monetary Planning in the USSR," *The American Slavic and East European Review*, December, 1950.

Davies, R. W. "Short-Term Credit in the USSR," *Soviet Studies*, May, 1953.

——— *The Development of the Soviet Budgetary System*. Cambridge, England: Cambridge University Press, 1958.

Dobb, M. H. "The Financial Plan in Soviet Economy," *American Review on the Soviet Union*, October, 1947.

——— *Soviet Economic Development Since 1917*, chap. xiv.

Garvy, G. *Money, Banking, and Credit in Eastern Europe*. New York: Federal Reserve Bank of New York, 1966.

Grossman, G. "Union of Soviet Socialist Republics," in Beckhart, B. H. (ed.) *Banking Systems*. New York: Columbia University Press, 1954.

Hodgman, D. R. "Soviet Monetary Controls through the Banking System," in Grossman, G. (ed.) *Value and Plan*. Berkeley, Calif.: University of California

Press, 1960.

Holzman, F. D. "Financing Soviet Economic Development," and comment by Powell, R., in National Bureau of Economic Research, *Capital Formation and Economic Growth*. Princeton, N.J.: Princeton University Press, 1955.

——— "Soviet Inflationary Pressures, 1928–1957: Causes and Cures," *Quarterly Journal of Economics*, May, 1960.

——— *Soviet Taxation: The Financial Problems of a Planned Economy*. Cambridge, Mass.: Harvard University Press, 1955.

Hubbard, L. E. *Soviet Money and Finance*. London: Macmillan, 1936.

Powell, R. P. "Soviet Monetary Policy," unpublished doctoral dissertation. Berkeley, Calif.: California University, 1952.

Reddaway, W. B. *The Russian Financial System*. London: Macmillan, 1935.

Varga, S. "Money in Socialism," *International Economic Papers*, No. 8, New York: Macmillan, 1958.

IV. Socialist Economic Models.

(11) Western Theories

Balassa, B. "Success Criteria for Economic Systems," *Yale Economic Essays*, Spring, 1961.

Baldwin, C. D. *Economic Planning, Its Aims and Implications*, Illinois Studies in the Social Sciences, Vol. XXVII, No. 1–2, University of Illinois, Urbana, Ill.: 1942.

Barone, E. "The Ministry of Production in the Collectivist State," in Hayek, F.A. (ed.) *Collectivist Economic Planning*. London: Routledge & Sons, 1938, Append.

Beckwith, B. P. *The Economic Theory of a Socialist Economy*. Palo Alto: Stanford University Press, 1949.

Bergson, A. *Essays in Normative Economics*. Cambridge, Mass.: Harvard University Press, 1966.

Dickinson, H. D. *Economics of Socialism*. London: Oxford University Press, 1939.

Dobb, M. H. *On Economic Theory and Socialism*. London: Routledge & Kegan Paul, 1955.

Hall, R. L. *The Economic System in a Socialist State*. London: Macmillan, 1937.

Halm, G. "Further Considerations on the Possibility of

Adequate Calculation in a Socialist Community," in Hayek, F. A. (ed.) *Collectivist Economic Planning.*

Hayek, F. A. "The Nature and History of the Problem," in Hayek, F. A. (ed.) *Collectivist Economic Planning.*

——— "Socialist Calculation: The Competitive Solution," *Economica,* May, 1940.

Heimann, E. "Literature on the Theory of a Socialist Economy," *Social Research,* 6, 1939.

Lange, O. "On the Economic Theory of Socialism," in Lippincott, B. E. (ed.) *On the Economic Theory of Socialism.* Minneapolis, Minn.: University of Minnesota Press, 1938.

Lerner, A. P. "Economic Theory and Socialist Economy," *Review of Economic Studies,* October, 1934.

——— "Statistics and Dynamics in Socialist Economics," *Economic Journal,* June, 1937.

——— *The Economics of Control, Principles of Welfare Economics.* New York: Macmillan, 1944, chaps. 1 and 5–11.

Meyer, G. "A Contribution to the Theory of Socialist Planning," *Plan Age,* 3, 1937.

Mises, L. "Economic Calculation in the Socialist Commonwealth" in Hayek, F. A. (ed.) *Collectivist Economic Planning.*

Mossé, R. "The Theory of Planned Economy," *Plan Age,* 3, 1937.

Taylor, M. F. "The Guidance of Production in a Socialist State," in Lippincott, B. E. (ed.) *On the Economic Theory of Socialism.*

Zassenhaus, H. "On the Theory of Economic Planning," *International Economic Papers,* No. 6, 1956.

(12) Soviet Theories

a. Economic Strategies

Brutzkus, B. *Economic Planning in Soviet Russia.* London: Routledge & Sons, 1935.

Domar, E. D. *Essays in the Theory of Economic Growth.* New York: Oxford University Press, 1957, chap. ix.

"Draft Program of the Soviet Communist Party" (Tass text), *The New York Times,* Aug. 1, 1961.

Erlich, A. *The Soviet Industrialization Debate 1924–28.* Cambridge, Mass.: Harvard University Press, 1960.

——— "Stalin's Views on Economic Development," in Simmons, E. J. (ed.) *Continuity and Change in*

Russian and Soviet Thought. Cambridge, Mass.: Joint Committee on Slavic Studies, 1955.

Gerschenkron, A. Review of A. I. Pashkov's *Economic Law Concerning the Faster Growth of Output of Producers' Goods*, in *American Economic Review*, September, 1959.

Kaser, M. C. "Welfare Criteria in Soviet Planning," in *Soviet Planning Essays in Honour of Naum Jasny*, edited by Degras, J., and Nove, A. London: Blackwell, 1964.

Lenin, V. I. *The Development of Capitalism in Russia* Moscow: Foreign Languages Publishing House, 1956, chap. vi.

Leontief, W. "The Decline and Rise of Soviet Economic Science," *Foreign Affairs*, January, 1960.

Spulber, N. *Soviet Strategy for Economic Growth*. Bloomington, Ind.: Indiana University Press, 1964.

b. Issues in Perspective Planning

Kaufman, A. "The Origin of the Political Economy of Socialism," *Soviet Studies*, January, 1953.

Lange, O. *The Political Economy of Socialism*. Lectures at the Belgrade Institute for International Politics and Economics. Warsaw: Polish Institute of International Affairs, 1958.

Lorwin, L. L. and Hinrichs, A. F. *National Economic and Social Planning, Theory and Practice with Special Reference to the United States*, National Planning Board, Washington, D.C., Part III, Soviet Planning. (Mimeo.)

Spulber, N. (ed.). *Foundations of Soviet Strategy for Economic Growth*. Bloomington, Ind.: Indiana University Press, 1964.

13) Other Socialist Theories

a. On Pricing

"A Note on the Introduction of Mathematical Techniques into Soviet Planning," *Economic Bulletin for Europe*, Geneva: June, 1960.

Bornstein, M. "Soviet Price Theory and Policy," *New Directions in the Soviet Economy*.

Campbell, R. W. "Marx, Kantorovich, and Novozhilov: Stoimost versus Reality," *Slavic Review*, Oct., 1961.

Dobb, M. *Marx As an Economist*. New York: International Publishers, 1935.

Ganczer, S. "Price Calculations and the Analysis of Proportions within the National Economy," *Acta Oeconomica Academiae Scientiarum Hungaricae*, 1, 1966.

Kantorovich, L. V. "Mathematical Methods of Organizing and Planning Production," *Management Science*, July, 1960.

Lange, O. "Marxian Economics in the Soviet Union," *The American Economic Review*, March, 1945.

Meek, L. *Studies in the Labor Theory of Value*. London: International Publishers, 1956, chap. 7.

Montias, J. M. "Producer Prices in a Centrally Planned Economy—The Polish Discussion," in Grossman, G. (ed.) *Value and Plan*.

Otis, B. "The Communists and the Labor Theory of Value," *The American Economic Review*, March, 1945.

"Problems of Planned Price Formation," in *Planning, Profit and Incentives in the USSR*, edited by Sharpe, M., *op. cit.*, pp. 122–159.

Stalin, J. *Economic Problems of Socialism in the USSR*. New York: International Publishers, 1952.

Sweezy, P. M. *The Theory of Capitalist Development*. Part II, The Accumulation Process, chap. 3.

"Teaching of Economics in the Soviet Union," *The American Economic Review*, September, 1944.

Ward, B. "Kantorovich on Economic Calculation," *The Journal of Political Economy*, December, 1960.

Zielinski, J. and Wakar, A. "Socialist Price Systems," in *The American Economic Review*, March, 1963.

Zauberman, A. "The Soviet Debate on the Law of Value and Price Formation," in Grossman, G. (ed.) *Value and Plan*.

b. On Decentralized Management

Dupont, C. and Keesing, F. A. J. "The Yugoslav Economic System and Instruments of Yugoslav Economic Policy: A Note," *International Monetary Fund Staff Papers*, November, 1960.

"Economic Planning and Management in Yugoslavia," *Economic Bulletin for Europe*, Geneva: November, 1958.

Holesovsky, W. "Problems of Transition to the New Model in Czechoslovakia," *The Aste Bulletin*, Fall,

1966, pp. 1–9.

Lange, O. "Outline of a Reconversion Plan for the Polish Economy," (Trans. from *Zycie Gospodarcze*, July, 1956) in *International Economic Papers*, No. 7, London: Macmillan, 1957.

Lange, O, *et al.* (eds.). *Problems of Political Economy of Socialism*. New Delhi, People's Publishing House, 1962.

Neuberger, E. "The Yugoslav Investment Auctions," *The Quarterly Journal of Economics*, February, 1959.

Nove, A. "The Politics of Economic Rationality," *Social Research*, Summer, 1958.

The Fiat-Soviet Auto Plant and Communist Economic Reforms. A Report for the Subcommittee on International Trade, Committee on Banking and Currency, House of Representatives, 89th Cong., 2nd Sess., Washington, D.C., 1967, Part II.

Ward, B. N. *The Socialist Economy. A Study of Organizational Alternatives*. New York: Random House, 1967.

Wiles, P. *The Political Economy of Communism*. Cambridge, Mass.: Harvard University Press, 1962, Part II.

V. Socialism v. Capitalism

(14) Problems of Socialist Cooperation

Allen, R. L. *Soviet Economic Warfare*. Washington, D.C.: Public Affairs Press, 1960.

Bornstein, M. "The Reform and Revaluation of the Ruble," *American Economic Review*, March, 1961.

Galenson, W. "Economic Relations between the Soviet Union and Communist China," in N. Spulber (ed.) *Study of the Soviet Economy*, Russia and East European Series, No. 25. Bloomington, Ind.: Indiana University Press, 1961.

Granick, D. "The Pattern of Foreign Trade in Eastern Europe and Its Relations to Economic Development Policy," *Quarterly Journal of Economics*, August, 1954.

Hoeffding, O. "Recent Trends in Soviet Foreign Trade," *Annals of the American Academy of Political and Social Science*, January, 1956.

——— "Soviet Economic Relations under the Orbit," in Bergson, A. (ed.) *Soviet Economic Growth*.

——— "State Planning and Forced Industrialization," *Problems of Communism*, November–December, 1959.

Hoffman, M. L. "Problems of Trade Between Planned Economies," *American Economic Review* (Proceedings), May, 1951.

Humphrey, D. D. "Some Implications of Planning for Trade and Capital Movements," in *National Economic Planning*, edited by Millikan, M. F. New York: Columbia University for the National Bureau of Economic Research, 1967.

Kaser, M. *Comecon, Integration Problems of the Planned Economies*. London: Oxford University Press for the Royal Institute of International Affairs, 1965.

Kovásznai, Gy. and Kozma, F. "On the Interrelations between the Socialist International Division of Labor and the Efficiency of Production," in *For the Progress of Marxist Economics*, Földi, T. (ed.). Budapest: Akadémiai Kiado, 1967.

Mason, E. S. "Competitive Coexistence and Economic Development in Asia," *International Stability and Progress: United States Interests and Instruments*. New York: Columbia University Press, 1957.

Mendershausen, H. "Terms of Trade Between the Soviet Union and Smaller Communist Countries 1955–57," *Review of Economics and Statistics*, May, 1959.

Spulber, N. and Gehrels, F. "The Operation of Trade within the Soviet Bloc," *The Review of Economics and Statistics*, May, 1958.

——— *The Economics of Communist Eastern Europe*. New York: Wiley and Technology Press M.I.T., 1957, chap. xi.

——— "The Dispute: Economic Relations Among Socialist States," in Benes, V. *et al.* (eds.) *The Second Soviet Yugoslav Dispute*, Russian and East European Series, Vol. 14, Indiana University Publications, Bloomington, Ind.: 1959.

Viner, J. "The Influence of National Economic Planning on Commercial Policy," *International Trade and Economic Development*. Glencoe, Ill.: Free Press, 1952.

(15) Competition and "Convergence"

Adler-Karlsson, G. "Functional Socialism: A Concept

for the Analysis of Convergence of National Economies," *Third European Peace Research Conference.* Vienna, Austria: Proceedings (mimeo.) 1966.

Comparisons of the United States and Soviet Economies, Parts I, II, III.

Dobb, M. *An Essay in Economic Growth and Planning.* London: Routledge & Kegan Paul, 1960.

Grossman, G. "Soviet Economy and Soviet World Power," *International Stability and Progress,* The American Assembly, Graduate School of Business, Columbia University, New York: June, 1957.

Hoeffding, O. "Substance and Shadow in the Soviet Seven-Year Plan," *Foreign Affairs,* April, 1959.

Kýn, O. "The Market Mechanism in a Socialist Economy," in *St. Antony's Papers Number 19. Soviet Affairs Number Four,* edited by Kaser, M. London: Oxford University Press, 1966.

Leontief, W. "The Second Industrial Revolution: The Economic Impact," *Automatic Control,* a *Scientific American* book. New York: Simon and Schuster, 1955.

Linnemann, H., Prowk, F. P., and Tinbergen, J. "Convergence of Economic Systems in East and West," in *Disarmament and World Economic Interdependence,* edited by Benoit, E., *et al.* Oslo and New York: Columbia University Press, 1967, pp. 246–258.

Nove, A. *Communist Economic Strategy: Soviet Growth and Capabilities,* Series: The Economics of Competitive Coexistence, Washington, D.C.: National Planning Association, 1959.

Soviet Economic Growth: A Comparison with the United States, a study prepared for the Joint Committee on the Economic Report, Washington, D.C.: 1955.

Wiles, P. J. D. "Convergence: Possibility and Probability," in *Planning and the Market in the USSR: the 1960's,* by Balinky, A., *et al.* New Brunswick, N.J.: Rutgers University Press, 1967.

——— "Fifty Years After: What Future for Communism?" in *Lloyds Bank Review,* Oct., 1967.

SOURCES IN OTHER LANGUAGES

I. The Economic Steering System

(1) Management of the Economy

Chambre, H. *Le Pouvoir Soviétique. Introduction a l' étude de ses institutions* [Soviet Power: Introduction to the Study of Its Institutions]. Paris: Librairie Generale de Droit et Jurisprudence, 1959, chap. v.

Cheliapov, I. B. *Osnovnye voprosy konstitutsii SSSR i sovetskogo zakonodatel'stva* [Basic Problems of the Constitution of the USSR and of Soviet Legislation]. Moscow: Uchebno-pedagog. izd., 1959.

Kurskii, A. A. *Ekonomicheskie osnovy narodnokhoziaistvennogo planirovaniia v SSSR* [Economic Foundations of National Economic Planning in the USSR]. Moscow: Gospolitizdat, 1959, chap. i.

Vlasov, V. A. *Sovetskii gosudarstvennyi apparat* [Soviet State Machine]. Moscow: Gosjurizdat, 1959.

(2) Plan Construction and Coordination

Bettelheim, C. *Problèmes théoriques et pratiques de la planification* [*Theoretical and Practical Planning Problems*]. 2d Ed., Paris: Presses Universitaires de France, 1951, Part II, La Théorie de la Planification, chap. i.

Bor, M. Z. *Voprosy metodologii planovogo balansa narodnogo khoziaistva SSSR* [Methodological Problems of the Planned Balance of the National Economy of the USSR]. Moscow: Akademiia Nauk SSSR, 1960, chaps. i–v.

Diekmann, K. *Wirtschaftsrechnung, Investitionen und Wachstum in einer Zentralverwaltungswirtschaft* [Economic Calculation, Investments, and Growth in a Centrally Administered Economy]. Berlin: Duncker & Humblot, 1960.

Efimov, A. N. (ed.). *Problemy optimal'nogo planirovaniia* [Problems of Optimal Planning]. Moscow: Ekonomika, 1966.

Evenko, I. A. *Voprosy planirovaniia v SSSR na sovremenom etape* [Current Planning Problems in the USSR]. Moscow: Gosplanizdat, 1959.

Les méthodes actuelles soviétiques de planification

[Current Soviet Planning Methods]. Paris: Institut de Science Economique Appliquée, Series G, No. 7, 1959.

Le plan septennal soviétique, Études et Documents [The Soviet Seven-Year Plan, Studies and Documents] (Introductory Notes by B. Kerblay and H. Chambre). Paris: Institut de Science Économique Appliquée, Series G, No. 10, 1960.

Marczewski, J. *Planification et croissance économique des Démocraties Populaires* [Planning and Economic Growth of the People's Democracies], 2 vols. Paris: Presses Universitaires de France, 1956, Vol. 2, chap. ii.

Nemchinov, V. S. *Primenenie matematiki v ekonomicheskikh issledovaniiakh* [Application of Mathematics in Economic Research]. Moscow: Sotsekonlitizdat, 1959.

Riabushkin, T. V. *Problemy ekonomicheskoi statistiki* [Problems of Economic Statistics]. Moscow: Akademia Nauk SSSR, 1959.

Smirnov, P. V. and Taras'iants, P. B. *Organizatsiia i planirovanie sbyta promyshlennoi produktsii v SSSR* [Organization and Planning of the Marketing of Industrial Output in the USSR]. Moscow: Gosplanizdat, 1960, chaps. ii, iii.

Wagenlehner, G. *Das sowjetische Wirstschaftssystem und Karl Marx* [The Soviet Economic System and Karl Marx]. Cologne-Berlin: Kiepenheuer u. Witsch, 1960, chaps. ii, iii.

(3) Pricing, Market Mechanisms, Controls

Belousov, R. A. (ed.). *Sovremennaia praktika tsenoobrazovaniia* [Current practice of price formation]. Moscow: Ekonomika, 1965.

Bogachev, V. N. *Srok okupaemosti. Teoriia sravneniia planovykh variantov* [The Recoupement Period. The Theory of Comparing Plan Variants]. Moscow: Ekonomika, 1966.

Denis, H., and Lavigne, M. *Le problème des prix en Union Soviétique* [The Price Problem in the Soviet Union]. Paris: Cujas, 1965.

Khachaturov, T. S. (ed.). *Ekonomicheskaia effektivnost' kapital'nykh vlozhenii i novoi tekhniki* [Economic Effectiveness of Capital Investment and New Technology]. Moscow: Sotsekonlitizdat, 1959.

Malafeev, A. N. *Istoriia tsenoobrazovaniia v SSSR, 1917–1963* [History of Price Formation in the USSR, 1917–1963]. Moscow: Mysl', 1964.

"Rationalité et calcul économiques en U.R.S.S." [Rationality and Economic calculations in the USSR]. *Cahiers de l'ISEA* (Series G, No. 19), Feb., 1964.

II. Sectoral Management and Planning

(4) Industry

Akademiia Nauk, Institut Ekonomiki. *Ekonomika promyshlenosti SSSR* [The Economics of Soviet Industry]. Moscow: Gospolitizdat, 1956.

Ekonomika sotsialisticheskikh promyshlennykh predpriiatsii [Economics of the Socialist Industrial Enterprise]. Moscow: Gospolitizdat, 1956.

Gusakov, A. D. and Maslov, N. S. (eds.) *Voprosy ekonomiki sotsialisticheskogo promyshlennogo predpriiatsiia* [Problems of Economics of the Socialist Industrial Enterprise]. Moscow: Profizdat, 1955.

Kamenitser, S., Kontorovich, V., and Pishchiulin, G. *Ekonomika, organizatsiia i planirovanie promyshlennogo predpriiatsiia* [Economics, Organization, and Planning of the Industrial Enterprise]. Moscow: Gospolitizdat, 1961, chaps. xv–xviii.

Mitel'man, E. L. *Finansirovanie i kreditovanie sotsialisticheskoi promyshlenosti* [Financing and Crediting Socialist Industry]. Moscow: Gosstatizdat, 1955.

Tatur, S. K. *Khoziaistvennyi raschet v promyshlennosti* [Economic Accounting in Industry]. Moscow: Gosfinizdat, 1959, chaps. v, viii.

Verre, E. *L'entreprise industrielle en Union Soviétique* [The industrial enterprise in the Soviet Union]. Paris: Sirey, 1965.

(5) Agriculture

Kovaleva, M. F., Karavaev, A. A., Tushunov, A. V. (eds.) *Voprosy Ekonomiki Sotsializma* [Problems of the Economics of Socialism]. Moscow: Akademiia Obshchestvennykh Nauk, 1959.

———, ———, ——— (eds.). *Sotsialisticheskoe sel'skoe khoziaistvo na sovremennom etape i voprosy agrarnoi teorii* [Socialist Agriculture in the Present Period and the Problems of Agricultural Theory]. Moscow: Akademiia Obshchestvennykh Nauk, 1960.

Khrushchev, N. S. "Itogi razvitia sel'skogo khoziaistva za poslednie piat' let i zadachi dal'neishego uvelicheniia proizvodstva sel'skokhoziaistvennykh produktov" [Results of the Development of Agriculture for the Past Five Years and the Tasks of Further Raising the Output of Agricultural Produce], *Plenum Tsentral'nogo Komiteta Kommunisticheskoi Partii Sovetskogo Soiuza, 15–19 dekabria 1958* g [Plenum of the Central Committee of the Communist Party of the Soviet Union, Dec. 15–19, 1958]. Moscow: Gospolitizdat, 1958.

"La Collectivization de l'agriculture soviétique et le régime des kolkhozes" [The Collectivization of Soviet Agriculture and the Collective-Farm System]. *La Documentation Française, Serie Économique et Financière*, CXXXV, April, 1952.

Nacou, D. *Du Kolkhoze au Sovkhoze* [From the Collective Farm to the State Farm]. Paris: Éditions de Minuit, 1958, chaps. iii, iv, v.

(6) Supply and Distribution

a. Domestic Trade

Ekonomika sovetskoi torgovli [Economics of Soviet Trade]. Moscow: Gospolitizdat, Fourth ed., 1965.

Riauzov, N. N. and Titel'baum, N. P. *Statistika sovetskoi torgovli* [Statistics of Soviet Trade]. Moscow: Gosstatizdat, 1956.

b. Foreign Trade

Karpich, V., *Bank sodruzhestva ravnykh* [The Bank of Cooperation among Equals]. Moscow: Mezhdunarodnoie otnosheniia, 1966.

Ramzaitsev, D. I. *Pravovye voprosy vneshnei torgovli SSSR* [Legal Problems of the Foreign Trade of the USSR]. Moscow: Vneshtorgizdat, 1954.

Spravochnik po vneshnei torgovli SSSR [Handbook of Soviet Foreign Trade]. Moscow: Vneshtorgizdat, 1958.

(7) Labor

Aganbegian, A. G. and Maier, V. F. *Zarabotnaia plata v. SSSR* [Wages in the USSR]. Moscow: Gosplanizdat, 1959.

Anstett, M. *La formation de la main d'oeuvre qualifiée en Union Soviétique de 1917 à 1954* [Training of Skilled Labor in the Soviet Union from 1917 to

1954]. Paris: Marcel Rivière, 1958.

Bellecombe, de, L. G. *Les Conventions Collectives de Travail en Union Soviétique* [Collective Labor Agreements in the Soviet Union]. Paris, The Hague: Mouton, 1958, chap. v.

Grigor'ev, A. E. *Ekonomika truda* [Labor Economics]. Moscow: Gosplanizdat, 1959, chaps. ii, vii.

Hofman W. *Die Arbeitsverfassung der Sowjetunion* [The Labor Organization of the Soviet Union]. Berlin: Duncker & Humblot, 1956.

Kuznetsov, A. D. *Trudovye resursy SSSR i ikh ispol'zovanie* [Labor Resources of the USSR and Their Utilization]. Moscow: Sotsekonlitizdat, 1960.

Prudenskii, G. A., Stepanov, A. P., Eidel'man, B. I. (eds.) *Voprosy truda v SSSR* [Labor Problems in the USSR]. Moscow: Gospolitizdat, 1958.

III. Social Accounting and Finance

(8) Income and Product Accounts

Calvez, J. Y. *Revenu national en USSR, problèmes théoriques et description statistique* [National Income in the USSR. Theoretical Problems and Statistical Description]. Paris: Société d'édition d' Enseignement Supérieur, 1956.

Kolganov, M. V. *Natsional'nyi dokhod* [National Income]. Moscow: Gospolitizdat, 1959.

Kronrod, Ia. A. *Sotsialisticheskoe vosproizvodstvo* [Socialist Reproduction]. Moscow: Gospolitizdat, 1955.

Kukushkin, M. S. *Narodnyi dokhod* [National Income]. Leningrad: Lenizdat, 1965.

Moskvin, P. M. *Voprosy statistiki natsional'nogo dokhoda SSSR* [Statistical Problems of the National Income of the USSR]. Moscow: Gosstatizdat, 1955.

(9–10) Finance

Allakhverdian, D. C.· *Nekotorye voprosy teorii sovetskikh finansov* [Some Problems of the Theory of Soviet Finance]. Moscow: Gosfinizdat, 1951.

Atlas, Z. V. (ed.) *Denezhnoe obrashchenie i kredit SSSR* [Monetary Circulation and Credit in the USSR]. Moscow: Gosfinizdat, 1957.

Birman, A. M. *Finansy otraslei narodnogo khoziaistva SSSR* [Finances of the Branches of the National Economy of the USSR]. Vol. I, Part II, The Finances of Socialist Industry; Vol. II, Part IV, The Finances of Agriculture. Moscow: Gosfinizdat, 1953, 1957.

Friebe, S. *Der Kredit in der Zentralverwaltungswirtschaft sowjetischen Typs* [Credit in a Centrally-Administered Economy of the Soviet Type]. Berlin: Duncker & Humblot, 1957, chaps. 1–6.

Garvy, G. * * *, and Bernard, Ph. "Planification, Banque et Gestion Economique en U.R.S.S." [Planning, Banking and Economic Management in the USSR]. *Cahiers de l'ISEA* (Series G, No. 18), Aug., 1963.

Ikonnikov, V. V. (ed.) *Denezhnoe obrashchenie i kredit SSSR* [Monetary Circulation and Credit in the USSR]. Moscow: Gosfinizdat, 1954.

Kovanoski, P. L. *Biudzhet SSSR: Istoriko-kriticheskii obzor* [The Budget of the USSR: A Historical-Critical Survey]. Munich: Institute for the Study of the USSR, 1956.

Liberman, Ia. G. *Gosudarstvennyi biudzhet i sotsialisticheskoe vosproizvodstvo* [State Budget and Socialist Reproduction]. Moscow: Finansy, 1966.

Plotnikov, K. N. *Finansy i kredit v SSSR* [Finance and Credit in the USSR]. Moscow: Izd. VPSh. pri TsK. KPSS, 1959.

Popov, V. F. (ed.) *Gosudarstvennyi Bank SSSR* [The State Bank of the USSR]. Moscow: Gosfinizdat, 1957.

Voprosy sovetskikh finansov [Problems of Soviet Finance]. Moscow: Gosfinizdat, 1956.

Zverev, A. G. *Voprosy natsional'nogo dokhoda i finansov SSSR* [Problems of Soviet National Income and Finance]. Moscow: Gosfinizdat, 1958.

IV. Socialist Economic Models

(11) Western Theories

Bettelheim, C. *Problèmes théoriques et pratiques de la planification,* chap. ii.

(12) Soviet Theories

a. Economic Strategies

Collette, J. M. *Politique des investissements et calcul economique. L'expérience soviétique.* Paris: Cujas, 1965, Part I.

Knirsch, P. *Die ökonomischen Anschauungen Nikolaj I. Bucharins* [The Economic Views of Nikolai Bukharin]. Berlin: Duncker & Humblot, 1959, Part E.

Lenin, V. I. "Po povodu tak nazyvaemogo voprosa o

rynkakh" [On the So-called Question of Markets], *Sochinenia* [Works]. 4th Ed.; Vol. I, Moscow: Gospolitizdat, 1951.

Levin, B. *Vsemernoe razvitie tiazhëloi industrii—general'naia liniia KPSS* [The Development of Heavy Industry in Every Possible Way—General Policy Line of the Communist Party of the Soviet Union]. Moscow: Gospolitizdat, 1956.

Pashkov, A. I. *Ekonomicheskii zakon preimushchestvennogo rosta proizvodstva sredstv proizvodstva* [The Economic Law of the Preferential Growth of the Production of Means of Production]. Moscow: Gosplanizdat, 1958.

Petrosian, K. A. *Sovetskii metod industrializatsii* [The Soviet Method of Industrialization]. Moscow: Gospolitizdat, 1951.

Preobrazhenskii, E. *Novaia Ekonomika* [New Economics]. 2d Ed., Moscow: Izd. Kom. Akad., 1926.

b. Issues in Perspective Planning

Bor, M. Z. *Voprosy metodologii planovogo balansa narodnogo khoziaistva SSSR*, chap. i.

Bobrowski, C. *Formation du système soviétique de planification.* [Formation of the Soviet Planning System]. Paris, The Hague: Mouton, 1956.

Pollock, F. *Die planvirtschaftlichen Versuche in der Sowjetunion* [Economic Planning Attempts in the Soviet Union]. Leipzig: Herschfeld, 1929, chap. v.

Popov, P. I. (ed.) *Balans narodnogo khoziaistva Soiuza SSSR 1923–24 goda* [Balance of the National Economy of the USSR, 1923–24]. Moscow: Trudy Tsentral'nogo Statisticheskogo Upravleniia, Tom XXIV, 1926.

Strumilin, S. G. *Na planovom fronte 1920–1930* [On the Planning Front, 1920–1930]. Moscow: Gospolitizdat, 1958, chaps. x–xiv.

(13) Other Socialist Theories

a. On Pricing

Bordaz, R. *La nouvelle économie soviétique, 1953–1960* [The New Soviet Economy, 1953–1960]. Paris: Bernard Grasset, 1960, chap. ii, iii.

Chandra, N. K. "Le Modèle de Kantorovitch et la méthode soviétique des balances" [The Kantorovich model and the Soviet method of balances]. *La Revue d'Economie Politique, mars–avril,* 1966.

Denis, H., Lavigne, M. *Le problème des prix en Union Soviétique* [The problem of prices in the Soviet Union]. Paris: Cujas, 1965.

Kantorovich, L. V. *Ekonomicheskii raschet nailushchego ispolzovaniia resursov* [Economic Calculation of Optimum Utilization of Resources]. Moscow: Akademia Nauk SSSR, 1960.

Kronrod, A. Ia. (ed.) *Zakon stoimosti i ego ispol'zovanie v narodnom khoziaistve SSSR* [The Law of Value and Its Utilization in the National Economy of the USSR]. Moscow: Gospolitizdat, 1959.

Maizenberg, A. *Tzenoobrazovanie v narodnom khoziaistve SSSR* [Price Formation in the National Economy of the USSR]. Moscow: Gospolitizdat, 1953.

Turetskii, Sh. Ia. *Ocherki planovogo tsenoobrazovaniia v SSSR* [Studies in Planned Price Formation in the USSR]. Moscow: Gospolitizdat, 1959, chaps. i, ii.

b. On Decentralized Models

Bobrowski, C. *La Yougoslavie Socialiste du plan quinquennal de 1947 au plan de 1955* [Socialist Yugoslavia from the Five-Year Plan of 1947 to the Plan of 1955]. Paris: Armand Colin, 1956, chaps. 5–8.

Centre d' étude des pays de l'Est, Institut de Sociologie Solvay, Université libre de Bruxelles. *Le régime et les institutions de la république populaire fédérative de Yougoslavie* [The Regime and the Institutions of the Federal People's Republic of Yugoslavia]. Brussels: Institut de Sociologie Solvay, 1959.

Dyskusja o polskim modelu gospodarczym [Discussion on the Polish Economic Model]. Warsaw: Ksiazka i Wiedza, 1957.

Meier, V. *Das Neue jugoslawische Wirtschaftssystem* [The New Yugoslav Economic System]. Zurich: Polygraphischer Verlag, 1956.

Weitzmann, I. *Das System der Einkommenstverteilung in der sozialisschen Marktwirtschaft Jugoslawiens* [The System of Income Distribution in the Socialist Market Economy of Yugoslavia]. Berlin: Duncker & Humblot, 1958.

V. Socialism v. Capitalism

(14) Problems of Socialist Cooperation

Agoston, I. *Le marché commun communiste. Principes et pratique du COMECON* [The Communist Common Market. Principles and Practice of the COME-

CON]. Geneva: Droz, 1964.

Gornov, V. P. (ed.) *Vneshniaia torgovlia SSSR s sotsialisticheskimi stranami* [Foreign Trade of the USSR with the Socialist Countries]. Moscow: Vneshtorgizdat, 1957.

Klinkmuller, E. and Huban, M. E. *Die Wirtschaftliche Zusammenarbeit der Ostblockstaaten* [The Economic Cooperation of the East Bloc States]. Berlin: Duncker & Humblot, 1960.

Kovrizhnykh, M. F., Frumkin, A. B., Pozdniakov, V. S. (eds.) *Vneshniaia torgovlia stran narodnoi demokratsii* [Foreign Trade of the People's Democracies]. Moscow: Vneshtorgizdat, 1955.

Pavel, T. "Pour un juste calcul de la rentabilité et de l'efficacité du commerce extérieur" [For an Accurate Calculation of the Rentability and of the Efficiency of Foreign Trade]. *Études Économiques,* No. 106–107, 1957.

(15) Competition and "Convergence"

Centre d'étude des pays de l'Est, Institut de Sociologie Solvay, Université Libre de Bruxelles. *L'Économie Soviétique en 1957* [Soviet Economy in 1957]. Brussels: Institut de Sociologie Solvay, 1958.

V(olmar), G. "Der isolirte sozialistische Staat" [The isolated socialist State] in *Jahrbuch für Sozialwissenschaft und Socialpolitik* (Zürich, Swiz.), 1879.

Kontrol'nye tsifry razvitiia narodnogo khoziaistva SSSR na 1959–1965 gody [Control Figures of the Development of the National Economy of the USSR for 1959–1965]. Moscow: Gospolitizdat, 1958.

Nauchno–issledovatel'skii ekonomicheskii Institut Gosplana SSSR: "Ob ekonomicheskom sorevnovanii mezhdu Sovetskim Soiuzom i Soedinennymi Shtatami Ameriki" [On the Economic Competition between the Soviet Union and the United States of America], *Planovoe khoziaistvo,* No. 7, 1958, supplement.

Narodnoe khoziaistvo SSSR, Statisticheski ezhegodnik [National Economy of the USSR, Statistical Yearbook]. Moscow: Gosstatizdat.

Index